Adventure Guide to

Kauai

Heather McDaniel

HUNTER

HUNTER PUBLISHING, INC.
130 Campus Drive, Edison, NJ 08818-7816
☎ *732-225-1900 / 800-255-0343 / fax 732-417-1744*
www.hunterpublishing.com
E-mail comments@hunterpublishing.com

IN CANADA:
Ulysses Travel Publications
4176 Saint-Denis, Montréal, Québec, Canada H2W 2M5
☎ *514-843-9882 ext. 2232 / fax 514-843-9448*

IN THE UNITED KINGDOM:
Windsor Books International
5, Castle End Park, Castle End Rd, Ruscombe
Berkshire, RG10 9XQ England, ☎ *01189-346-367 / fax 01189-346-368*

ISBN 978-1-58843-633-7

This guide focuses on recreational activities. As all such activities contain elements of risk, the publisher, author, affiliated individuals and companies disclaim any responsibility for any injury, harm, or illness that may occur to anyone through, or by use of, the information in this book. Every effort was made to insure the accuracy of information in this book, but the publisher and author do not assume, and hereby disclaim, any liability for loss or damage caused by errors, omissions, misleading information or potential travel problems caused by this guide, even if such errors or omissions result from negligence, accident or any other cause.

Cover photo: Na Pali Coast (© Jacques Jangoux / Alamy)
Other photos by the authors and courtesy of shorediving.com, hawaiianimages.com and others.

Maps © 2007 Hunter Publishing, Inc.
Index by Nancy Wolff

4 3 2 1

Contents

Maps

Introduction

IN THIS CHAPTER

Kaua`i is one of the most beautiful places on earth. With its lush, green mountains, clear waters, and once-in-a-lifetime views, there's a reason why it's called "The Garden Island." You'll be sure to leave refreshed, rejuvenated and enchanted by an island that has so much to offer. It really is unforgettable.

From the moment you step off the plane, you'll notice that you're in a unique place, and it will captivate you. It's hard to believe that a mere 20-minute flight from Honolulu can bring you to a place so different, like being in a different country. Even though it's only about 100 miles from Honolulu, Kaua`i is literally a world away from the up-tempo city life.

As you drive around the island, you'll be sure to notice a few things right away. First, the chickens. Seriously, Kaua`i is full of chickens. Not in a bad way, but rather in a quaint and amusing way. They're at the airport, they're probably at your hotel (not in your room, of course), and you can see them cross the road. Don't worry; they won't bite.

Second, you'll notice the extreme heart-stopping beauty of the island. The natural beauty that's been refined over literally millions of years ranges from Waimea Canyon to the majestic Na Pali cliffs. Mark Twain dubbed Waimea Canyon "The Grand Canyon of the Pacific," and for good reason. Seeing the canyon stretch for miles is absolutely amazing.

You'll also notice that Kaua`i is quite rural. It has a laid-back style and feel all on its own. The residents of Kaua`i have worked hard to maintain its plantation town past. Streetlights are few and far-between. Highrises are non-existent.

Opposite: Na Pali Coast

Waimea Canyon

Kaua`i's residents are rare in that they have really fought to ke`ep its natural beauty, at the expense of development.

If you think that means there's nothing to do, you're wrong. Dead wrong. Kaua`i has so much to offer. Whether you visit for a quiet getaway, a great adventure or even to get married, Kaua`i does have it all. You can sit at the beach and read a good book, enjoy a massage, learn about Kaua`i's past at a museum or, if you're the adventurous type, kayak to the Na Pali cliffs, snorkel the crystal clear waters, explore caves and beaches, or hike around Waimea Canyon. There's something for everyone on this tropical island in the middle of the Pacific Ocean.

KAUAI QUICK FACTS	
Kaua`i size	553 sq mi
Population	62,000
Average Temperatures	75-85°
Island Flower	Mokihana
Official Color	Purple
Highest elevation	5243 ft (Kawakini)

■ The Hawaiian Islands

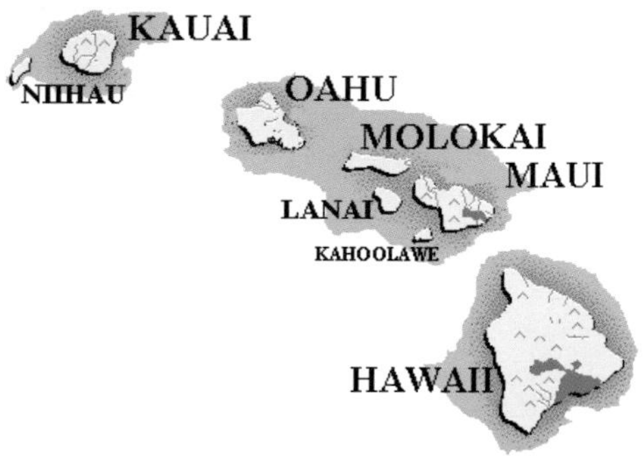

The Hawaiian island chain is among the most isolated in the world. It's about 2,550 miles from Los Angeles and 3,850 miles to Tokyo. Its isolation has played a huge part in the development of this unique culture.

The chain consists of as many as 132 islands, atolls, shoals and reefs, which stretches over 1,600 miles in the Pacific. This archipelago began to form millions of years ago, and is still growing, as evidenced by the 20-year eruption of Kilauea on the Big Island of Hawai`i. Of these 132 islands, eight of the most southeastern are inhabited and are considered to make up the State of Hawai`i.

In June 2006, President Bush signed the Northwestern Hawaiian Island Marine National Monument, which created the largest protected marine monument in the world. It covers almost 140,000 square miles and is home to more than 7,000 species, one-quarter of which are found only in this area. More important, it's also home to the critically endangered Hawaiian monk seal. There are only between 1,200 and 1,400 left of this amazing animal in the world and most reside here. This area also serves as the breeding ground for 90% of the Hawaiian green sea turtle population.

The northernmost inhabited island, **Ni`ihau** is located 17 miles off the west coast of Kaua`i. Ni`ihau is the smallest of the main Hawaiian Islands, with a land area of 70 square miles and a population of about 250, almost all of whom are Native Hawaiian. You can see Ni`ihau from the south and west shores of Kaua`i.

The island was offered for sale by King Kamehameha IV in 1863 and was purchased by Elizabeth Sinclair for $10,000. Mrs. Sinclair turned the entire island into a cattle and sheep

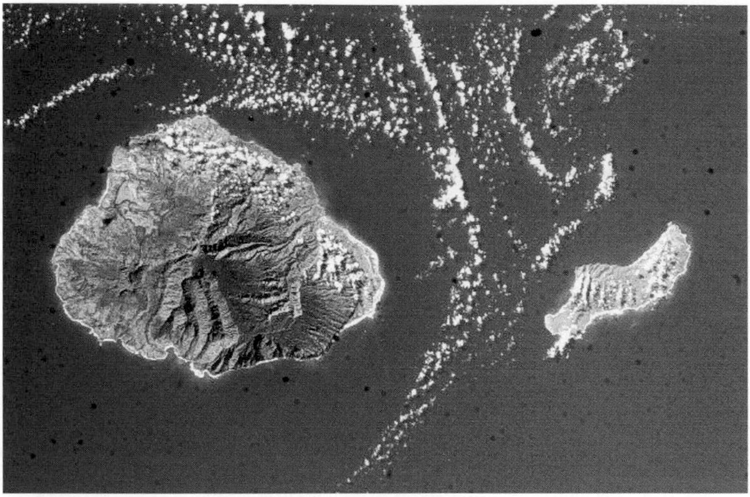

Ni`ihau (at right) and Kaua`i from space (NASA)

ranch, before moving back to Kaua`i. Today, Ni`ihau is still privately owned by the descendents of Helen Sinclair Robinson, with the US Navy also keeping a presence there for weapons testing.

Because of the limited access, the island has remained immune to the influences of "modern civilization." Hawaiian is the primary language here and there are none of the modern conveniences – no paved roads, cars, hotels, restaurants. Each family grows their own fruits and vegetables and the ranch still raises beef and mutton.

What Ni`ihau is well-known for is the incredibly rare Ni`ihau shell-lei. These intricate necklaces are hand-sewn from tiny shells that are found only on this island. These are the only shells that are considered to be gems. The shells come in a variety of colors, including white, yellow, orange and blue.

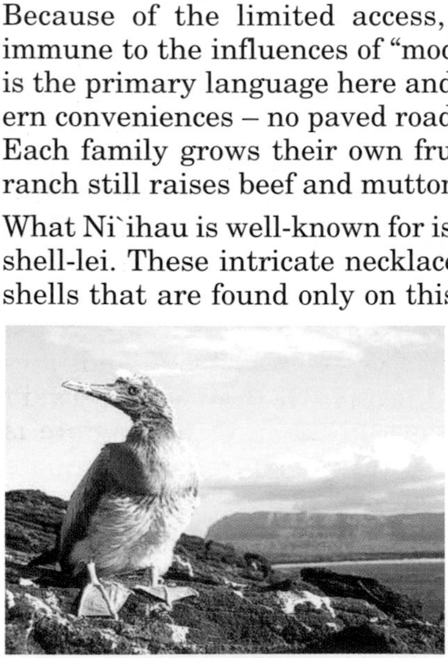

Birdlife on Ni`ihau

Want to see Ni`ihau for yourself? There's a reason why Ni`ihau is known as "The Forbidden Island." Access is extremely limited. People who have lived on Kaua`i for years and grew up in the shadows of Ni`ihau have never set foot on the island. Access to the island is restricted to only family members, US Navy personnel, government officials and invited guests.

But there are ways to visit Ni`ihau. **Ni`ihau Helicopters** (www.niihau.org, ☎ 1-877-441-3500) offers three-hour helicopter tours on a very limited basis for $300. You can also go on a full-day hunting excursion, shooting at pigs and sheep. Prices start at $1,650, not including a Hawai`i hunting license and rifle rental.

There are snorkeling and diving tours off the coast of Ni`ihau as well, but those do not make landfall. **Hololo Charters** also offers snorkeling off the northernmost tip of Ni`ihau (☎ 1-877-678-7333 or 808-572-7333, adventureinhawaii.com/kauai_niihau.htm).

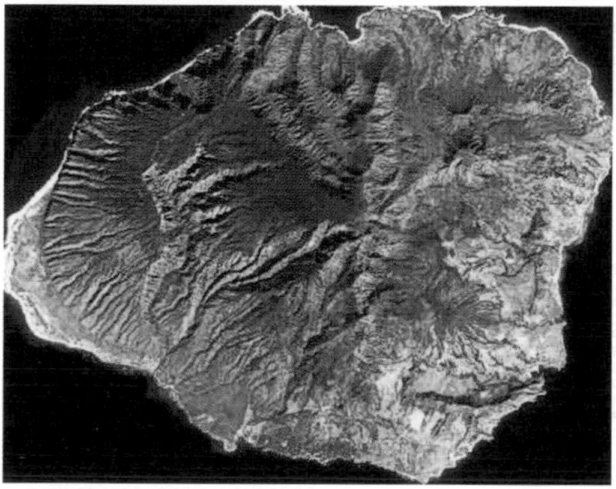

Kaua`i (NASA)

**Kaua`i** itself is the second-oldest inhabited Hawaiian Island, with a population of approximately 62,000. Kaua`i is considered to be a rather rural island, as it's kept its focus on preserving the natural beauty of the island, as opposed to the major development seen on other islands over the past few years. That's the primary reason residents of the other islands consider Kaua`i their favorite. However, like the rest of Hawai`i today, it's growing at an astronomical pace. Real estate is booming and tourism is way, way up.

The Island of **O`ahu** is the third-oldest island and geographically, the third-largest at 607 square miles. It's home to nearly three-quarters of the state's 1.275 million residents, most living in and around the city of Honolulu. Honolulu serves as the county seat, the state capital, and the center of business and industry in the Islands. Honolulu Harbor is the lifeline for all

Maui (NASA)

the Islands. Most of Hawai`i's food and manufactured goods must be imported and distributed through this port. O`ahu is also home to Waikiki beach, the world-renowned waves of the North Shore and military bases such as Pearl Harbor.

Next is **Maui**, with a population of 126,000. The second-largest of the populated Hawaiian Islands, Maui also boasts the second-largest population in the state, behind O`ahu. Haleakala, which translates as "house of the sun," is the largest dormant volcano in the world. Not yet extinct, it is expected to erupt sometime in the next 200 years (it last erupted in 1790).

Formed by six, possibly seven, different volcanoes, the islands of Maui, Moloka'i, Lana'i and Kaho'olawe were once a single island called Maui Nui. Rising sea levels eventually separated the islands, though, as a group, they are still called Maui County. The valleys that once connected Maui, Moloka`i Lana`i and Kaho'olawe are shallow, which makes for a great marine environement. It's also a major spot for tourists, especially for folks from the mainland US and Canada. The "Valley Isle" boasts several fun towns, such as Lahaina (especially on Halloween), Ka`anapali and Wailea.

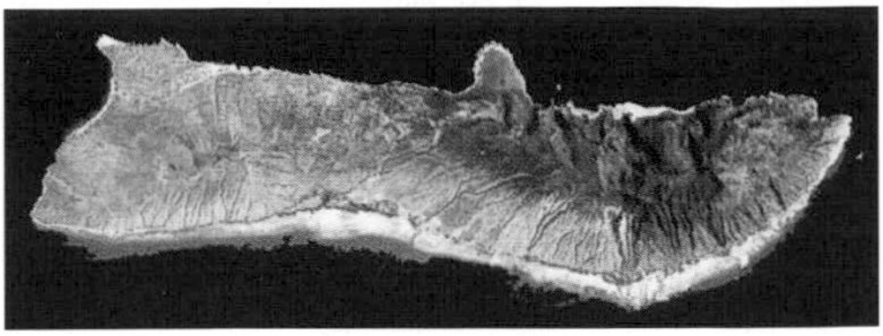
Moloka`i (NASA)

Moloka`i is the "Friendly Isle." Located nearly at the center of the Hawaiian Island chain, it is about two million years old. From the eastern end of the island, it's only eight miles across the Pailolo Channel to Maui. The population is estimated at 8,000 residents, half of whom live in or near the primary town of Kaunakakai. Nearly 40% of the residents of Moloka`i are of Hawaiian descent.

The island is probably best-known as a former leper colony. In the mid-1800s leprosy (today called Hansen's Disease) was brought to Hawai`i by Chinese who came to labor in the sugar cane fields. Many Hawaiians were stricken with the disease and, since there was then no cure for the disease, strict isolation was the only means available to keep the it from spreading.

In 1866 the first sufferers were banished to Kalaupapa, a small peninsula on the north side of Moloka`i. A Belgian priest named Father Damien came to Moloka`i in 1873 to minister to the needs of the dying. Through his ministry and labors, order was created where there had been only suffering and chaos. Father Damien succumbed to the disease himself in 1889.

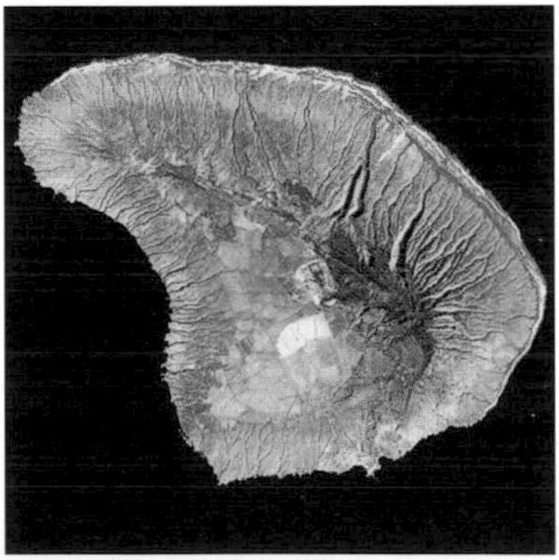
Lana`i (NASA)

**Lana`i** is appropriately named the "Pineapple Island" – a throwback to its days as an island-wide pineapple plantation. Jim Dole bought the island for $1 million in 1888 from the Hawaiian Kingdom. Lana`i is the sixth-largest of the eight main Hawaiian Islands with an area of 140 square miles. It is home to a mere 5,000 residents, most of whom live in Lana`i City. Although agriculture and ranching are still a vital part of Lana`i's economy, the island is now primarily known as an upscale tourist destination, offering two five-star resorts – The Manele Bay Hotel and The Lodge at Ko`ele. Nowadays, the pineapple crops have waned and tourism has taken over.

Kaho`olawe

Off to the southwest of Maui is **Kaho`olawe** (pronounced ka-ho-oh-lahv-eh). It's the smallest of the eight main islands. There are no permanent residents, nor are visitors permitted on the island. Kaho`olawe is a prime example of the sometimes contentious relationship between the Native Hawaiian movement and the US government. Once a penal colony in the mid-1800s, Kaho`olawe became a ranch in the late 1800s. The ranch was failing and, in May of 1941, the ranch owners leased the land to the US Navy. Of course, Pearl Harbor happened the following December, at which point the US declared martial law and took outright control of the island.

In 1993, the US government approved a $400 million clean-up fund for Kaho`olawe, and in 1994 the island was officially returned to Hawai`i. However, the federal government retained control of access to the island. It wasn't until 2003 that the State of Hawai`i gained complete control of the island. In April of 2004, the Navy ended the 10-year clean-up of the island and the Kaho`olawe Island Reserve Commissions (KIRC). The island is still contaminated, however, and still contains an unknown amount of unexploded devices.

Last but certainly not least, there's the island of **Hawai`i**. The Orchid Isle covers 4,028 square miles, roughly the size of Connecticut. To alleviate any confusion between the State of Hawai`i and the island of Hawai`i, the island is referred to as the Big Island. When most folks visit Hawai`i, they think of O`ahu as being the Big Island. While O`ahu does hold most of the state's population, the Big Island earned its name by sheer size. It's twice the size of size of all of the other major islands combined and it's still growing due to the volcanic eruption of Kilauea. The Big Island is home to the Ironman Triathlon in Kona, which is held every October. Kilauea Caldera is the longest continuously erupting volcano in the world, with the present eruption going back to 1983.

Hawai`i (NASA)

■ History

In the beginning, there was water. About 20 million years ago, the Hawaiian archipelago was formed by a hot spot beneath the Pacific Tectonic Plate. Islands rise and fall as the archipelago moves slowly to the northwest. As the chain moves, the oldest islands erode and fade into their roots in the ocean, while the newest island, Loihi, is slowly forming 15 miles from the Big Island.

Did you know? The Hawaiian Island Chain moves about 3½ inches per year.

Kaua`i was formed approximately five million years ago. No one can say when the first plants arrived on the island, but it's suspected that, over a period of a million years, roughly 240 species of plants bloomed on the island. The spores and seeds arrived via birds or wind currents. They evolved to the point that, by the time the first Polynesians arrived, there were some 1,300 species.

Polynesian Settlers

It's widely believed that the first settlers came to Kaua`i in canoes from the Marquesas Islands. No one knows for sure why they left, but it is widely believed that they were unaware of the existence of the Hawaiian Islands until they arrived. Along the Na Pali coast, there is archaeological evidence of human existence that dates back to 500 AD through 600 AD.

These first settlers brought several staples of life with them for survival – taro, breadfruit, pigs, and other plants used for food clothing, shelter and medicine. They lived mostly on taro and fish. Over time, the society developed and flourished.

Travel between the Marquesas and Hawai`i developed and became fairly regular. Then the Tahitians learned about Hawai`i, and eventually they conquered the Marquesans in 1000 AD.

As in all societies, a class system eventually developed. At the top of the hierarchy were the ali`i or ruling chiefs. The chiefs were separated according to lineage. At the bottom were the commoners, farmers, builders and those who performed the physical labor. This system was enforced by the kapu (pronounced KAH-poo) system or set of laws. According to the kapu system, it was against the law if your shadow should cross the shadow of an ali`i. It was also a violation for a man and woman to eat together. The penalty of violating kapu was usually death.

Arrival Of The British

The Polynesians on Kaua`i were left alone until 1778, when Captain James Cook landed the ships *Resolution* and *Discover* at Waimea. This is considered to be the major turning point in the history of the islands.

Captain Cook

Even though Captain Cook is credited with discovering the islands, some historians now believe that he wasn't the first European to come here. Spanish Captain Gaetan in 1592 was trying to find his way to Mexico, was blown off course and arrived at Kaua`i. Finding no gold or other riches, Gaetan left and never returned to the islands.

Captain Cook meets with the Hawaiians

Captain Cook's arrival on Kaua`i opened the door for other Westerners – missionaries, businessmen and laborers who brought new ideas, materials and foods. They also brought diseases that were unknown to Hawaiians and in turn decimated the native population.

Hawaiian Monarchy

Kamehameha the Great

Hawai`i is the only state in the country to have had a monarchy. This period in Hawaiian history is considered to have begun after **Kamehameha the Great** unified the Hawaiian Islands once Kaua`i's ruler, **King Kaumuali`i**, vowed his allegiance to Kamehameha.

Kaua`i takes pride in being the only island not to have been defeated by Kamehameha. Kamehameha fought savage battles from the Big Island all the way through O`ahu, conquering each island. On his way to Kaua`i, there was a storm, forcing him to turn back.

Kamehameha's son, **Liholiho** succeeded him to become Kamehameha II. Even though Liholiho held the title of king, the power of the monarchy remained with **Queen Ka`ahumanu**, wife of Kamehameha I. She was a bit of a feminist, and she encouraged Kamehameha II to break several kapu restrictions on women's power in Hawaiian society. She even convinced Kamehameha II to sit down and eat with

Queen Ka`ahumanu

women. After seeing that kapu could be broken without retaliation, Kamehameha II ordered the destruction of heiaus and an end to the kapu system, abolishing the traditional Hawaiian laws and religion. This left a great void in Hawaiian society.

The next three monarchs were also a part of the Kamehameha Dynasty. They were **Kauikeaouli** (Kamehameha III), **Alexander Liholiho** (Kamehameha IV) and **Lot Kamehameha** (Kamehameha V). When **Kamehamea V** died in 1872, he left no heirs to assume the throne. A struggle of power ensued between William Lunalino and David Kalakaua to take over the kingdom. The conflict was resolved by an informal vote in the legislature, declaring **Lunalilo** to be the next reigning monarch.

In 1874, David Kalakaua was elected king under Hawai`i's constitution. **King Kalakaua** was an established songwriter, and revived the hula and other Hawaiian arts and traditions.

King Kalakaua

During his rule, he was forced to sign what's called the **Bayonet Constitution**. This document was drafted and backed by businessmen and lawyers. They just happened to have their own paramilitary force to convince the king to sign the constitution. The Bayonet Constitution eliminated the king's power and made the Hawaiian-controlled legislature accessible to those with significant wealth or land.

King Kalakaua died during a trip to San Francisco in 1891. His sister, **Queen Liliuokalani**, took over the throne to become Hawai`i's last monarch. She drafted a new constitution that restored power to the monarchy.

In 1893, a number of Caucasian businessmen, seeking to protect their economic interests and backed by American troops, overthrew Queen Liliuokalani. She was imprisoned in Iolani Palace for nine months. In 1900, Hawai`i became a Territory of the United States, and Hawai`i was allowed a delegate to the US Congress.

Queen Liliuokalani

It wasn't until 1993 when President Clinton signed a joint resolution on the 100th anniversary of the overthrow of the Hawaiian Kingdom. In it the United States acknowledged and apologized for its part in the overthrow.

THE GREAT MAHELE

Land was traditionally divided into several districts called moku. The moku were further divided into ahupa`a, and were controlled by ruling chiefs. The land was divided like a slice of pie from the mountain to the ocean so that everyone had access to fish, rainwater in the mountains and could grow plants and taro to survive. Even though the ruling chiefs controlled the land, access was open to everyone.

By the time King Kamehameha II died in 1824, demand for land had increased. The demands came from ruling chiefs and from businessmen, who were accustomed to owning land outright. They objected to the way the king and other chiefs distributed land and evicted them at will.

In the 1830s, King Kamehameha III initially proposed the Great Mahele (division of the land). In 1845, a land commission was established to preside over cases where land claims were disputed.

In 1848, the king signed a division of the land into four categories: land belonging to the king, land belonging to the ali`i or chiefs, land that could be purchased by the foreigners who lived in Hawai`i, and land worked by the commoners or maka`ainana.

Arrival Of The Missionaries

Samuel & Mercy Partridge Whitney, who sailed in the first company of missionaries to Hawai`i (portraits by Samuel F.B. Morse)

The missionaries came at a critical time for Hawaiians. Once Queen Ka`ahumanu and Kamehameha II destroyed the kapu system, a huge void was left. This turned out to be great timing for the missionaries who arrived in 1820. Hawaiians were becoming disillusioned in their own deities as Ka`ahumanu and then Kamehameha II defied kapu without retribution. They were ripe to accept the ideas of Christianity.

The Congregational Church (now the United Church of Christ) sent the first missionaries to Hawai`i in 1819. These missionaries had to endure a seemingly endless voyage from Boston, sailing for 164 days around Cape Horn and South America through the Pacific to reach Hawai`i. The first missionaries on Kaua`i established the mission station at Waimea in 1820. Those that survived were shocked by what they found – a relatively free culture where people were often nude. The missionaries quickly established and enforced their own rules. Women had to wear long gowns. The hula was also banned.

Ironically, while the missionaries are blamed for destroying Hawaiian culture, they are the ones that began to record it. Hawaiian history and language were solely oral traditions, until the missionaries created Hawaiian as a written language. They used this written language to translate the bible into Hawaiian.

Children of the missionaries established themselves in a number of different professions. Many became land and sugar plantation owners.

■ The Economy

Once Westerners came to Hawai`i, they began to commercialize crops such as sugar and pineapples. In 1835, the first sugar plantation was started in Koloa by Ladd and Company.

The first harvest in 1837 produced 30 tons of sugar and 170 barrels of molasses, which sold for approximately $200.

Sugar was the main source of revenue until the early 1900s. This is when the pineapple industry developed on Kaua`i. First, the Kaua`i Fruit and Land Co. began operations in 1906. These canneries were the main employers on Kaua`i until the mid-1960s.

When the sugar and pineapple industries declined, tourism quickly replaced them. In 1927, there were only 668 visitors to Kaua`i. The number grew steadily, hotels and resorts began to pop up and tourism quickly became the island's main source of revenue.

Even though the economy of Kaua`i was virtually wiped out by Hurricane Iniki, it has since bounced back with a vengeance. Today, Kaua`i is in the midst of an economic boom. There has been an increase in tourism, mostly due to the large influx of visitors from Japan. But one of Kaua`i's biggest employers isn't a hotel or resort. It's the Pacific Missile Range Facility, which employs about 935 people.

While tourism has replaced sugar and pineapples as the leading source of revenue, Kaua`i still sees agriculture as a vital part of the economy. Papaya, beef, coffee and guava are important and Kaua`i also produces more than 60% of Hawai`i's taro.

■ Statehood

Not only is Hawai`i the only state within the US that had a monarchy, Hawai`i also had the only royal to serve in the U.S. Congress. Once Hawai`i became a territory, it was permitted to have a non-voting delegate in the House of Representatives. That delegate was Prince Jonah Kuhio Kalanianaole, a Kaua`i native who was the grandson of the last king of Kaua`i, King Kaumuali`i. Prince Kuhio served in Congress for 19 years.

Many people throughout Hawai`i believed that statehood would further protect their interests. In 1954, there was a petition for statehood signed by 120,000 people in just two weeks. This 250-lb document was sent off to Washington, to the Office of then Vice President Richard Nixon.

In March 1959, the Admission Act was passed by Congress and signed by President Eisenhower. On August 21, 1959, statehood became official. Hawai`i became the 50th state in the union and people across Hawai`i celebrated well into the night.

HAWAIIAN HISTORY

400-600 AD: The earliest settlers from the Marquesas Islands arrive.
1778: Captain James Cook and the crews of the *HMS Resolution* and *HMS Discovery* land in Waimea, Kaua`i.
1779: Captain Cook is killed in Kealekekua Bay on the Big Island by Hawaiians.
1782: Kamehameha I begins his campaign to unify the islands.
1795: Kamehameha I conquers Maui, Lana`i, Moloka`i, and O`ahu.
1796: Kamehameha I attempts to invade Kaua`i. A storm forces him to turn back.
1809: King Kaumuali`i of Kaua`i goes to O`ahu to meet with Kamehameha I and arrange cession of Kaua`i.
1810: Kaua`i is ceded to Kamehameha I, thus unifying all of the Hawaiian Islands.
1819: Kamehameha I dies; Liholiho becomes King Kamehameha II.
1820: Arrival of the first missionaries.
1824: Kamehameha II dies; Kauikeaouli becomes Kamehameha III.
1848: The Great Mahele, or division of the land, is signed by King Kamehameha III.
1854: Kamehameha III dies; Alexander Liholiho becomes Kamehameha IV.
1863: Kamehameha IV dies; Lot Kamehameha becomes Kamehameha V.
1872: Kamehameha V dies, leaving no heir to the throne. William Lunalilo becomes King of Hawai`i through an informal vote in the legislature.
1874: King Lunalilo dies; David Kalakaua is elected King.
1891: King Kalakaua dies; Liliuokalani becomes Queen.
1893: Queen Liliuokalani surrendered the kingdom to the United States under protest.
1898:President McKinley signs the Newlands Resolution, which annexed Hawai`i to the United States.
1900: Sanford B. Dole becomes first territorial governor of Hawai`i.
1959: Hawai`i becomes the 50th US state

■ Politics & Government

The State of Hawai`i is comprised of five counties. The **City & County of Honolulu**, which is the Island of O`ahu. Honolulu is also home of the State Capitol. **Maui County** contains the islands of Maui, Moloka`i, and Lana`i.

Hawai`i County** is comprised of the Big Island and, finally, **Kaua`i County includes Kaua`i and Ni`ihau.

Each county has its own mayor and county council. The mayor of Kaua`i County is elected with a four-year term and the seven-member council is elected for two-year terms.

■ The Land

It's widely believed that Kaua`i first began to form around 10 million years ago, formed by the Olokele Volcano. Over time, the volcano eroded to form Mt. Wai`ale`ale, Mt. Kawikini and Waimea Canyon. Over the years, cliffs and beaches were able to form throughout the island. The terrain along the coast is flat, with an occasional rolling hill. However, farther inland the land is rugged and downright treacherous, which is why most of the island is inaccessible by road.

The Napali Coast

Ecosystems

Since it's one of the oldest Hawaiian islands, Kaua`i combines a number of ecosystems. You can find rainforests, valleys in places like Hanalei and Waimea, dry canyons in Waimea, Alakai Swamp and, of course, miles and miles of beaches and reefs. The 20 bogs that make up the Alakai Swamp are incredibly fragile, as native species are slowly being eradicated by centuries of use and through the introduction of invasive species. Kaua`i's ecosystems are among the most fragile in the world. Hawai`i has the highest rate of extinction of all of the tropical ecosystems in the world.

Climate

Kaua`i's location in the northern pacific, along with its extraordinary mountain formations creates this fascinating variety in climate conditions. Since Kaua`i is located in the tropics, it's a safe bet to assume that Kaua`i has a tropical climate to boot. The weather on Kaua`i can be as much an adventure as anything you do on the island. It's home to the wettest spot on the planet – Mt. Wai`ale`ale – which averages an incredible 486 inches of rain each year. Fortunately, the rest of the island doesn't experience this kind of weather. Princeville on the North Shore tends to average 85 inches per year, and Waimea on the West Shore averages 21, while the rest of the island comes in at 40 inches a year.

Since Kaua`i is a tropical island, it has its own micro-climates, so the weather will differ according to where you're at, even if it's only a few miles away. On the North Shore, for instance, the weather is typically wetter than the rest of the island, especially during the rainy winter season. It's also rains a bit on the eastern or windward side of the island. The rainy season runs between November and April.

On the Western or leeward side of the island, it's considerably hotter and drier. On the south shore, you'll find the most sunshine.

Even though the temperatures seem hot, the tradewinds create a cooler climate. On days when the tradewinds aren't blowing, you can certainly feel the difference. It can be downright oppressive. Although this is a very general overview of Kaua`i's weather, note that conditions can change frequently and can vary dramatically from one part of the island to another on the same day. It's often raining in places such as the north shore, while it's hot and sunny in Po`ipu. The trade winds provide cooling fresh air and brief rain showers in the early morning and evening.

Temperature

The average high temperature on Kaua`i during January is in the mid- to upper 70s, while in late August to early September the temperature ranges from the mid- to upper 80s. Late August through early September is the hottest time of the year and the sun is blazing hot in the middle of the day. Even though there are periods during the year that are warmer and cooler, Kaua`i doesn't experience extreme swings in temperature.

TEMPERATURE RANGES	
January-April	78-66°
May-August	86-72°
September-December	85-70°
Ocean temperatures	71° to 81° year-round

For the current Kaua`i weather forecast, visit the National Weather Service website at www.prh.noaa.gov/hnl/pages/zone.php?zone=HIZ002. Another great resource for beach and surf conditions is www.kauaiexplorer.com. You can also call ☎ 808-245-6001 for current weather conditions. Marine conditions can be found by calling ☎ 808-245-3564. For Kaua`i's surf forecast, call ☎ 808-241-7873 or visit www.surfnewsnetwork.com.

Hurricanes

Hurricanes rarely hit Hawai`i, but there are two that did have a direct impact on Kaua`i.

In 1982 Hurricane Iwa formed south of Hawai`i and moved north to brush Kaua`i, O`ahu, and Ni`ihau with wind speeds of 80-90 mph and gusts over 100 miles per hour. At the time, it was considered one of the costliest hurricanes to hit the United States, with over $200 million in damage.

Just a few weeks after Hurricane Andrew leveled South Florida in 1992, Hurricane Iniki formed southeast of Hawai`i and was heading north when it made landfall near Waimea on September 11 with winds estimated at 130 mph and gusts up to 160 mph. Iniki's winds caused widespread damage and storm surge and high waves did extensive damage on both Kaua`i and O`ahu. Over 14,000 homes were either damaged or destroyed. The economy also took a hit as sugar cane, banana, and papaya plants were either stripped or severely set back. Electric power and telephone service had also been lost, and those took months to be restored.

In March of 2006, Windward O`ahu and Kaua`i were hit with seemingly never-ending rainstorms for almost the entire month. It caused a tragic dam failure in the town of Kilauea. Three people died in the dam burst and four are still missing. The failure temporarily washed out Kuhio Highway, which is the main road that connects Hanalei, Princeville and Kilauea to the rest of the island.

The dam break did make international headlines and there have been concerns as to whether or not this could be repeated. Since then, all 54 dams on Kaua`i have been inspected by the US Army Corps of Engineers and are managed in accordance with the weather. State authorities have also assured residents that there is no immediate threat and they will continue to monitor the level to assure that these are manageable.

Flora & Fauna

Kaua`i certainly lives up to its Garden Isle nickname. You're sure to find a wide variety of plants, including kiawe trees, guava, eucalyptus, bamboo, sugar cane and pineapple. However, it's important to keep in mind that there are more endangered species per square mile throughout Hawai`i than any other place in the world.

Since Kaua`i began as an isolated volcano, nothing is truly native to Kaua`i. Plants don't grow easily on lava rock. It's believed that the seeds, spores and insects were originally carried by wind currents and in birds' feathers. Over millions of years, these plants, birds, and insects adapted to the environment.

Once the Polynesians came to Kaua`i, they brought their own staple foods to survive. They brought tara, breadfruit, ti, sugar, ginger and other plants that were used for food and medicinal purposes.

Western contact in the late 18th century increased the introduction of other species. Plants such as mango, guava, pineapple were brought here and eventually commercialized.

Caution: The mango is from the same family as poison oak and poison ivy. The mango's skin and sap contains a chemical called urushiol, which can cause an allergic reaction in some people.

You are no doubt already familiar with plants such as **papaya**, **mango**, **banana** and **coconut**. These can be found in abundance on Kaua`i. You may not be familiar with some of the plants mentioned below.

First off, there's Kaua`i's official plant, the **mokihana**. This plant can be found only on Kaua`i. It's a tree that can grow from six to 25 feet tall. It has thin leaves that have an aroma similar to anise when they're crushed. Its primary use is in making leis.

Mokihana

Breadfruit was originally brought to Kaua`i by the settlers from the Marquesas Islands. It is thought to have originated in New Guinea and was a staple food throughout Polynesia. When the flesh of the fruit is roasted, it smells like fresh baked bread.

Guava

Guava made its way to Kaua`i from the Americas in the late 1700s. The plant thrived in the tropical climate and it soon became the most common wild fruit throughout the islands. Today, Kaua`i is home to the largest guava plantation in the world – the Guava Kai Plantation in Kilauea. There, the fruit is processed to create jams, sauces and juices.

Did you know that guava is good for you? Guavas contain more vitamin C than oranges.

The **lychee** came to Kaua`i from China. These hardwood trees can grow to 40 feet tall and produce a fruit that is very popular in Hawai`i. At first, you'll see a round, red fruit with

Lychee

bumpy skin that looks unappealing. Once you peel the skin, you'll find the white fruit that's similar to a grape, but much sweeter.

Two trees that are indigenous and are revered in Hawaiian culture are the **koa** and **o`hia**. Koa is thought to have come to Hawai`i from Australia and was used by Native Hawaiians for outrigger canoes, paddles, spears and surfboards. Today, it's an increasingly rare tree that is used for furniture and musical instruments such as `ukuleles.

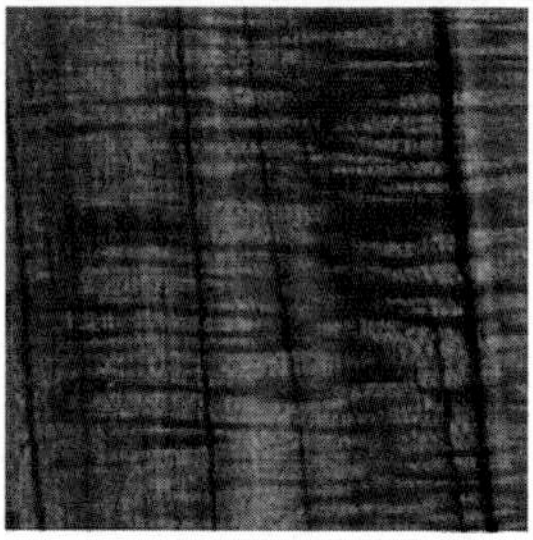

Koa wood

The o`hia's leaves and flowers were used in lei-making. The wood was sturdy enough to be used in construction. The o`hia is so beloved in Hawaiian culture that there are songs, chants and legends about the plant.

Kukui

Another important tree is the **kukui** or **candlenut tree**. The official state tree of Hawai`i was brought here by the Polynesians because of its many uses. The plant was used for medicinal purposes, fertilizer and to produce dye. The kukui nut contains an oil that can be burned and it was used to produce light. The flowers and nuts were also used to make leis.

Out of all of the islands in Hawai`i, Kaua`i is the place to come for **bird-watching**. Some credit the great bird-watching to the lack of **mongoose**s on Kaua`i. With the introduction of Western contact and eventually the commercialization of sugar, there was one critter that came along for the ride in ships – the rat. To eradicate the rats that were terrorizing the sugar fields, it was thought that the mongoose would do the job.

So mongooses were brought to the islands and it was then found that the rats were generally nocturnal and the mongoose were not. Mongooses did kill some rats, but certainly not enough to eradicate them. The mongoose did find a host of eggs and native birds to feast on. On some islands, the mongoose virtually destroyed the bird populations.

Fortunately, Kaua`i was spared most of this disaster. According to the story, a dock worker was bitten by a mongoose in a cage that was on its way to Kaua`i. In a fit of rage, the worker threw the cage into the water.

You can find the **nene**, a Hawaiian goose that's also the Hawaiian state bird. It is still an endangered species, but is growing in population, especially on Kaua`i.

Nenes

Other birds that you'll be able to spot are the **albatross**, **frigate birds**, the **red-tailed** and **white-tailed tropicbird**.

Kilauea Point

Great places to go for bird-watching are the **Kilauea Point National Wildlife Refuge**, **Hanalei National Wildlife Refuge** and **Koke`e State Park**.

The only mammals that came to Kaua`i on their own are the **Hawaiian monk seal** and the **hoary bat**. Both species are endangered today.

One thing that you're sure to find on Kaua`i is an abundance of marine life. There's nothing like snorkeling a few feet from shore and seeing a huge, graceful turtle peacefully swimming underneath you.

The **green sea turtle**, or **honu**, feeds on limu (algae). They can be four feet long and weigh up to 400 pounds. The average honu lives to be about 80 years old.

Honu

The honu is protected by the Endangered Species Act of 1979. If you see them in the water, you're required to give them 10-15 feet of space and it is against the law to touch or harass them.

If you happen to be on Kaua`i between the months of November and April, you will probably have at least one opportunity to see the majestic **humpback whale**. Whale-watching is one of the most popular activities on Kaua`i during this time as folks love to see whales blow, breach and slap various parts of their bodies against the water.

Humpback whale

Humpback whales spend the summer in waters off Alaska then they migrate to the warmer tropical waters, where they breed and nurse their calves.

The **Kilauea Point National Wildlife Refuge**, the **Kalalau hiking trail**, and **Po`ipu Beach** are great spots to see humpback whales from land. On a few days during this season, the National Marine Sanctuary records the number of whales sighted from certain points on shore. If you're lucky enough to see the Sanctuary Count, volunteers are available to answer questions about the count and about the whales. You can find out more by visiting www.hawaiihumpback-whale.noaa.gov.

The **Hawaiian monk seal** is a critically endangered animal that makes its primary home in the Northwestern Hawaiian Islands. Some also make their way to Kaua`i and are occasionally found lying on the beach.

Hawaiian monk seal (Kaua`i Visitors Bureau)

The Hawaiian monk seal population plummeted 50% between the 1950s and early 1970s In 1976, it was placed on the endangered species list. Their population is now about 1,200. If you see a monk seal, observe it from a safe distance – at least 50 yards. It's illegal to harass, touch or play with them. For more information about this special animal, visit www.kauaimonkseal.com.

Humuhumunukunukuapua`a

There are also approximately 680 species of fish in the Hawaiian Island chain. You can see quite a few of them in the water. You can find colorful reef fish like the **humuhumunukunukuapua`a**, Hawai`i's state fish, **octopi**, **crabs**, **sea urchins** and **lobsters**.

■ The People & Culture

The people of Hawai`i have a rich culture dating back to ancient times. Today, we see a rebirth of this culture and a resurgence in the use of the Hawaiian language as people get in touch with what it means to be Hawaiian.

The Lei

A symbol of Hawaiian culture is the lei. Thw word means garland or wreath. The history of the Hawaiian lei dates back to the ancient Hawaiians who offered them to each other and to their gods as a symbol of love and friendship.

From the 1800s the arrival of a ship was cause for celebration and for social events; family and friends meeting guests, press and photographers, music and hula. Lei sellers, arms draped with stands of ginger, ilima and carnations sold their leis for a quarter each on the pier.

Throughout the islands, that tradition continues. It's common to give leis for birthdays, speaking engagements, special performances, graduations, and virtually every other special occasion. If you're visiting a friend, odds are they'll greet you with a lei at the airport. If you watch a high school graduation, it's typical for graduates to be covered in leis up to their eyeballs.

A lei can be made from just about anything – flowers, leaves, there are even candy leis. The most popular leis tend to be made from plumeria, lehua blossoms, kukui nuts, orchids, or maile, shells. On Kaua`i, there's one special lei, the mokihana lei, which is made from mokihana berries, found only on this island.

The most common leis you're likely to see are plumeria, which have a lasting fragrance. There's also awapuhi (ginger flower). It is common for men to wear leis as well. They wear maile leis at weddings; it's an open lei made from the rare green maile leaves. Other common leis are tuberose and gardenia.

The correct way to wear a lei is draped over the shoulders, hanging down both in front and in back. If you are given more than one lei for the same occasion, wear them all. It's commonplace to wear multiple leis on your birthday or graduation. If you want to preserve your lei, wrap it in a paper towel and put it in the refrigerator.

Little girls with leis (Kaua`i Visitors Bureau)

On Kaua`i, culture consists of festivals, history, museums. During most weekends, you're likely to find festivals with music and hula. Later in this chapter, you'll find a list of annual festivals. Also check out the nightlife sections later on in the book.

The Population

In Hawai`i everyone is a minority. Hawai`i truly is a melting pot of cultures and ethnicities. The population of Hawai`i totals roughly 1.275 million people. Here's how it breaks down:

- 6.6% Native Hawaiian.
- 24.3% Caucasian, including Portuguese.
- 41.6% Asian, including 0.1% Asian Indian, 4.7% Chinese, 14.1% Filipino, 16.7% Japanese, 1.9% Korean and 0.6% Vietnamese.
- 1.3% Samoan, Tongan, Tahitian, Maori or Micronesian.
- 21.4% a mixture of two or more races/ethnic groups.
- 1.8% Black or African-American.
- 0.3% Native American or Alaska Native.

The population of Kaua`i County (Kaua`i and Ni`ihau) at time of publication was 62,640. Kaua`i County's ethnic population broke down as follows:

- 33.5% Caucasian.
- 0.4% African-American.

- 0.4% American Indian or Alaska Native.
- 35.6% Asian.
- 8.6% Native Hawaiian and other Pacific Islander.
- 21.5% mixed race.
- 8.6% Hispanic or Latino origin.

An influx of visitors also has an impact in the population. In 2005, Kaua`i hosted over 1.1 million visitors, a 6.8% increase from 2004. Kaua`i's top US visitor markets are Los Angeles, San Francisco, New York, Chicago, Seattle, San Diego, Phoenix, Denver, Sacramento and Dallas. Internationally, Kaua`i's top visitor market is Japan.

The Aloha Spirit

The most familiar aspect of the Hawaiian culture is the aloha spirit. In Hawaiian, the word aloha can mean many things, such as hello, goodbye, love, respect, even joyfully sharing life.

The aloha spirit is unique. It exemplifies friendliness, a spirit of hope and giving among the people of Hawai`i. It is shared with friends, family and guests alike. You'll be sure to feel the aloha spirit as soon as you step off the plane. It really is a way of life on Kaua`i and it's something you have to experience to believe and understand.

The aloha spirit means so much to the Hawaiian culture, that it's even a law in the state legislature. Well, it might not be an enforceable law, but it does serve as a guideline for all state representatives and it serves as a reminder of how legislators should conduct themselves. Here's what the "law" states:

THE ALOHA SPIRIT LAW

(a) The Aloha Spirit is the coordination of mind and heart within each person. It brings each person to the Self. Each person must think and emote good feelings to others. In the contemplation and presence of the life force, Aloha, the following unuhi laulâ loa (free translation) may be used:

- Akahai, meaning kindness, to be expressed with tenderness;
- Lôkahi, meaning unity, to be expressed with harmony;

- `Olu`olu, meaning agreeable, to be expressed with pleasantness;
- Ha`aha`a, meaning humility, to be expressed with modesty;
- Ahonui, meaning patience, to be expressed with perseverance.

These are traits of character that express the charm, warmth and sincerity of Hawai`i's people. It was the working philosophy of native Hawaiians and was presented as a gift to the people of Hawai`i.

Aloha is more than a word of greeting or farewell or a salutation. Aloha means mutual regard and affection and extends warmth in caring with no obligation in return.

Aloha is the essence of relationships in which each person is important to every other person for collective existence. Aloha means to hear what is not said, to see what cannot be seen and to know the unknowable.

(b) In exercising their power on behalf of the people and in fulfillment of their responsibilities, obligations and service to the people, the legislature, governor, lieutenant governor, executive officers of each department, the chief justice, associate justices, and judges of the appellate, circuit, and district courts may contemplate and reside with the life force and give consideration to The Aloha Spirit.

Island Time

Hawai`i Standard Time is +10 hours Greenwich Mean Time (GMT). Hawai`i Standard Time is in effect year-around, as we don't observe Daylight Savings Time. When the mainland observes standard time from November through March, Hawai`i is two hours behind Pacific Standard Time and five hours behind Eastern Standard Time. In other words, when it's noon in Hawai`i, it's 2 pm in California and 5 pm in New York. During Daylight Savings Time, Hawai`i is three hours behind California and six hours behind New York. So between April and October, when it's noon in Hawai`i, it's 3 pm in California and 6 pm in New York.

One aspect of Hawaiian culture you're almost guaranteed to experience during your visit is affectionately known as "island time." It's a nod to the laid-back culture throughout the islands. If you're a prompt person, you may have a bit of an adjustment ahead of you. My advice – you're on vacation – leave your watch at home. This is just a fair warning. Some things start right on time. Some things don't. There's no hurry, as most people don't really need to get anywhere. Relax, you're on holiday. Don't be shocked if the schedule says that an event starts in 15 minutes, but actually takes 30 minutes to get underway. It's just part of that laid-back island style.

Kaua`i In Films

During your stay in Kaua`i, you might think that certain mountains or landscapes look familiar, even though you've never been here before. It's very possible you've seen it in a film or TV show. Kaua`i has appeared in more than 75 movies and television shows. The powers that be in Hollywood, ranging from Steven Spielberg to Elvis Presley, agreed that Kaua`i is a shooting great location.

Jurassic Park Velociraptor

MOVIES MADE ON KAUA`I	
2005 Band of Pirates Komodo vs Cobra Stitch-The Movie	1980 Seven
2003 Tears Of The Sun	1979 Last Flight of Noah's Ark
2002 Dragonfly Finding Brandon The Time Machine Lilo & Stitch	1978 Deathmoon Acapulco Gold

2001 Jurassic Park III Manhunt Moolah Beach The Time Machine	1977 Fantasy Island Islands in the Stream
2000 To End All Wars Dinosaur The Testaments	1976 King Kong
1998 6 Days / 7 Nights Mighty Joe Young	1974 Castaway Cowboy
1997 George of the Jungle The Lost World: Jurassic Park	1970 The Hawaiians
1995 Outbreak	1969 Lost Flight
1994 North	1968 Yoake No Futare Lovers at Dawn
1993 Jurassic Park	1966 Lt. Robin Crusoe, U.S.N.
1992 Honeymoon in Vegas	1965 Operation Attack None but the Brave Paradise Hawaiian Style
1991 Hook	1964 Gilligan's Island
1990 Flight of the Intruder Lord of the Flies	1963 Donovan's Reef
1989 Millennium	1962 Diamond Head Sanga Ari
1988 Lady in White	1961 Blue Hawai`i Seven Women from Hell
1987 Throw Momma from the Train	1960 The Wackiest Ship in the Army
1986 Islands of the Alive	1959 Forbidden Island
1983 The Thorn Birds Uncommon Valor Body Heat Raiders of the Lost Ark	1958 South Pacific She Gods of Shark Reef

Most of the tours on Kaua`i are bound to reference various film locations, whether it's the familiar scenery in Raiders of the Lost Ark or the Jurassic Park series. If you are interested in a tour of different movie locations, there are a few companies that provide them. **Hawai`i Movie Tours**, www.kauaimovietours.com, ☎ 800-628-8432 or 808-822-1192, offers tours that take you around the island in a mobile theater, so you can visit the locations while you're watching the scenes from the films in which they appear. They offer three different types of tours daily. They're open from 7:30 am to 6 pm daily.

If you want to go at it on your own, you can purchase the ***Kaua`i Movie Book***. It's by Chris Cook and David Boynton and is a driving guide to movie locations. It's pretty detailed and has movie location maps. It illustrates how different locations throughout the island were chosen to substitute for places like Africa, or a South American rainforest and it includes great photographs. You can also check out the **Kaua`i Film Commission**'s website at www.FilmKaua`i.com.

Music

When most people think of Hawaiian music, they immediately think of the `ukulele or Elvis. Many influences are involved due to the immigrant population. For instance, did you know that the `ukulele isn't a native Hawaiian instrument? It's actually from Portuguese immigrants who brought the instrument to here. These different styles blended with religious chants to create the melodic sounds of Hawaiian music today.

Hawaiian music has its own distinct feel and sound. There's certainly a laid-back element to it. There are several kinds of local music. There are ancient chants or mele (songs) that you'll hear during a kahiko (ancient) hula. There's the hapa-haole style that is reminiscent of Elvis or Bing Crosby. The hapa-haole songs will probably seem more familiar as they blend Hawaiian music with English lyrics. Then there's today's popular style, which is referred to as Jawaiian. It's a fusion of Hawaiian music and Reggae. Then of course, there's that Hawaiian institution – the legendary Don Ho. Tiny Bubbles, anyone?

Today, groups like Hapa and Na Leo Pilimehana are popular throughout the islands. Ukulele virtuoso Jake Shimabukuro is taking the `ukulele to new heights with his blazing speed and rock/pop influence. He has a following not only in Hawai`i, but in Japan as well. He's gaining popularity in the mainland US too after a major tour there and an appearance on the David Letterman show. Another popular artist is Israel "Bruddah Iz" Kamakawiwo'ole, whose music lives on even though he passed away in 1997. His cover of *Over the Rainbow* has been heard in films like *Finding Forrester* and on the TV show *E.R.*

Jake Shimabukuro

One of the more popular and familiar standard songs in Hawai`i is *Aloha Oe* (Farewell to Thee). It was written by the last reigning monarch of Hawai`i, Queen Lilioukolani.

Hawaiian music even has its own category at the Grammy Awards. *Slack Key Guitar, Volume 2*, a compilation of slack key guitar greats, brought home the first-ever Grammy for Hawaiian Music at the 2005 awards ceremony. In 2006, slack key guitar won again with *Masters of Hawaiian Slack Key Guitars - Vol. 1*.

Hula

Hula dancers in the 1890s

How can you think of Hawai`i and not think of the hula? Pretty impossible, right? There are considered to be two types of hula: modern and kahiko, or ancient-style. Hula is for everyone – women, men, and children. Further along in the book, I'll show you places where you can learn hula during your stay on Kaua`i.

Hula girls 1910

More than just a swaying island dance in a grass skirt, the hula began as a means of worship and storytelling through chants. Hula is a language as much as a dance. All parts of the body tell stories of gods, ali`i (chiefs or royalty) and nature. Kaua`i was once the site of the most prestigious hula school in all of the islands and people would travel from all over Hawai`i to Kaua`i to learn hula.

Kahiko hula has it roots in ancient times. This is learned in halau (hula schools) across the islands and even across the world. Kahiko hula has a primal and intense energy on its own as a team of dancers share stories of Hawaiian myths through chants and primal rhythms.

Modern hula is what you typically think of when you imagine hula: a lone, lovely woman with long, flowing hair, flower behind her ear, backed up by a standing bass player, guitarist, and `ukulele player. This harkens back the relaxed pre-World War II days or Waikiki, at the beginning of its tourism boom.

Hula actually almost disappeared completely in the early 1800s. The missionaries banned it because they didn't understand its significance to the Hawaiian people and because it was deemed sinful.

Later on in the century, King David Kalakaua – The Merrie Monarch – formed his own dance company and encouraged others to learn the hula. This began the resurgence of hula. King Kalakaua's efforts are still recognized with the Merrie Monarch Festival, an international hula competition held every April in Hilo on the Big Island.

Myths & Legends

Hawaiian folklore is steeped in mythical gods and goddesses. Much as with the ancient Greek and Roman pantheons, Hawaiians had a god for everything. Maui was the god of the sun, Pele was the goddess of fire. The most popular stories that live on today are the stories of Maui and Pele.

Tiki woodcarvings

Pele is known as the volcanic goddess with a fiery temper. There are a few stories that tell how Pele wound up in Hawai`i. One tells how she was born into a family of 13 siblings, her parents the Earth mother Haumea and Moemoe, god of the sky in Tahiti. She was exiled from Tahiti by her father and her sister, Namakaokahai, for seducing her sister's husband. Pele first landed on Kaua`i and was considered to be among the first to come to here. She tried to dig a home for herself, but found it difficult as her sister Namakaokahai kept filling the holes with water. Having no luck on Kaua`i, she traveled to O`ahu, Moloka`i, Maui, until she finally found a home for herself in Kilauea on the Big Island.

There is a legend about taking rocks from The Big Island's Hawai`i Volcanoes National Park. Visitors are warned not to take lava rocks from the land, or else you have a sting of bad luck upon your return home. This was actually the creation of a park ranger. The park receives a large number of packages every year containing lava rocks taken from previous trips to the Big Island.

Maui is another god you may hear of during your visit to Kaua`i. Maui is said to have created the Hawaiian Islands. He was fishing with his brothers and his hook was caught on the ocean floor. He told his brothers that he had a big fish and the brothers needed to paddle so Maui could pull this big fish up. The brothers paddled and paddled but, instead of a fish rising from the ocean, it was an island. Maui was able to trick the brothers several more times in the same way, and that's how the Hawaiian Islands were created. Today, Maui's fishhook can be seen in the night sky as part of the constellation Scorpius.

There's another story about Maui that involves the sun. Maui's mother Hina once complained that the sun moved to fast. Maui went to the top of Haleakala on the island of Maui, lassoed the sun with a rope and made it promise to go slower.

Kaua`i has its own legends of the Menehune or little people. Even though this legend is throughout the Hawaiian Islands, it's on Kaua`i where the Menehune are most at home. The Menehune are similar to elves, fairies or leprechauns, with a mischievous reputation. Even today, if your keys have mysteriously disappeared or if your car won't start, it's pretty common to say that the Menehune had something to do with it.

Not only are the Menehune a fun people, they're also great builders. This legendary race is credited with building the Alekoko Fishpond near Nawiliwili harbor, just outside of Lihu`e. This structure was built from a stone wall measuring 900 feet long and five feet high. The most amazing part about this story was that the Menehune completed construction in just one night. It was built to honor the prince and princess of Kaua`i.

The Menehune are also credited for building the Menehune Ditch in Waimea. Also built in one night, it was created upon request from the island's high chief to get water to his people's taro fields. It's an aqueduct made by cutting and dressing the stones, transporting them, and fitting them into place, using a fireman's bucket brigade-type system.

The Menehune are afraid of owls. When they get out of control and cause too much chaos, the owl god, Paupueo, sends all the owls to chase them back into the forest.

Some historians suggest that the Menehune are an actual race of people. It is thought that they are descendants of the first settlers of Hawai`i from the Marquesas Islands. These descendants were then overtaken by the larger Tahitians when they arrived.

Some stories say that there were once over a half-million Menehune on Kaua`i. A census taken in the 1800s found 65 people in Wainiha that considered themselves to be Menehune and put that as their nationality.

waiian Language

English and Hawaiian are the two official languages. eryone speaks English on Kaua`i, but if you listen local music or if you hang out long enough at the local restaurants, you're bound to hear Hawaiian, as well as the unofficial language of the islands – pidgin.

Even though English is the primary language throughout the islands, there has been a resurgence of the native language in the past 25 years and Hawaiian words are interspersed in daily life and conversation.

In 1984, the first Hawaiian-language pre-school opened on Kaua`i. Now, there are a dozen pre-schools and over 20 Hawaiian-language immersion schools and charter schools throughout the state. Hawaiian is often spoken by people of all ages and backgrounds.

The Hawaiian language was an oral tradition until the missionaries helped make it a written language in the early 1800s. It consists of five vowels –a, e, i, o, u – and seven consonants – h, k, l, m, n, p and w.

It tends to be easier to pronounce Hawaiian words if you remember to pronounce all the vowels. In that sense, it's similar to Spanish or Italian.

In some schools of thought, there is an eighth consonant – the okina. The okina (`), is a glottal stop where your breath stops briefly between the two parts. For example, in English, it's like saying oh-oh.

Consonants are pronounced the same way in English, with the exception of the letter w, which can sometimes be pronounced as v. Here are some words and phrases you'll probably come across during your trip:

A hui hou . . . . Until we meet again
Ahupua`a Division of land stretching from mountains to sea
Aina . . . . Land, earth
Akamai . . . . Smart, clever
Ali`i . . . . Hawaiian royalty
Aloha . . . . Hello, goodbye, respect, love
Ewa . . . . Westward
Halau . . . . Hula school
Hale. . . . . House or building
Hana . . . . Work
Hana hou . . . . To work again, encore
Haole . . . . Caucasian, foreigner
Hapa . . . . Half, also refers to person of mixed ethnicities

Heiau . . . . Ancient Hawaiian religious temple
Honu . . . . Green sea turtle
Hula . . . . Hawaiian dance
Humuhumunukunukuapua`a . . . . State fish
Huhu . . . . Angry, agitated
Imu . . . . Underground pit oven used in luau
Kai . . . . Ocean, ocean water
Kalo or taro . . . Type of starch, staple of the Hawaiian diet
Kama'aina . . . . One of this land, long time resident
Kahuna . . . . Priest, expert in a field
Kane. . . . . Man
Kapu . . . . Forbidden, restriction
Koa. . . . . Native tree
Kokua . . . . Help
Kuleana . . . . Responsibility
Lei . . . . Necklace made of flowers, leaves, or shells
Lolo . . . . Crazy, stupid
Luau . . . . Feast
Mahalo . . . . Thank you
Mahimahi . . . . Dolphinfish
Makahiki . . . . Annual Hawaiian celebration
Mana . . . . Spiritual energy
Mauka. . . . . Toward the mountains
Moana . . . . Ocean, sea
Nene . . . . State bird, a type of goose
Ohana . . . . Family
Ono . . . . Delicious
Paniolo. . . . . Cowboy
Pau hana . . . . End of the work day, done with work
Puka. . . . . Hole
Pupu. . . . . Hors d'oeuvre, appetizer
Wahine . . . . Woman
Wikiwiki . . . . Quickly

Pidgin

In Hawai`i, you'll hear the colorful local slang, called pidgin – a cross between Hawaiian and English. The majority of the words and phrases are versions of English slang, with words from the other languages that make up pidgin, making it sound like very poor use of English.

Hawaiian Pidgin came about when sugar cane was the dominant industry in Hawai`i. The native Hawaiian population was nearly decimated by diseases introduced through Western contact, and the plantation owners recruited cheap labor from places like China, Japan, Korea, Portugal and the Philippines.

With so many people from so many different cultures and languages, Pidgin evolved as a way for the laborers and plantation owners to communicate with each other. It's made up of mostly Hawaiian and English, along with words from every ethnic group in the plantation work-force.

It can be hard to understand at first, but if you stay on Kaua`i for any time, it's sure to rub off on you. You might find yourself saying things like "talk story" or "bummers" before your journey ends.

Here are a couple of examples of Hawaiian pidgin.

No can . . . . Cannot
Stink eye . . . . Dirty look, evil eye
Talk stink . . . . Speaking bad about someone
Wat doing? . . . . What are you doing?
An Den . . . . What happened next, "And then"
Brah/bruddah . . . "Brother" or "pal." Example: "Eh, brah!"
Broke da mout' . . . . Delicious tasting
Bumbye . . . . Later on
Bummahs . . "Bummer" – term expressing disappointment
Bussum Out . . . . I what some, share with me
Bussup . . . . Broken, worn out, or screwed up
Check U'm Out . . . . Check it out
Chicken skin . . . . Goose bumps
Choke . . . . Plenty, lots
Da kine . Typically used when you're referring to something or someone you can't remember.
Eh, brah! . . . . Heh!
Fo' What . . . . Why? How come? "For what"
Fo' Real . . . . Are you sure? "For real"
Give 'um . . . . Go for it dude, try your hardest
Grind . . . . To eat

Grinds	Good food
Hana Hou	One more time, do it again
Hawaiian Time	To be late
Hele On	Let's go, get moving
Howzit	How are you? How've you been?
Like dis; like dat	Like this or like that
(What) Like Beef	Do you want to fight? You better run if someone says this to you.
Lolo	Dumb, slow, crazy, does not make sense
Lua	Bathroom
Moke	Big, tough local
Nevah	Never
Okole	Buttocks, Butt
Pau	Finished
Pilau	Dirty
Shoots	Alright, of course
Talk story	Conversation at length

There are a couple of books out there the can help decode this mysterious language. Among them are *Pidgin to Da Max* by Douglas Simonson, Pat Sasaki, Ken Sakata. Oh yeah, there's even a translation of The New Testament in Pidgin, called *Da Jesus Book*.

Dining

Dining in Hawai`i can be a pleasant and unique experience. Sometimes, a local meal can be an adventure in itself. Dining experiences tend to be a melting pot of flavors and influences, particularly American, Chinese, Filipino, Japanese, Korean, Polynesian and Portuguese, the same way the population in Hawai`i is a melting pot of cultures.

There are a number of local favorites that you must try while you're here. They range from a plate lunch, shave ice, lau lau, malasadas, and the one thing have to try at least once while you're in Hawai`i – poi.

First and foremost, you'll find the local staple – the **plate lunch**. The plate lunch typically consists of a large serving of meat, which could be anything ranging from mochiko chicken, teriyaki chicken, or teriyaki beef. Add two scoops of rice (one scoop of rice if you order a mini-plate) and a scoop of macaroni salad and you're all set.

For breakfast, there's also the **loco moco**. This heart attack special is a hamburger patty with a fried egg on top, two scoops of rice and Spam or Portuguese sausage. It may not be the healthiest thing in the world, but it is something to try at least once. After all, when in Rome....

Loco moco

Shave ice

Shave ice is very much like a snow cone you'd see on the mainland. Since we don't have snow here, we had to resort to a different name. Shave ice (note that it's not "shaved ice") is made up of, you guessed it, shaved ice tightly packed and covered in flavored syrup. You can get the typical flavors such as strawberry and grape, but I'd recommend going for something a bit more adventurous. Try tropical flavors such as banana, mango, guava, lilikoi (passion fruit), pineapple, coconut or papaya.

Malasadas tend to make a great breakfast, snack or even dessert. They're fried dough balls rolled in sugar or cinnamon and served hot. Malasadas were introduced by Portuguese immigrants who were working the plantation fields in the late 1800s and the tasty treat has been here ever since.

Malasadas

Poke

Another local favorite is **poke**, a traditional Hawaiian dish that contains cubed raw fish or seafood mixed with seaweed, sea salt, chili peppers and shoyu (soy sauce).You're most likely to find ahi (tuna) poke or tako (octopus) poke. Don't worry, the tako is cooked, so it won't be slimy.

For more traditional Hawaiian fare, nothing can beat the **lu`au**. This celebratory feast got its current name from the taro leaves, also called lu`au, that are served at the festivities. Taro leaves are cooked with squid and coconut milk, and are also used to wrap meats and fish, which are then steamed to make laulau. **Kalua pig**, slow-cooked in an imu – a traditional underground pit oven – and **poi**, a dish of mashed, cooked taro root, are both classics.

If you're looking for fine dining, there are also plenty of options. Chefs such as Sam Choy, Roy Yamaguchi and Alan Wong, among several other chefs, in 1991 created a "**Hawai`i Regional Cuisine**" in 1991, which put Hawai`i on the international fine dining map.

Hawai`i Regional Cuisine uses fresh Hawaiian-grown ingredients and may include items such as herb-crusted onaga, green curry Keahole lobster, seared Hawaiian ahi with lilikoi shrimp butter, guava-smoked Kahua ranch lamb, blackened ahi summer rolls, Pahoa corn cakes, gourmet Waimanalo greens and vine-ripened tomatoes.

Still, strangely enough, Hawai`i is the **Spam** capital of the United States. Hawai`i consumes more Spam per capita than any place in the US. That amounts to four cans of Spam per capita per year. No one's really sure how or why Spam became so popular, but it's believed that during World War II, when fresh meat was scarce, the locals loaded up on Spam, which has the half-life of kryptonite. Spam's so popular throughout the islands that some McDonald's added Spam to their breakfast menu. The most popular way to eat spam is Spam musubi, a slice of Spam on top of rice wrapped in nori (seaweed).

Shoreline from Hanalei to Ke`e Beach, with protective reef

Travel Information

■ When To Go

There are two types of seasons in Kaua`i, one just for tourists and the other according to climate. The peak tourist seasons are from mid-December to Easter, then again from mid-June to Labor Day. Prices increase for hotel rooms, rental cars become harder to reserve and everything moves a bit faster. You'll want to shop around online. Package deals that include discounts on published rates are available.

IN THIS CHAPTER

Here are a few questions you should ask yourself that will help determine the ideal time for you to visit:

- **What do you really want to do on Kaua`i?** If you want to get away from the cold mainland and don't care what you do on Kaua`i, then by all means, show up in the winter months. Be aware that it is Kaua`i's rainy season. It doesn't mean that every day is rainy, but there's a higher chance of rain. For the most part, it's still sunny and warm and you'll go back home with a nice tan.
- **Do you want to see the humpback whales?** If this is what you're on Kaua`i for, then the months from Novem-

ber-March are for you. The peak of whale season tends to be mid-January through mid-February.

- **Do you want to spend a lot of time in the water snorkeling, surfing, or just plain old horsing around?** If so, I recommend coming during the summer months. The waters tend to be calmer than in winter. The water is also a bit more refreshing, especially if you've been walking around on a rather hot day.
- **Would you prefer to be here when there aren't that many other people?** The peak seasons for tourists are during the summer months and from mid-December to Easter. There are fewer people at other times. For many, the off-season is the best time to visit. The camping sites, hiking trails and other attractions are much less crowded.

No matter when you decide to come, make your reservations well in advance – especially if you plan to visit during the peak tourist seasons. Rental agencies do run out of cars during busy times of the year such as 4th of July weekend and other major holidays. If you have special needs, definitely make reservations in advance.

■ What To Pack

How to Dress

Leave your suit and tie at home! If you must bring a suit, make it the Hawaiian three-piece suit: slippers (most people call them flip-flops or thongs), shorts and an aloha shirt. Even in the finer establishments on the island, resort wear is acceptable. When packing your suitcase, start off with clothes that are comfortable and light and are appropriate for the activities you want to do while you're here.

For daytime activities, you certainly don't want to leave home without your swimsuit and sunglasses. If you wear a hat to block the sun, be sure to bring it with you. For exploring around town and going to a restaurant for lunch, you'll be just fine with shorts, slippers and a short-sleeve shirt. You're probably going to do quite a bit of walking, exploring the different towns on the island. Be sure to bring comfortable shoes.

If you plan on doing some hiking, bring hiking shoes or shoes that will be comfortable in rocky terrain. Don't plan on hiking in sandals; they probably won't cut it on certain rough trails. Also bring a light, long-sleeve shirt and long pants in case the trail is overgrown or for the cooler weather in higher elevations.

If you're planning on stepping out in the evening, casual pants or jeans and a casual shirt are standard in most places. If you plan to spend an evening in one of the finer restaurants, then go with casual pants and a sport coat for men and for women a dress or skirt and top.

Tip: It's custom in Hawai`i to take off your shoes when entering a home. This doesn't apply to most hotel rooms, but is mostly practiced at bed & breakfasts, vacation rentals and condominiums.

What Can I Bring?

Despite what you might have seen in the film *Snakes on a Plane*, the snakes could not have possibly been from Hawai`i. Hawai`i does not have snakes. Geckos, yes. Snakes, frogs and other reptiles, no. These reptiles can cause irreparable harm to Hawai`i's incredibly sensitive environment. For this reason, you have to go through some unusual precautions when flying to and from Hawai`i. During your flight, you will be required by state law to complete an agricultural declaration form. This is handed out by your flight crew toward the end of your flight.

You have to declare items such as fresh fruits and vegetables, plants and animals, virtually anything agricultural, and submit them for inspection to a Hawai`i Plant Quarantine Inspector in the baggage claim area.

When you leave Hawai`i, you have to put your bags through an agricultural inspection. You'll see the inspection stations just before the check-in lines. This is only if you're taking fruit, vegetables and plants that are not approved for travel. If you want to take pineapples home, you can purchase boxes at the airport that are already approved, boxed and ready for you to take home.

For further information on bringing plants and animals into the state, be sure to visit the Hawai`i State Department of

Agriculture's Quarantine Office website: www.hawaiiag.org/hdoa/doa_importing.htm.

In terms of federally mandated security, the items you can and cannot take on board changes frequently. Can you take liquids and gels with you on the plane or not? Your best bet is to check out the Department of Homeland Security website, www.dhs.gov, and the Transportation Security Authority, www.tsa.gov, for the latest information.

Accommodations

For a small island, Kaua`i offers a wide variety of accommodations, from a five-star resort to a quiet bed and breakfast or even a hostel. Before making your reservations, you should think about what you want from the place where you stay. Do you want to just show up and have everything done for you? Are you traveling on a budget? Do you want extreme privacy? Are you going to spend a lot of time in the unit, or will you spend most of your time sightseeing? Here's a quick rundown of the types of accommodations you'll find on Kaua`i.

Hotel prices given in this guide are based on double-occupancy, not including taxes or added fees.

Hotels

A hotel in Hawai`i is pretty much the same as a hotel anywhere else. Most hotels offer daily maid service, a pool, restaurant and bar and concierge services, as well as a few shops. Hotels are generally convenient, but you also might have to put up with the occasional loud high school volleyball team visiting during spring break. They do offer some privacy, but not too much. Hotels work if you don't plan on staying for a long time or if you plan on eating out during your stay.

Resorts

Resorts are great if you want the best of everything and everything done for you. All you have to is show up. Golf and tennis won't be too far away and some resorts provide activities just for kids. You'll usually see a day-spa, fitness center, beach access, room service, multiple restaurants and bars. The conveniences are great, but you certainly will get what you pay for. Some places do call themselves resorts, but they do not provide everything for you. Check before you make your reservations.

Condos

Condos are a wonderful option if you plan on staying for a long period or you have a sizeable group. Condos tend to be more private than hotels and come with fully stocked kitchens, and enough space to accommodate quite a few people. Most properties do not have daily maid service but do offer some sort of housekeeping services for an additional fee. Condos are more cost-effective than hotels or resorts, especially if you're with a lot of people. A lot of condo units are individually owned, so you won't find the same furniture and kitchen equipment in the different units.

Bed & Breakfasts

Bed & breakfasts on Kaua`i are like those you'd find anywhere else. They offer several rooms in a home, with breakfast served at a specific time in the morning. There are a couple of places that call themselves bed and breakfasts but that are really vacation rentals with everything you need to make your own breakfast. B&Bs are great if you want to meet other visitors, and you want an inexpensive option. There is a lack of privacy and you do have to share space with others, perhaps a bathroom.

Vacation Rentals

Vacation rentals are homes that owners rent out to others who want a home away from home. They're great if you want privacy. It can be a condo unit in a high-rise complex or an entire house. Most vacation rentals have parking, fully stocked kitchens, laundry facilities, TV, VCR/DVD player and stereo. It's a great option if you're on the island for a wedding or family reunion or if you plan to stay on the island for a while. Vacation rentals tend to be ideal if you want plenty of privacy.

No matter when you book your accommodations, be sure to ask about additional charges. Some places might charge a resort fee or a housekeeping fee. There's also a 7.25% accommodations tax, plus a 4.166% general excise tax.

Hawai`i does not have a sales tax; instead, we have the general **excise tax**, assessed on all business activities, including retail sales, commissions, rental income, and services at 4.166%. This tax, of course, is passed on to you, the consumer.

Dining

Dining experiences here tend to be a melting pot of flavors and influences, particularly American, Chinese, Filipino, Japanese, Korean, Polynesian and Portuguese.

Don't' forget to tip! If the service was good, a 15-20% tip is standard. If the service was excellent, then tip 20-25%.

I'm sure you've heard that Hawai`i is a pretty expensive place. You may suffer from sticker shock upon your first trip to the grocery store. You'll find that everything – gas, food, milk and even movie tickets – is more expensive here than most places. That's just the "Price of Paradise."

Restaurant prices given in this guide include pupu (appetizer), entrée and dessert. Drinks, taxes and tip are extra.

MONEY SAVER

If you're looking for an easy way to get discounts on tours, adventures and meals, look no further than the **Activity and Attractions Association of Hawai`i** (A3H). It's a nonprofit trade association of almost 200 activity and tour operators throughout the Hawai`i. A3H offers opportunities to get discounted adventures.

If you're a Hawai`i resident, go to www.kama`aina.org, where you can get discounts of up to 50%. Proof of residency is required.

So how do you get these discounts? A3H offers its own gold card. It's like a credit card and it costs $30, which will give you and up to three others a 10%-25% discount on activities from A3H members. You can see a list of the vendors at www.hawaiifun.org. If you're a gold card member, you can make your reservations online before you leave for your trip.

Let's say that you're on Kaua`i with your sweetheart. You buy the card for $30 and you book a tour for kayaking that costs $100. Assume that you get 20% off per person. That's $20 each. The card already saved you $10 . And that's from only one tour. If you're there with your family, you must buy this card. It will pay for itself time and time again.

If you're also going to places like Maui or O`ahu during your trip, this card is a must. A3H has more vendors on these islands than on Kaua`i, so it makes a lot of sense to purchase the card if you plan to take a few tours and adventures.

For more information, visit the websites mentioned above or contact A3H at ☎ 808-871-7947 or info@hawaiifun.org.

■ Banks

$ The main banks on Kaua`i are Bank of Hawai`i, First Hawai`i Bank, Central Pacific Bank, and Territorial Savings Bank. Banks are open Monday through Friday, 8:30 am-4:30 pm. Some banks are open later on Fridays and Saturdays. If you need to exchange currency, you can go to the main branches of the banks.

You'll find branch offices in the main towns on the island and ATMs everywhere.

■ Post Offices

Post offices are located in the main towns throughout Kaua`i. They're generally open from 8-4 and some are open on Saturdays from 9-12.

If you absolutely need to get something in the mail, another option is the **Mail Service Center** in the Princeville Shopping Center. They provide postal services, shipping, packaging supplies and services, e-mail access and copy machines.

■ Libraries

Hawai`i's State Library System is probably onc of the state's best-kept secrets. Want to rent a movie? Forget Blockbuster, take a trip to your local library. For $1 a week, you can rent DVDs and VHS tapes. Most libraries have a pretty current selection to choose from, but the it does vary from location to location. You can also access the Internet from the library.

For visitors, there are two non-resident cards available. There's the $25 non-resident card good for five years. You have the option to renew it for an additional $25. There's also a $10 visitor card that's good for three months but it can't be renewed.

You can apply for a library card by visiting any public library. You'll fill out an application and present your identification to the staff member. They'll give you a card on the spot, which will enable you to take out books and videos. You can go to www.librarieshawaii.org for membership information, location information and hours. You can also access the state library system's catalog from here as well to request items. On Kaua`i, you'll find libraries in Hanapepe, ☎ 808-335-8418, Kapa`a, ☎ 808-821-4422, Koloa, ☎ 808-742-8455, Lihu`e, ☎ 808-241-3222, Princeville, ☎ 808-826-4310, and Waimea, ☎ 808-338-6848.

■ Holidays

During your stay on Kaua`i, you might find that banks are closed on odd days that are holidays only here in Hawai`i. Here's a rundown of public holidays.

New Year's Day	January 1
Martin Luther King Day	Third Monday in January
President's Day	Third Monday in February
Kuhio Day	March 26 (birthday of Prince Jonah Kuhio Kalanianaole)
Memorial Day	Last Monday in May
Lei Day	May 1
Kamehameha Day	June 11
Independence Day	July 4
Admissions Day	Third Friday in August (when Hawai`i became the 50th state)
Veteran's Day	November 11
Thanksgiving	Last Thursday in November
Christmas	December 25

Festivals On Kaua`i

A great way to explore the culture of Hawai`i is by taking a look at any of the festivals that occur throughout the year. You'll get a feel for local living on Kaua`i, plus these festivals tend to be very family-friendly.

The festivals incorporate many cultures and influences. There are festivals that focus on Native Hawaiian traditions and Hawaiian monarchs. There are also music concerts, lei contests, and hula competitions. Japanese festivals include bon dances at Buddhist temples, cultural and art fairs, and events centered on Okinawan culture.

The Kaua`i Visitors Bureau recently launched a web-site that gives you up-to-date information about Kaua`i's festivals. You can get the latest information about what's happening on Kaua`i at **www.kauaifestivals.com**.

January

The **Inspiration Wellness Expo** is a resource for learning about holistic living through lectures and workshops. Health professionals throughout Kaua`i gather for two days so you can learn how to combine Eastern and Western medicine to lead a healthy and balanced life. In 2006, *New York Times* best-selling author Barbara DeAngelis gave the keynote address. It takes place at the Kaua`i War Memorial. ☎ 808-652-4328 or visit www.inspirationjournal.com.

February

The **Waimea Town Celebration** is sponsored by the West Kaua'i Business & Professional Association and serves as a fundraiser for local groups, including the Hawaiian Civic Club, Waimea high school clubs, Lions and Rotary clubs and area sports groups. You'll find plenty of events associated with the festival, including Lappert's Ice Cream Eating Contest, Kilohana Canoe Race, a 5K Fun Run, a Ukulele Contest and a silent auction. It's held every year on the Friday and Saturday following President's Day weekend. Contact PO Box 903, Waimea, Kaua`i, Hawai`i 96796, or visit www.wkbpa.org. You can also e-mail info@wkbpa.org to request more information.

March

The **Prince Kuhio Festival** is dedicated to one of Kaua`i's favorite sons. Every year, there are festivities held in several locations throughout the island. The largest is held at the Grand Hyatt in Po`ipu.

Prince Kuhio

In Lihu`e, Prince Kuhio Park hosts a series of games, a 10K run and a royal ball in period dress. In the morning, The Order of Kamehameha typically conducts a commemorative festival in the morning. Members of the order wear semi-formal suits with symbols of royalty, including colorful capes, while the Order's women's auxiliary wear long, white dresses.

The **Garden Island Orchid Society Spring Fantasy Show** is held in mid-March at the United Church of Christ in Hanapepe. In addition to the floral displays, there is a plant and craft sale. There is no entrance fee.

April

Buddha Day is also known as Wesak and is celebrated on the Sunday closest to April 8. The Kaua`i Buddhist Council (comprised of the nine Buddhist temples on the island) sponsors events ranging from dances and flower shows to pageants. Offerings of tropical flowers are placed at temple altars for the Buddha's birthday.

**Kaua`i Historical Society Royal Paina** works to perpetuate the history of Kaua`i and Ni`ihau. This is an evening full of food, history, and entertainment. There's a silent auction, dinner and dancing. There is an admission fee and advance purchase of tickets is recommended. www.kauaihistoricalsociety.com, ☎ 808-245-3373 or e-mail info@kauaihistoricalsociety.org.

The **Hapa Haole Hula Competition** features talent from the hospitality industry. It's an annual fundraiser for the Kaua'i Mokihana Festival and the Visitor Industry Charity

Walk. Groups and solo performers compete in three divisions: Halau, Hotel and Business. There is an admission fee. For more information, check out the Kaua`i Mokihana Festival's website at mokihana.kauai.net.

May

May Day is **Lei Day** in Hawai`i. Traditional lei-making takes place all over the islands and the best place to view the intricate craftsmanship is at the Kaua`i Museum. They hold a lei contest every Lei Day. And it's a great opportunity to give a lei and get lei'd. www.kauaimuseum.org, ☎ 808-245-6931.

Lei Day

Kilauea Point & Lighthouse

Lighthouse Day celebrates the anniversary of Kilauea Lighthouse with entertainment, activities and the unveiling of a new NOAA geodetic marker. Sponsored by the Hawaiian Islands Humpback Whale National Marine Sanctuary, Kilauea Point National Wildlife Refuge, and Kilauea Point Natural History Association. It's held at Kilauea Point National Wildlife Refuge. For more information, contact ☎ 246-2860.

Mother's Day Orchid Show displays hundreds of varieties of orchids. Orchids are also for sale and there are plenty of lectures and demonstrations about orchid culture. It's held at the Kukui Grove Shopping Center.

The four-day **Kaua`i Polynesian Festival** starts with a dinner and Polynesian entertainment on the first evening; on the following days you can check out Polynesian entertainment, crafts, dance competitions, food, and more. Admission fee. For information, ☎ 808-335-6466 or www.kauaipolynesian-festival.org.

Banana Poka Festival is named after the banana poka vines that threaten native Hawaiian plants and trees. You can learn quite a bit about the environment on the west side of Kaua`i. There are crafts workshops, exhibits, family-oriented activities and entertainment. Free. ☎ 808-335-9975, www.koke`e.org

Visitor Industry Charity Walk is a huge fundraiser put on by those in the tourist industry – hotels, airlines, etc. It's the largest one-day fundraiser in the state, with similar walks taking place simultaneously on O`ahu, Maui, Kaua`i and the Big Island. Monies raised go to various charities. On Kaua`i, the walk is about three miles long, with several checkpoints. Each checkpoint offers refreshments and food from local hotels as well as entertainment. Hawai`i Hotel and Lodging Association, ☎ 808-246-5149, www.charitywalkhawaii.org.

June

Taste of Hawai`i is dubbed "The Ultimate Sunday Brunch"' and for good reason. This is the one opportunity each year to try out the best creations from chefs all over the state. There are also several stages with entertainment. It's normally held on the first Sunday of June and it's sponsored by the Rotary Club of Kapa`a. There is a fee for tickets. You can purchase them in advance. For more information, ☎ 808-246-6983, www.kapaa.rotary-site.org/toh.html.

At **Bon Dance and Carnival** the Japanese Obon dance season (June 1-August 31) pays respect to ancestors through dance and music. It's held throughout the summer at various Buddhist temples all over the island. Check newspapers for current schedules and times.

Prince Albert Music Festival. Why is there a music festival for Prince Albert of Monaco on Kaua`i? It's actually not for that Prince Albert, but for Prince Albert Kauikeaouli Lei o Papa a Kamehameha, son of Queen Emma and King

Kamehameha IV. Prince Albert was also the last child born to a Hawaiian monarch and the namesake of Princeville, where the festival is held. Here you can witness classical and Hawaiian music and dance, hula, exhibitions of antique quilts and artifacts, lei contests, silent auction, demonstrations, and workshops. Sponsored by the Prince Albert Foundation.

King Kamehameha Celebration Floral Parade and Hoolaulea, one of the highlights of the annual festival calendar, is full of colors and aloha. Marching bands, gorgeous Pau units on horseback and decorated vehicles make their way through Lihu`e. The parade usually starts in Lihu`e at the Vidinha Stadium, makes its way down Rice St, ending at the county building. There's a festival on the lawn of the county building with music, hula, crafts and, of course, lots of local food. For more information, ☎ 808-821-6895.

At the King Kamehameha Celebration

Hanapepe Folk Festival brings together a variety of artists to raise money for the historic Storybook Theatre in Hanapepe. Admissions fee. ☎ 808-651-1090.

Na Hula o Kaohikukapulani Exhibition. You can enjoy hula from Hawaiian and Polynesia performed by people of all ages – ranging from four-year-old keiki to the elderly kupuna. Held in Lihu`e. Fee for admission.

July

Billed as the single largest family event on Kaua`i each year, **The Concert in the Sky** brings together people from all walks of life to celebrate the 4th of July. The festival kicks off in the middle of the afternoon with live music, bounce houses and games for the kids, silent auction and, of course, food booths. The food is provided by local hotels, so you can definitely try out some good food with a local flair. The largest fireworks show on the island caps it all off. It's held at Vidinha Stadium in Lihu`e as a fundraiser for Kaua`i Hospice. Fee for admission. ☎ 808-245-7277.

Koloa Plantation Days is a week-long festival celebrating the sugar plantation heritage of Hawai`i and the immigrant cultures. It's held where Hawai`i's first sugar plantation was founded in 1835. Highlights include sports tournaments, entertainment, traditional Hawaiian games, a rodeo, parade and block party. www.koloaplantationdays.com, ☎ 808-822-0734.

Bon Dance and Carnival (June 1-August 31) contiues during the summer at Buddhist temples throughout the island. Check newspapers for schedules.

**Kaua`i Family Ocean Fair**. Spend the day at Kilauea Point Lighthouse and National Wildlife Refuge and learn about Hawai`i's marine environment. There are games, arts, crafts, and activities for kids. Sponsored by the Hawaiian Islands Humpback Whale Marine Sanctuary, Kilauea Point National Wildlife Refuge and the Kilauea Point Natural History Museum. Admission is free. ☎ 808-246-2860.

**Hanama`ulu Town Celebration**. This tiny hamlet on the outskirts of Lihu`e celebrates its plantation heritage. Here you'll find a parade to kick off the celebration, flower and produce show, live entertainment, classic car displays, crafts and rides and games for the kids, as well as workshops and lectures about the area's culture and history. ☎ 808-245-5359 or visit www.htcelebration.org.

Hanama`ulu Town Celebration

August

**The Kaua`i County Farm Bureau Fair** is held in Lihu`e at Vidinha Stadium. The weekend event has a host of carnival rides, food booths, games, entertainment and more. ☎ 808-274-3471.

Bon Dance and Carnival (June 1-August 31) contiues during the summer at Buddhist temples throughout the island. Check newspapers for current schedules and times.

September

**Kaua`i Mokihana Festival**. Named after Kaua`i's famed Mokihana flower and berry plant, this weeklong celebration features lectures and workshops about Hawaiian culture, a local composers' competition, cultural workshops and three nights of hula competition. Events are held in various locations on the island. Fee for admission to most events. Call ☎ 808-822-2166 or 808-652-1249, or visit www.mokihana.kauai.net for a complete schedule of events and locations.

Kaua`i Mokihana Festival

Aloha Festivals began back in 1947 as a way to honor the cosmopolitan heritage of Hawai`i through music, dance and history. Today, Aloha Festivals are huge events on all of the islands with parades and Hoolaulea or block parties. On Kaua`i, there are events happening throughout the month, including a colorful parade, Hoolaulea and luau. For a complete schedule of locations and events, ☎ 808-322-7778, www.alohafestivals.com, info@alohafestivals.com.

**Matsuri Kaua`i**. Celebrate the Japanese culture with a day of traditional music and dance performances, exhibitions and demonstrations. There are events such as mochi pounding, oshibana (creating pictures with pressed plants), a tea ceremony, and kimono dressing, games, crafts and food. It's held at the Kaua`i War Memorial Convention Hall. For more information, ☎ 808-822-5353. Presented by the Japanese Cultural Society. Free admission.

October

Coconut Festival. This is one of only two festivals on the planet that celebrate the coconut. Learn about the many uses of coconuts and check out the food, cooking demonstrations, music and activities. Presented by the Kapa`a Business Association. www.kbakauai.org. Fee for admission.

Eo E Emalani Festival celebreates the journey Queen Emma took from her house in Lawai to see the views of Waimea Canyon and the bogs of Alakai Swamp in 1871. Activities include a royal procession, photographic exhibits and craft demonstrations, such as lauhala weaving and Ni`ihau shell lei-making. ☎ 808-335-9975, Koke`e State Park, www.koke`e.org.

November

The **Hawai`i International Film Festival** showcases some of the finest films from the Pan Pacific region. Notable screenings in the past have included *Crouching Tiger, Hidden*

Travel Information

Dragon in 2000 and *Brokeback Mountain* in 2005. Screenings are held throughout the islands. On Kaua`i, they take place in early November at Waimea Theatre and Kukui Grove Cinema. Admissions fee. ☎ 808-528-FILM, www.hiff.org. kauai@hiff.org.

December

Festival of Lights and Annual Lights on Rice Parade. Kick the Christmas season off Hawaiian-style with an evening parade, entertainment and Christmas caroling. Watch the lighting of the Christmas tree and decorations on the grounds of the Historic County Building. The parade goes down Rice St. in Lihu`e and ends at the Historic County Building. The Festival of Lights lasts until New Year's. Admission is free.

Waimea Christmas Parade

Waimea Lighted Christmas Parade. Enjoy a small-town Christmas parade here in Waimea. Floats are lit up and decorated, as are the storefronts. The first Christmas celebrated in Hawai`i was in Waimea over 200 years ago. Come to town early to see the decorated storefronts and spend the day. Free to the public. Contact the West Kaua`i Business & Professional Association at www.wkbpa.org.

Audubon Christmas Bird Count. Bird lovers must not miss this opportunity to see Kaua`i's native birds. Don't worry if you've never participated in a bird count before. Koke`e Musuem will train you as a volunteer to participate. Koke`e Museum, www.koke`e.org. For more information, ☎ 808-335-9975.

Getting Here

By Air

Flying to Kaua`i is a pretty simple affair. The main airport is centrally located in Lihu`e. There's also a smaller airport in Princeville on the North Shore, and in Port Allen on the South Shore, both of them used for smaller commuter and private planes. Be sure you have a window seat for your arrival into Kaua`i; there will be amazing and dramatic views of the island.

AIRLINES

Aloha Airlines, ☎ 1-800-367-5250, 808-484-1111, www.alohaair.com

American Airlines, ☎ 1-800-433-7300, 808-833-7600, www.aa.com

ATA, ☎ 800-435-9282, www.ata.com

Continental, ☎ 800-523-3273, www.continental.com

Delta, ☎ 800-221-1212, www.delta.com

go! Airlines, ☎ 888-435-9462, www.iflygo.com

Hawaiian Airlines, ☎ 800-367-5320, 808-838-1555, www.hawaiianair.com

Island Air, ☎ 800-652-6541, www.islandair.com

Northwest, ☎ 800-225-2525, www.nwa.com

United, ☎ 800-241-6522, www.united.com

If you're flying to Kaua`i from O`ahu, you have plenty of options. It's only a 25-minute flight from Honolulu International Airport. Hawaiian Airlines, Aloha Airlines, and Island Air all have regularly scheduled flights every day. With the entry of go! Airlines into the interisland travel market, prices have come down dramatically for an interisland flight. A price war ensued in June of 2006 and the airlines are competing harder for your travel dollar.

Another cost-effective way to reach Kaua`i is aboard charter flights that include hotel and car packages. Check with your travel agent or local newspaper for the best deals.

If you're coming from the mainland, you have a few options available to you. Most major carriers serve Honolulu International Airport, so you can fly to Honolulu and then hop on one of the many flights to Lihu`e from there.

Depending on where you're flying from, you may be lucky enough to get a direct flight to Lihu`e. United Airlines offers direct service to Kaua`i from Los Angeles and San Francisco and American Airlines offers service to Lihu`e from Los Angeles. America West/US Airways also offers a non-stop flight from Phoenix.

It takes about 10 hours to get to Lihu`e from New York, eight hours from Chicago, five hours from Los Angeles, and 15 hours from London, not including layovers.

By Sea

It is possible to get to Kaua`i by sea other than as a stowaway. **Norwegian Cruise Line**, ☎ 800-555-5555, www.ncl.com, recently began its interisland cruises with the *Pride of Aloha, Pride of Hawai`i* and the *Pride of America*. These ships start out from Honolulu Harbor and venture to all of the neighbor islands. Cruises range from seven to 10 days.

In 2007 Honolulu is expected to get ferry service to the neighbor islands. The **Hawai`i Superferry** is expected to launch in July 2007 with service from Honolulu to Kaua`i and Maui. The trip to Kaua`i is expected to take about three hours from Honolulu. Preliminary prices from Honolulu to Kaua`i start at $42. One advantage that's being touted by the company is that you'll be able to bring an SUV (with surfboards or canoes on top), pickup, minivan, motorcycles, bikes, scooters, surfboards or canoes. All of these will cost extra and prices have yet to be determined. Check out www.hawaiisuperferry.com for more information.

■ Getting Around

By Car

Getting around Kaua`i is a pretty easy affair. There are two main roads that almost form a complete circle around the island. Coming from Lihu`e and heading north, you'll take Kuhio Highway (Hwy. 56). This road goes up the east coast through Kapa`a, Wailua, Anahola and then heads around the north through Kilauea, Princeville, Hnalei, finally ending at Ke`e Beach.

Driving west from Lihu`e, you'll take Kaumuali`i Hwy. This is pretty hard to pronounce, so it's OK to refer to the road as Highway 50. This will take you to Po`ipu, Kalaheo, Port Allen, Hanapepe and Waimea.

Upon arriving on Kaua`i, you'll find a few options to get around the island. You can rent a car, take a hotel shuttle or a taxi. Kaua`i offers limited bus service as well.

While it is pretty easy to get around Kaua`i, there are a few rules of the road you should know beforehand. First of all, all front seat occupants, as well as passengers in the back seat under 18 must wear a seat belt or you'll be hit with a $92 fine. Children under the age of four must be in a child safety seat. Pedestrians always have the right of way, even if they're not in the crosswalk. You can turn right on red at intersections unless there's a sign that says otherwise.

We tend to "Drive with Aloha" on Kaua`i. This means that we're slower, we actually do yield to pedestrians, and we even yield to oncoming drivers. And you won't see tailgating. Speed limits are lower than what you're probably used to. By driving slower, we tend to appreciate the scenery around us.

A fun and slightly odd feature of Kaua`i is the one-lane bridge. You'll find these bridges mostly as you're driving through the north shore between Hanalei and Ha`ena. It takes a few tries to get a feel for the flow of traffic. When you approach the bridge, look and see if there are cars coming in your direction or waiting to cross the bridge. If there are no cars, then go ahead and cross the bridge. If there are cars approaching, let them cross until it's clear or someone stops to let you cross.

Because there has been considerable growth on Kaua`i in terms of residents and visitors, there has been an increase in traffic as well. There actually is a "rush hour" on Kaua`i.

Rental Cars

This is by far the best way to get around the island. Almost all visitors to Kaua`i choose this method for sheer convenience. You can do what you want, go where you want on your schedule. Rental car prices are competitive since the major rental car companies all have a presence on Kaua`i. You can also find great rates on the Internet at web sites such as www.

priceline.com. A little research before you make your reservation can save you money.

Be sure to make your rental car reservations in advance, especially if you have special needs. It's not uncommon for car companies to run out of cars.

Once you get to Lihu`e Airport, you'll find rental car company booths across the street from the main terminal. Each company has a shuttle that will take you directly to the cars.

In order to rent a car in Hawai`i, you must be at least 25 years of age and have a major credit card and valid driver's license. If you're from outside the United States, you'll need an international driver's license as well as a foreign driver's license.

If you're between the ages of 21 and 25, you can get a rental car through Alamo, Avis, Budget, Dollar, National. Depending on who you rent with, you may not be able to rent a minivan, SUV or luxury vehicle.

If you're 18 and over, you can rent a car from Rent-A-Wreck of Kaua`i. You do need to fax over proof of insurance before making your reservation. Call prior to making your reservations. They're on Rice Street in Lihu`e and provide free drop-off and pick-up services.

At Lihu`e Airport you'll find these car rental booths:

- **Alamo Rental Car**, ☎ 808-246-0645, 800-327-9633, www.goalamo.com
- **Avis Rent A Car**, ☎ 808-245-3512, 800-331-1212, www.avis.com
- **Budget**, ☎ 808-245-9031, 800-527-0700, www.budgetrentacar.com
- **Dollar**, ☎ 866-434-2226, 800-800-4000, www.dollarcar.com
- **National**, ☎ 808-245-5636, 800-227-7368, www.nationalcar.com
- **Hertz**, ☎ 808-245-3356, 800-654-3011, www.hertz.com
- **Rent-A-Wreck of Kaua`i**, 3501 Rice St. Suite 112A, Lihu`e, ☎ 808-632-0741, www.rentawreck.com
- **Thrifty**, ☎ 866-450-5101, 800-847-4389, www.thrifty.com

On top of the actual rental fee, you must pay an airport access fee, airport concession fee, and general excise tax. These add up quickly, so be sure to verify the total cost when making your reservations.

Insurance

Rental car companies do offer insurance for your vehicle for an extra fee. This isn't required and a lot of credit card companies offer rental car insurance. You might even be covered under your personal insurance policy as well. Be sure to double-check with your insurance company and your credit card company before you make your rental car reservations.

Hawai`i is one of 12 states that is a no-fault state when it comes to auto insurance. This means that if you're uninsured, you're liable for all damages whether the accident was your fault or not, and whether you live here or not.

No matter what insurance you have, check to see if you're covered on unpaved roads or beaches, especially if you plan to visit places like Polihale Beach or you like to do off-road driving. Also check to see if they'll cover four-wheel-drive vehicles and Jeeps. Some policies do, others don't.

By Taxi

If you couldn't get a rental car or prefer to take a taxi everywhere, expect to pay dearly for it. Here's a rundown of taxi companies that operate on Kaua`i.

- **Kaua`i Taxi Company**, ☎ 808-246-9554
- **Akiko's Taxi**, ☎ 808-822-7588
- **City Cab**, ☎ 808-245-3227
- **North Shore Cab**, ☎ 808-639-7829

If you need to take a taxi from the airport, expect to pay about $55 to Princeville, $80 to Ha`ena, $24 to Kapa`a, $30 to Po`ipu, and $55 to Waimea.

By Bus

Kaua`i Bus offers service Monday-Friday from 5:15 am-7:15 pm and on Saturdays from 7:15 am-3:15 pm. The Bus services the main towns of the island.

A round-trip on the bus runs at $1.50 for adults, 75¢ for children under 18 and 75¢ for those over 60. Children six years or under travel free when accompanied by an adult passenger. You can purchase a frequent rider pass for $15.

Most of the buses on Kaua`i have a bike rack in front, so you can load your bike, take the bus to a trail that you might want to explore and come back. Just let the driver know you're loading and unloading the bike.

There are some items that you cannot take on the bus. You cannot take oversized backpacks with you, surfboards or anything larger than 10 x 17 x 30 inches. You can bring folding baby strollers, guitars, `ukuleles, and body boards, however.

For a complete schedule, check www.kauai.gov or call ☎ 808-241-6410.

By Motorcycle

There are a couple of places to rent motorcycles on Kaua`i, and these places are geared for the Harley-Davidson set.

- **Two Wheels in Lihu`e**, 3846 Rice St, near Nawiliwili Harbor, ☎ 808-246-9457, rents Harleys starting at $75 for three hours. If you want to keep the bike overnight, it'll be about $170.
- **Street Eagle of Hawai`i**, 3-1866 Kaumuali`i Hwy, ☎ 808-241-7120, also specializes in Harley Davidson rentals. You can find them across from Kaua`i Community College. They're open from 7 am to 7 pm.

DRIVE TIMES FROM LIHU`E AIRPORT	
Waimea Town	45 minutes
Hanapepe	40 minutes
Po`ipu	30 minutes
Kapa`a	20 minutes
Kilauea	45 minutes
Princeville	50 minutes
Hanalei	1 hour
Ha`ena	1 hour 25 minutes

By Bicycle

To really appreciate Kaua`i's beauty, sometimes it's best to go slow. A great way to enjoy Kaua`i's scenery is by bicycle. There's a new 4.3 mile bike path that starts at Lihi Park in Kapa`a town to Ahihi Point in Kealia. This is scheduled to be completed by early 2007. You'll go through coastal neighborhoods and along bluffs overlooking two popular Kaua`i beaches. The path is a part of a 16-mile project that will eventually connect Anahola and Nawiliwili. There's also a 2½-mile path around Lydgate State Park.

There are a few other options for road biking on the island. There is little or no debris on the shoulders, but they aren't that wide in a lot of spots and traffic can be heavy.

You can bring your own bike to Kaua`i. Just note that most airlines will charge about $75 to take a bike on the airplane.

Bike Rentals

**Outfitters Kaua`i**, 2827 Po`ipu Rd, Po`ipu, ☎ 808-742-9667, www.outfitterskauai.com. A cruiser bike goes for $20 a day and a mountain bike for $30 a day. Children's mountain bikes rent for $20 a day. Baby seats are $5 a day

Pedal 'N Paddle offers tandem bikes, as well as mountain and road bikes for rent. Daily rentals start at $10 a day and weekly rentals at $30 a day. Car racks are also available. They're located at the Ching Young Village center in Hanalei. ☎ 808-826-9069, http://pedalnpaddle.com.

> **Tip:** For activities and adventures, it is customary to tip 15-20% of the tour cost to your guide.

■ Staying Safe

General Safety

Hawai`i is generally a safe place to visit, but that doesn't mean you can throw all caution to the winds. Visitors to Kaua`i do become victims of crime, so stay aware of your surroundings and use common sense.

The most common crime against visitors is car theft, especially at tourist destinations such as beaches and resort areas. It's pretty common to hear stories about car theft where people have left valuables in their rental cars and there's not much that can be done. Do not leave valuables such as your wallet, camera, or anything of value, in your car or unattended at the beach.

It's also common sense to stay in well-lit areas after dark and keep a limited amount of cash on you. Your best bet is to keep your valuables locked in the hotel safe or in another safe place.

In the event of an emergency, such as an accident, medical emergency, or if you're the victim of a crime, the **Visitor Aloha Society of Hawai`i** can help you out. You have to have a police report if you're the victim of a crime in order to receive VASH services. After filing a police report, VASH services are provided on Kaua`i by calling ☎ 808-482-0111.

Hospitals

If you're on vacation and you need medical attention, there are a number of options. Of course, for medical emergencies, dial ☎ 911.

Kaua`i's main hospital and medical facility is **Wilcox Memorial Hospital**, 3420 Kuhio Highway, ☎ 808-245-1100. Wilcox provides emergency room and intensive care services, as well as full in-patient and out-patient medical services, obstetrics, and laboratory services.

If you're on the west side of the island, **West Kaua`i Medical Center/Kaua`i Veteran's Memorial Hospital** at 4643 Waimea Canyon Road in Waimea, ☎ 808-338-9431, is also available for 24 hours for emergencies.

Hale Le'a Family Medicine, 2460 Oka St. Kilauea, ☎ 808-828-2885, www.kauai-medical.com, also offers medical services. It's open Monday-Friday from 8:30 am-5:30 pm and on Saturdays from 8:30 am to noon.

North Shore Clinic and **North Shore Pharmacy**, Kilauea and Oka Rds, Kilauea, ☎ 808-828-1418, are open 8:30 am to 5 pm, Monday to Friday, and 8:30 am to noon on Saturday.

Mahelona Medical Center in Kapa`a, ☎ 808-822-4175, offers a walk-in clinic that's open weekdays from 9 am to 5 pm.

If you want healthcare on the go, **Dr. Harold Spear** offers diagnosis, treatment, phone consultations and prescriptions. His office is in Hanapepe, ☎ 808-335-0915 or call 866-437-3425.

If you need the **Poison Control Center**, they can be reached at ☎ 800-362-3585.

To get a prescription filled, you have options. You can go to **Southshore Pharmacy** in Koloa, ☎ 808-742-7511; **Westside Pharmacy** in Hanapepe, ☎ 808-335-5342; **Menehune Pharmacy** in Waimea, ☎ 808-338-0200; or **North Shore Pharmacy** in Kilauea, ☎ 808-828-1844. There's also **Long's Drugs** in the Kukui Grove Shopping Center in Lihu`e, ☎ 808-245-7771, or in Kaua`i Village in Kapa`a, ☎ 808-822-4915.

Police

The Kaua`i Police Department is headquartered in the Public Safety Building at 3990 Ka`ana Street in Lihu`e, Kaua`i. There are also substations in Hanalei and Waimea. In an emergency, you should dial ☎ 911. For non-emergency situations, you can call ☎ 808-241-1711.

Water Safety

Kaua`i's beaches are renowned for their pristine beauty. It's easy to forget that within the beauty lies a potential beast of a disaster. Each beach has its own risk factors and can change dramatically between winter and summer.

It can be easy to underestimate the power of the ocean. Once you're out there, you might quickly realize that you're in over your head, literally.

One of the first things most people think of when it comes to the ocean is **sharks**. There are millions of people in Hawai`i's waters every year. But only three or four shark bites occur each year. To learn more about the various sharks in the water, be sure to check out **www.hawaiisharks.org**. It's a great resource that will educate you and put your mind at ease when you're entering the water.

> **Reef shoes** are popular for protecting your feet in the water. But just because you're wearing reef shoes you don't have a free license to walk on top of a reef. First of all, Kaua`i's reef environment is very fragile and you can cause incredible damage. Not only that, coral is very sharp and can cut right through your shoes.

According to the Hawai`i State Department of Health, **drowning** is the second leading cause of injury and death. Most of these incidents do happen to visitors. Here are a few basic tips so you and your family can stay safe throughout your journey.

- Always get in the water with other people, whether you're swimming, surfing or snorkeling.
- Avoid the water at dusk, dawn and nighttime. This is prime feeding time for sharks. You don't want to be mistaken for shark bait.
- Swim or surf at beaches patrolled by lifeguards, and follow their advice.
- Check with lifeguards for conditions
- If fish or turtles start to behave erratically, leave the water. Be alert to the presence of dolphins, as they are prey for some large sharks.
- If you have younger children, keep a close eye on them and hang onto them, even if they are using flotation devices.
- Stay out of muddy or murky waters, especially after a heavy rainfall. Sharks do feed in these areas.
- Never turn your back on the water, because waves can some up unexpectedly.
- Seven to 10 days after the full moon, on the south shores of all islands you may see an influx of box jellyfish. Check with lifeguards if there's a jellyfish problem after the full moon.
- In surf over waist high, use caution, especially during the winter. Waves can surge and sweep you away, even if you're just observing from the rocks.
- If in doubt, don't go out!

Another great resource about Kaua`i's beaches and ocean safety can be found online at **www.kauaiexplorer.com**. It's a guide that further details safety precautions, surf trends, and it provides a printable version of the day's surf reports.

Other risks are shorebreaks, rip currents and undertows.

Shorebreaks are where waves break one-three feet from shore. While the waves are tempting for body surfing, they can be so powerful enough to slam you down hard on the ocean bottom, potentially causing neck and back injuries.

Rip currents are strong currents that flow from the beach out to sea. If you get caught in a rip current do not panic. If you're swimming with someone, signal to them and make them aware of the situation. Don't swim against the current. You'll only waste your energy. The best thing to do is to ride it out, as they typically last for only 50-100 yards; swim parallel to shore to get out of the current then swim back to safety.

An **undertow** is basically a rip current that travels right into incoming surf. The surf goes over and the current goes under, pulling the swimmer underneath.

Sun Safety

Remember that you're in the tropics and the sun is powerful. Even on cloudy days, you can get severe sunburn. That's why sunscreen is an absolute necessity. Use sunscreen of at least SPF 15. If you have fair skin, then you'll need a stronger sunscreen of SPF 30 or higher. The sun's strength peaks between 10 am and 2 pm, so plan your day accordingly.

Hiking Safety

Kaua`i is a dream if you're an avid hiker. There are trails that are easy to access for all levels of fitness and experience. It's also a great way to see Kaua`i's beautiful flora and ecosystems up-close. However, like everything else, it definitely has its potential dangers. By taking a few precautions and knowing what to do in an emergency, you can keep yourself and your family out of harm's way.

Dressing appropriately for hiking is a great place to start. If you're hiking in cooler elevations, you're going to want to wear a long-sleeve shirt and long, light pants, with comfortable shoes, preferably hiking boots for ankle support and traction. Even if you're not in cooler elevations, you might be hiking on trails that are somewhat overgrown with branches and thorns. They can tear your arms and legs up after a while. Don't forget the sunscreen.

It's been mentioned a number of times how fragile Hawai`i's ecosystem is. Did you know that invasive weeds could spread just by having seeds mixed with mud on your hiking boots and gear? Help protect Kaua`i's environment by scrubbing your boots and gear before and after your hike.

Hydrate, hydrate, hydrate. Bring plenty of water with you, at least half a gallon. It can get hot on the trails, even if you're at high elevations. It's important to stay hydrated to keep a clear head.

It's a bad idea to hike on deserted trails alone. If you're a novice hiker and you're not that familiar with the trails, you might want to consider hiking with a group like the Sierra Club or a tour group. And it's a good idea to know your limits and choose trails that suit your fitness level. Let someone know where you're going and, if possible, carry a cell phone.

Before you go and during your hike, check the weather. The weather on Kaua`i does change frequently

Get an early start. If you start out late, watch the time. Sunset happens quickly here and you don't want to get caught on the trail after dark. If that does occur, stay still unless you're very familiar with the trail or have a flashlight.

The there are the dangers you cannot see, mainly bacteria and water contamination. No matter how tempting it is, do not drink fresh water from streams and pools. Bacteria such as salmonellae, salmonella typhi, and e coli can put a real damper on your vacation. There are other water-borne illnesses that are also found in fresh-water ponds and streams.

Leptospirosis is one of the more common illnesses. You can be infected if the bacteria come in contact with your eyes, nose or mouth. Exposure can occur by swimming or walking in freshwater streams or puddles, or by coming into contact with wet soil or plants contaminated by infected animal urine, blood or tissues. Symptoms usually begin within one to two weeks, and can include fever, headache, chills and sweating, muscle pain, red eyes and vomiting.

Giardiasis is usually a mild intestinal illness, caused by the Giardia parasite and passed through feces of people or animals to the mouth of another person, either through your hands or indirectly through drinking water or food. Symptoms begin to surface seven to 10 days after exposure, and include cramps, fatigue and weight loss.

Don't expose your cuts, sores or face to stream or pond water. If you do become ill and suspect it may be a waterborne disease, see your medical provider. Antibiotics or other treatments may reduce the severity or length of illness.

A great resource you can send away for before your trip is the ***The Kaua`i Recreational Trail Map***. Mail a cashier's check or money order in US currency for $6 domestic or $7 for foreign mailings. Send your money to Division of Forestry & Wildlife, 3060 Eiwa Street, Rm 306, Lihu`e, Hawai`i 96766. Call the Kaua`i Forestry Office at ☎ 808-274-3433 for any notices. Another option is to go right to the Kaua`i Forestry and Wildlife Office in Lihu`e and buy the map for $5. Hey, it saves a buck, plus the fee to purchase a cashier's check.

■ Getting Married on Kaua`i

Approximately 20,000 non-resident marriages are performed in the state every year. If you're one of the lucky couples coming to Kaua`i to get married, congratulations. You've made an excellent choice. There are a couple of ways to get married on Kaua`i: you can do it yourself or you can have someone else plan it for you.

If you go at it yourself, all you really need is a license and someone to perform the ceremony. It's relatively easy to obtain a marriage license in Hawai`i. You don't have to be a resident of the state of even an American citizen and blood tests are not required.

All you need is proof that you're 18 years of age or older. If you're 16 or 17, then you need the written consent of both parents, legal guardians or family court. You do have to appear in person and by appointment at the Department of Health, which is on 3060 Eiwa St in Lihu`e. The Department of Health is open Monday-Friday 8:30 to 11:30 am and 1:30 to 3:30 pm. Call for an appointment at ☎ 808-241-3498.

Assuming that you're over the age of 18, you both have to bring proof of age, fill out the application form and pay $60 cash for the license. You can get that at the Department of

Health or download it from the Department of Health's website at www.hawaii.gov/health/vital-records/vital-records/marriage/index.html.

You'll get your marriage license as soon as it's approved. Your license is valid within the State of Hawai`i for 30 days.

If you're a couple that's considered to be "Kissing Cousins," you're in luck. Cousins may marry in Hawai`i. The relationship between the two can't be closer than first cousins.

If you have someone plan the wedding for you, you have a few options. A great resource is the **Kaua`i Wedding Professionals Association**, www.kauaiwedpro.com. Or **The Hawai`i Visitors and Convention Bureau**, www.gohawaii.com, can provide information for wedding coordinators. You'll find that the larger resorts usually have their own coordinators on staff or they work with their own wedding planners. Many planners have private estates available for ceremonies. The wedding can be a small and simple affair on the beach or a big wedding where friends and family fly in. They can arrange a Hawaiian minister, musicians, hula dancers, appropriate leis, flower petal carpet, even an archway of orchids.

If you want a traditional wedding, you might want to consider getting married at the **Waioli Church** in Hanalei. It's a beautiful old church that would be perfect for a traditional setting. For the downright adventurous, **Kaua`i ATV** offers weddings in the mud. **Safari Helicopters** does weddings in the air, but you'll have to wait if you want to join the mile-high club.

■ Kaua`i Wi-Fi

It's pretty easy to stay in touch with people during your stay – get caught up with your e-mail, or e-mail your friends and family back home to brag about the beauty of the island. You know what it's like, you're in paradise, and your friends and family are stuck elsewhere.

Nowadays, most hotels and condominiums have high-speed Internet access. Kaua`i does have a number of places where you can park your laptop and check your e-mail or surf the Web.

Akamai Computers, ☎ 808-823-0047, has an Internet café at Kapa`a. They're open from 9 to 5:30 Monday-Friday.

Starbucks in Lihu`e, **Java Kai** (a coffee shop with locations in Hanalei and Kapa`a) and **Borders Books** have access for a fee.

If you aren't into paying for Internet access, you're in luck. There are a handful of places on Kaua`i where you can surf the Web for free. Free access is provided at **Koloa Coffee Roasters** in Koloa and **Small Town Coffee Company** in Kapa`a. If you don't care for coffee shops, **The Shack** in Kapa`a and the **Tradewinds Bar** in Coconut Marketplace offer free wireless Internet access.

You can find a pretty accurate list of Wi-Fi hotspots at **www.JWire.com**.

■ Cell Phone Service

Cell phone service is OK throughout the island. Verizon does tend to have the best coverage. Sprint, Cingular, and T-Mobile also have a presence on Kaua`i. No matter what carrier you have, you'll be able to get coverage in and around Po`ipu and Lihu`e. As you move farther away from these areas, coverage becomes questionable. Don't expect to get coverage in areas like Polihale, Waimea Canyon, and Ha`ena.

Hawai`i is affectionately called the 808 state because the area code for the entire state is 808. If you're calling interisland, you have to dial 1-808 and then the rest of the number. If you're calling the mainland, you have to dial 1 then the area code and number. All calls within Kaua`i are considered local calls.

■ Gay Kaua`i

Now that you've made it to paradise, you may be wondering "Where do they keep the gays and lesbians?" They're pretty hidden, actually. It's not that Kaua`i isn't a tolerant place for gays, it's just that there's not much of a community, such as you'd see on O`ahu or Maui. You have to do a little digging around. When you get to Kaua`i, make sure your first call is to **Lamba Aloha Bisexual, Transgender, Gay, Lesbian**

Community Bulletin Board, ☎ 808-823-6248. It's a recorded line with GLBT events and information. You can also check out Lambda Aloha's website at www.lambdaaloha.com to see a list of weekly events, such as tennis, movie nights, and various hikes. You can also sign up on their e-mail list to get information sent straight to your inbox.

■ Important Numbers

Ambulance, Fire, Police	☎ 911
Non-Emergency Police	☎ 808-241-1711
Wilcox Memorial Hospital	☎ 808-245-1100
Camping permits (County Parks)	☎ 808-241-4463
Camping Permits (State Parks)	☎ 808-274-3444
Hawai`i Division of Forestry & Wildlife	☎ 808-274-3433
Fishing Licenses	☎ 808-274-3344
Kaua`i Bus	☎ 808-241-6410
Kaua`i Visitors Bureau Information Hotline	☎ 800-262-1400
Hawai`i Visitors & Convention Bureau	☎ 808-923-1811
Visitors Aloha Society of Hawai`i	☎ 808-482-0111
Lifeguard Services	☎ 808-241-6506
Marine Forecast	☎ 808-245-3564
Time of day	☎ 808-643-8463
Weather	☎ 808-245-6001
Surf Forecast	☎ 808-241-7873
Lihu`e Airport Information	☎ 808-246-1448

■ Top Attractions - Best Of Kaua`i

Kaua`i has so much to see and do, it can be difficult to decide what to do each day. Do you go shopping? Do you hit the beach? Which ones are really worth seeing? Here's a quick top-20 list of Kaua`i's best activities and attractions so you can make the most of your stay, no matter how long it is.

■ *Take a helicopter ride*

The only way to really see Kaua`i is by helicopter. Roughly 70% of the island is inaccessible by road. If you want to get a bird's-eye view of untouched waterfalls and Kaua`i's rugged terrain, this is the way to go. Most tours fly out of Lihu`e Airport and there are a couple of tours that fly out of Princeville as well.

■ *See the Na Pali Cliffs*

The beauty of the Na Pali cliffs, shown on the previous page, is a breathtaking sight that you will see nowhere else. There are a number of ways to get to the cliffs. You can see them via helicopter. You can also take a boat tour, kayak tour, kayak on your own or hike the Kalalau Trail. No matter what you choose, your unforgettable adventure around the Na Pali cliffs will leave you breathless.

Waimea Canyon

■ *Visit the Grand Canyon of the Pacific*

Drive up to Waimea Canyon in the early morning or at sunset. The different shades of red and brown that line the canyon look spectacular at those times. For a more exciting journey, **Outfitters Kaua`i**, ☎ 808-742-9667, takes you to the top of the canyon for a 12-mile downhill bike ride at sunrise or sunset. The tour costs $94 for adults and $75 for children.

■ *Spend the Day in Hanalei*

Spend part of the day at the beach. You can hang out at Black Pot Beach, Hanalei Bay, snorkel Hanalei Bay, pick up lunch at Hanalei Mixed Plate and shop at Ching Young Village. There are plenty of interesting stores, but my favorite thing to do is to sit at Java Kai and people-watch. Hanalei is such a laid-back town, you're very likely to strike up a conversation with one of the locals and get a real local feel for the Hawaiian lifestyle.

■ *Hike the Kalalau Trail*

Get down and dirty on this 11-mile trek through Na Pali State Park. The trail begins at the end of the road at Ha`ena Beach State Park on the north shore. For a nice day-trip, you can do the two-mile hike to Hanakaipai Beach. For a more intense experience, hike the remaining nine miles through Hanakoa Valley, ending at Kalalau Beach.

■ *Polihale Beach*

Polihale Beach

This isolated beach on Kaua`i's west shore is one of the world's most beautiful and the best place to watch a sunset. Once you walk up the short path, you'll find the seemingly endless and pristine beach. The sand is soft and hot on your feet, the water is blue like a mysterious gem. You just want to stand there, sink in the sand and take it all in.

■ *Whale-Watching*

If you're going to be on Kaua`i between November and March, you'll be there at the peak of whale-watching season. From land, good viewing spots are Kilauea Point National Wildlife Refuge, the Kalalau Trail, Po`ipu Beach and Kukui O Lono Park in Kalaheo. If you want to get up-close, take a boat tour. The types of tours vary with the boat company, from exciting zodiac boats to stable catamarans.

Whale diving

■ *Sunday Brunch at Princeville Hotel*

If you'd like to check out a Sunday brunch, you might as well do it right – at **Café Hanalei** in the Princeville Hotel. Outdoor seating is available, affording the best views of Hanalei Bay, which are spectacular. The food is as good as the view. The menu is pretty standard, but it is well-executed. Brunch is $46 per person and $49 with champagne.

■ *Celebrate Hawaiian Culture at a Luau*

How can you be in Hawai`i and not go to a luau? It's a great way to experience Hawaiian food, music and dance in one evening. No matter what luau you choose, there will be Kalua pig, poi, sweet potatoes, chicken, fish, and no shortage of desserts. You will not leave hungry.

■ *Allerton Gardens*

Allerton Gardens

The beauty and the history of the Allerton Gardens is worth the money and the time. The tours are 2½ hours long, but they leave you wanting more.

■ *Shopping Kaua`i Style*

For gifts and crafts, check out the weekend craft fair in Kapa`a. If you're on the west side, don't worry. The West Kaua`i Craft Fair is also excellent. The farmers' markets throughout the island are also good bets for shopping.

■ *Try a Plate Lunch*

For a quick bite to eat in the afternoon, look no further than the plate lunch. This is a serving of meat, two scoops of rice and a scoop of macaroni or potato salad. The meat can be anything – teriyaki chicken, chicken katsu (a version of fried chicken) or fish. You can get a mini-plate, which only has one scoop of rice. It's one of the better values in terms of food.

■ *ATV Ride with Kipu Ranch Adventures*

Get down and dirty on an ATV tour with Kipu Ranch Adventures (www.kiputours.com). You'll ride out onto dirt roads through the ranch and see where scenes were shot from movies like *Raiders of the Lost Ark*, *Jurassic Park The Lost World* and *Six Days Seven Nights*.

■ *Kaua`i Museum*

You'll find Native Hawaiian artifacts, photographs dating back to 1890, quilts and World War II memorabilia, all telling the fascinating history of Kaua`i. ☎ 808-245-6931, www.kauaimuseum.org

■ *Queen's Bath*

This swimming area is off the beaten path in Princeville. It's a popular place to swim because it's protected from the sometimes pounding surf and it's also a great place to snorkel.

Queen's Bath

■ *Surfing*

Surfing lessons

You'll never forget your first time standing up on a wave, the rush that comes with standing on the board, looking down and seeing the water part beneath your feet. On the North Shore, favorite spots include Hanalei Bay, Tunnels and Cannons. On the South Shore, Po`ipu Beach, Lawai Beach and Shipwrecks are great places to learn. To the East, start off at Kalapaki Beach. In the West, Salt Pond is a good place for beginners. Lessons are available all over the island.

■ *Snorkeling*

Snorkeling is the best way to see Kaua`i's marine life up-close. There are plenty of places to snorkel, and one of the best places on the island is Tunnels on the North Shore. Just rent some gear and get in the water.

■ *Have a drink at Stevenson's Library*

This bar inside the Grand Hyatt in Po`ipu was named after Robert Lewis Stevenson. They have the best selection of Scotches and Ports. There's also live jazz every night, plus pool tables.

■ *Walk around Koloa Town*

Pick up a brochure about the Koloa Heritage Trail and walk around town. Travel back in time. While you're there, have a look at the Koloa History Center, where you can see old photographs and artifacts.

■ *Friday Art Night in Hanapepe*

Hanapepe turns into a party every Friday night. The shops and galleries stay open and there's live music as well. This happens every Friday from 6 to 9 pm.

The North Shore

What to See

IN THIS CHAPTER

When locals on Kaua`i talk about their favorite area of the island, the North Shore almost always comes up, and for good reason. To call this area quaint and idyllic doesn't do it justice. Watching the sunrise or sunset is majestic. The locals are friendly and more than willing to tell you where the good places to go are.

As you drive up the east coast or windward side of the island, it can be very easy to pass through the town of Kilauea and not even know you passed anything special. There are few shops along the highway that would indicate you're in a major town. You won't find any strip malls or a lot of traffic.

At the Shell gas station near mile marker 23, make a right turn and you'll find Kilauea Town.

Kilauea was once home to Kilauea Sugar Plantation. Today, it maintains its rural charm, a sleepy town and the gateway to the North Shore.

There are a couple of things that you can do here. You can stop by the **Kong Lung Center** for shopping and good eats. Down the road from there is the **Kilauea Lighthouse** and **National Wildlife Refuge**. There are also a number of farms and nurseries that sell fresh flowers and produce along the roadside.

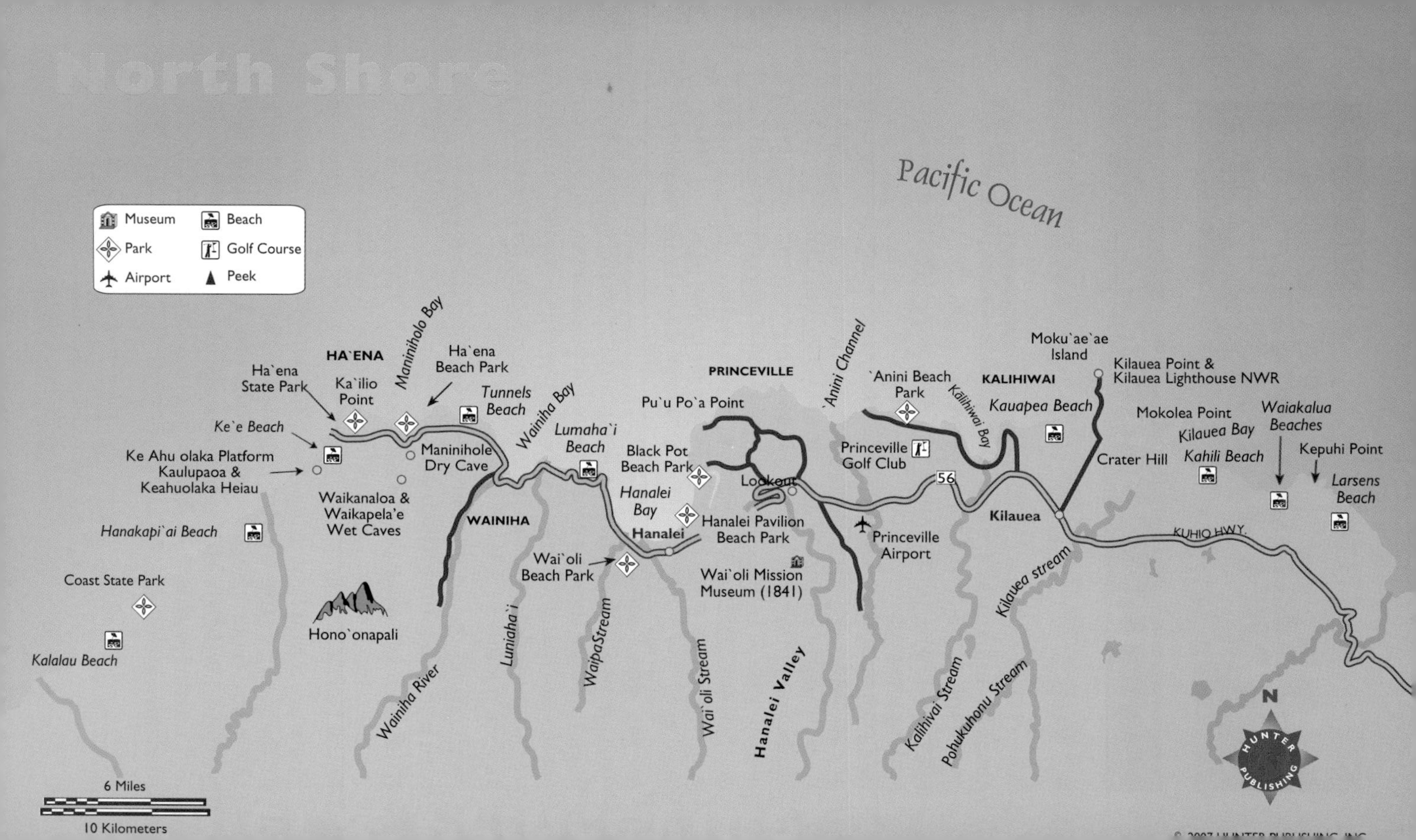
North Shore
Pacific Ocean
Museum
Beach
Park
Golf Course
Airport
Peek
HA`ENA
Ha`ena State Park
Ka`ilio Point
Maniniholo Bay
Ha`ena Beach Park
Tunnels Beach
Ke`e Beach
Ke Ahu olaka Platform Kaulupaoa & Keahuolaka Heiau
Maninihole Dry Cave
Waikanaloa & Waikapela'e Wet Caves
Hanakapi`ai Beach
Coast State Park
Kalalau Beach
Hono`onapali
WAINIHA
Wainiha Bay
Wainiha River
Lumaha`i Beach
Luniaha`i
Wai`oli Beach Park
WaipaStream
Black Pot Beach Park
Hanalei Bay
Hanalei
Hanalei Pavilion Beach Park
Wai`oli Mission Museum (1841)
Wai`oli Stream
Hanalei Valley
PRINCEVILLE
Pu`u Po`a Point
Lookout
`Anini Channel
`Anini Beach Park
Princeville Golf Club
Princeville Airport
56
Kalihiwai Bay
KALIHIWAI
Kauapea Beach
Kalihivai Stream
Pohukuhonu Stream
Kilauea
Kilauea stream
Moku`ae`ae Island
Kilauea Point & Kilauea Lighthouse NWR
Crater Hill
Mokolea Point
Kilauea Bay
Kahili Beach
Waiakalua Beaches
Kepuhi Point
Larsens Beach
KUHIO HWY.
6 Miles
10 Kilometers
N
HUNTER PUBLISHING

Hanalei & Princeville

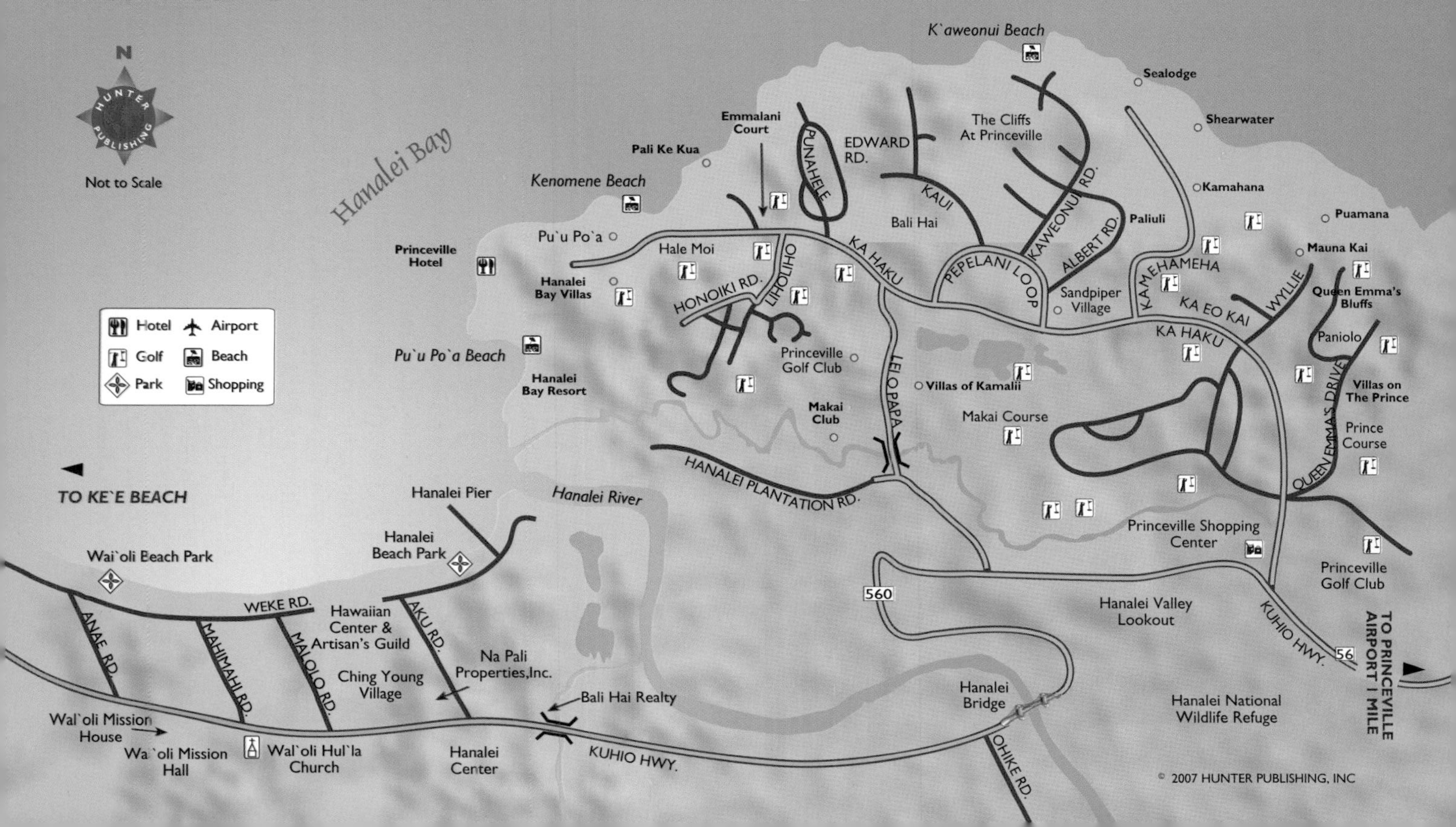

After your stop in Kilauea, get back on Kuhio Highway and continue north. After about 10 minutes, you'll come across **Princeville**. Princeville was once home to Hawaiian heiaus and was revered by ancient Hawaiians as a place of great spirit, or mana.

Captain Cook's arrival opened the door for other Westerners and they came in droves. In 1815, Georg Scheffer forged an alliance with King Kaumuali`i in order to regain lost cargo for the Russian-American Company. Scheffer promised manpower and weapons to help Kaumuali`i take control of the Hawaiian Islands. In return, Scheffer would get the right to construct factories throughout all of the Hawaiian Islands and half of O`ahu.

Scheffer then went to work. In 1816, he began to build the foundation of Fort Elizabeth in Waimea as well as Fort Alexander in Princeville and Fort Barclay near the Hanalei River. Scheffer was forced to abandon his efforts a year later, when King Kamehameha learned of this plan. Very little remains of Fort Alexander, which can be seen in front of the Princeville Hotel.

In 1853, Robert Wyllie, Hawai`i's former foreign minister, bought land near Hanalei and started a sugar plantation. He named the area Princeville seven years later. It was named in honor of a visit by King Kamehameha IV, Queen Emma and their two-year old son, Prince Albert. Sadly, the prince died in 1862 at the age of four. Albert Wilcox bought the land in 1895 and converted the plantation into a ranch. Princeville Ranch still exists as a working cattle ranch.

The Princeville of today can be described as a master-planned luxury resort. Princeville does at times feel over-planned, almost like a Disney resort. It doesn't have the charm or character of Hanalei, but it still has incredible beauty and opulence within its well-manicured area. Princeville's draws are the incredibly elegant Princeville Hotel, which sits hundreds of feet above the cliffs and the resort's two world-class golf courses.

Keep driving along Kuhio Highway past Princeville Shopping Center and you'll see taro fields on either side of you. Once you cross the one-lane bridge into **Hanalei**, you might feel as if you've been transported to a timeless wonderland where old hippies, surfers, tourists and even the occasional celebrity mix and mingle. The town is charming and maintains a laid-back feel. You can sit at a coffee shop and people-watch, have a drink at any of the establishments and find its easy to strike up a conversation with just about anyone.

You can walk around town and around the two shopping centers, **Hanalei Center** and **Ching Young Village**. Hanalei Center was once an old schoolhouse and now houses several shops and restaurants. Hanalei is also where you'll find some of the glorious beaches around Hanalei Bay.

Past Hanalei are several one-lane bridges that will take you to stunning beaches and the island's best snorkeling. After a few miles, you'll come to the end of the road in Ha`ena. **Ha`ena** is where you'll find dry and wet caves and it's also the start of the magnificent **Na Pali Cliffs**, which tower over the beach. The area is also the beginning of the 11-mile **Kalalau Trail**, which runs through Na Pali State Park.

If you're a history buff, there's plenty to keep you busy on Kaua`i. Here's a sample of historic sights you can check out while you're on the North Shore.

Kilauea

Guava Kai Plantations, ☎ 808-828-6121-4900, Kuawa Road, Kilauea, www.guavakai.com. Open daily from 9 am to 5 pm, including holidays. Guava Kai Plantation considers itself to be the guava capital of the world. With 450 acres of guava orchards under commercial cultivation, it's certainly earned the right to bill itself as such. Stop by the Visitor Center, where you'll learn how guava is grown, processed and how they make those sweet jams and jellies. They do offer the opportunity to pick guava for yourself, so get ready to be put to work.

There's a free self-guided tour that shows you how the fruit is processed. Don't forget to stop by the snack shop for a guava smoothie or guava ice cream.

Kilauea Point Lighthouse is open daily from 10 am to 4 pm. Closed national holidays. It's a 52-foot-tall structure built in 1913. The lighthouse has the world's largest clam-shell lens, which can send out a beacon of light reaching 90 miles. It was built in France at a cost of $12,000. And the view is something else. It's on the northernmost point of the island,

Kilauea Lighthouse

with a view of the Pacific Ocean and Mokuaeae Island below. It was decommissioned in 1976 and there are exhibits that detail the history of the lighthouse and wildlife you can see from the area. There are binoculars that you can borrow from the exhibit area to view the frigate birds and humpback whales in the winter.

Kilauea Point National Wildlife Refuge, ☎ 808-828-0168, was established in 1985 after its transfer from the US Coast Guard to the US Fish & Wildlife Service. The area consists of 200 acres of protected land. This is a great place to come and watch humpback whales, dolphins and honu. You might even catch a glimpse of the Hawaiian monk seal.

A number of native species of birds call this area home. The nene was reintroduced here in the 1960s. There's a one-mile walking trail from Kilauea Point to Crater Hill and it's used solely for tours led by refuge volunteers. The tour is at 10 am sharp Monday-Friday.

AUTHOR'S CHOICE ★ **Na Aina Kai Botanical Gardens**, 4101 Wailapa Road, Kilauea, ☎ 808-828-0525, www.naainakai.org. Na Aina Kai offers only guided tours at 9 am and 1 pm Tuesday-Thursday and 9 am on Friday. Reservations are highly recommended. Closed to the public on weekends and holidays. This 240-acre garden is actually comprised of 13 different gardens, each of which has its own unique character. As you walk through the gardens, you'll see as many as 70 bronze sculptures to admire. There are any number of tours you can take, ranging in length from 1½ hours to five hours. The tours are offered at specific times throughout the week and reservations are highly recommended. If you plan to bring children under the age of 13, then the only tour you can take is the Children's Garden Family tour. Tour fees range from $25 per person to $70 per person.

In the Na Aina Kai Botanical Gardens

In Ha`ena at the end of the road, there is an ancient hula site that dates back over 1,000 years. **Ka Ulu A Paoa Heiau** can be found off of Ke`e Beach. You'll see a trail that leads up to it. You'll come to the altar dedicated to Laka, the godess of hula. This site is said to be the birthplace of hula. You might see offerings such as maile leis left by hula dancers hoping for a successful dance competition. These leis are made of maile leaves, a vine-like plant native to the islands.

Also at Ha`ena are the **caves**. The caves are the result of the ocean pounding the lava rock for thousands of years. The best-known is the **Maniniholo Dry Cave**, which is 300 yards deep. To get there, go to Ha'ena Beach Park

Maniniholo Dry Cave

and look for the cave on your left.

A little farther down the road, just before mile marker 10, is a trail that leads uphill to the **Waikapalae** and **Waikanaloa Wet Caves**. There is no swimming allowed, but a few brave souls do enter the water at Waikapalae to observe a phenomenon that turns everything blue when sunlight reflects off the water. That's how it got the name "The Blue Room." The water is ice cold and there is nothing to hang on to, so be careful.

Christ Memorial Church

Christ Memorial Episcopal Church, ☎ 808-826-4510, 2509 Kolo Rd, Kilauea. Christ Memorial Episcopal Church is one small simple church that you can't help but notice as you drive through Kilauea. It's a small stone building that's nice to look at from the outside. But, once you enter, you'll notice the stunning glass windows and the mahogany altar. It's the history of the church that's as fascinating as the stained glass windows. Worship services were held in Kilauea as early as 1888, but they really didn't have a place of worship. They used a simple building owned by the Hawaiian Congregation Church, but it wasn't until 1939 that the church was built. Like almost everything else on the island, the church was built by the sugar industry. Kilauea Sugar Company deeded the land and donated the stone to Christ Memorial Church.

There's a graveyard surrounding the church that dates back approximately 100 years. Quite a number of the graveyards are unmarked and no one knows for sure how many people are buried there. Christ Memorial Episcopal Church does hold Sunday Service at 8:30 am. The church is on Kolo Road, just before you turn on Kilauea Road.

St. Sylvester's Roman Catholic Church, 2390 Kolo Road, Kilauea, is down the road from Christ Memorial Episcopal Church – another classically simple church. It was built around 1880 and it's far from your typical Roman Catholic

Church. First off, it's octagonal in shape. Second, it was made from lava rock and wood. The frescoes inside the church are work a look. They were painted by artist Jean Charlot. Worship Services are held on Saturdays at 5 pm and Sundays at 7 am.

Hanalei

The **Hanalei Bridge** is one of seven one-way bridges that connect Hanalei and Ha`ena State Beach Park (the end of the road). The bridge was originally built in 1912 and underwent a renovation in 2003. It is on the National Register of Historic Places. Remember when driving across this or any other one-way bridge that proper road rules apply.

When the Hanalei River reaches six feet or above, the bridge will close. Be aware of this fact during periods of heavy rains, especially if you're staying in Ha`ena and need to get to town or if you're planning on spending the day in Ha`ena.

This 917-acre **Hanalei National Wildlife Refuge** was established in 1972 to protect endangered Native Hawaiian waterbirds, including the Hawaiian stilt, coot, moorhen, and

Hanalei Valley

duck. Over 45 species of birds call the refuge home. You won't be able to find mammals or reptiles in the refuge, but the Hawaiian hoary bat is rumored to have a presence there. The Hanalei River flows through this area and it is also home to most of Hawai`i's taro farming. Hanalei National Wildlife Refuge is closed to the public but can be viewed from the Hanalei Valley Scenic Overlook.

Hanalei Valley Scenic Overlook Drive is north along Kuhio Highway (Highway 56). The Hanalei Valley Scenic Overlook is across the street from the Princeville Shopping Center. This area offers incredible views of the valley and taro farms below. The different shades of green and the taro patches look like a patchwork quilt from above. You can also catch amazing views of the mountains that back the valley. Bring your binoculars, for you might be able to catch a glimpse of the native birds that live in the Hanalei National Wildlife Refuge.

Hanalei Pier

Hanalei Pier. In the early 1900s, Hawai`i was one of the largest rice producers in the country, with towns like Hanalei and Wailoi leading the way. The Hanalei Pier was originally built in 1892 and extended in 1912, responding to the need to transport rice grown in nearby Hanalei Valley. It was one of the main ports on the island until 1933, when Nawiliwili Harbor was established. Since then, it was used primarily as a recreational pier where locals would come to fish. The pier shot to fame in 1957 when it was featured in South Pacific.

The Hanalei River was designated an American Heritage River by President Bill Clinton in 1998.

**Waioli Hui`ia Church**, Kuhio Highway, Hanalei, ☎ 808-826-6253. This area is a National Register Historic District. In 1921, three granddaughters of Hanalei Missionaries Abner and Lucy Wilcox restored the meeting hall that was originally built between 1837 and 1841. The Waioli Hui`ia Hawaiian Church choir still sings hymns in the Hawaiian language, which is remarkable to hear. Sunday Services are held at 10 am and are a must, even if you're not terribly religious. It's the green church on Kuhio Highway next to the soccer fields.

Waioli Hui`ia Church

Waioli Mission House, Kuhio Highway, Hanalei, ☎ 808-245-3202. Open Tuesday, Thursday and Saturday from 9 am to 3 pm. Closed on major holidays. Admission is free. Located right behind the Waioli Hui`ia Church, this former missionary home and the surrounding grounds give you a glimpse of what life was like in that era. The home was built in 1837. The house has been restored and contains furnishings and plants from that era. You can just walk in and you'll be greeted by a guide who will show you around the property.

Harigruchi Rice Mill, ☎ 808-651-3399, 5-5070 Kuhio Hwy, Hanalei www.haraguchiricemill.org. Office hours are Monday through Saturday 10 am to 5 pm. Tours are held only on Saturdays at 8 am. Admission $65. The Haraguchi Rice Mill is the only remaining rice mill in Hawai`i. The mill dates to the 1880s. It is on the W.T. Haraguchi Farm in the Hanalei National Wildlife Refuge. Learn about Hawai`i's agriculture and cultural history, view endangered native waterbirds, and explore the cultivation and uses of taro. Then have a picnic lunch featuring items prepared with taro grown on the farm. Tours include a sandwich or a smoothie (you can opt for the tasty Polynesian Papaya Kooler). In 1983, the Haraguchi family formed a nonprofit organization to restore the mill. It is now listed on the National Register of Historic Places.

Ha`ena

Limahuli Botanical Garden

Limahuli Botanical Garden and Preserve, Kuhio Highway, Ha`ena, ☎ 808-826-1053, www.ntbg.org. Open Tuesday through Friday and Sunday from 9:30 am to 4 pm. For guided tours that last about two hours, the cost is $20 per person. For a self-guided tour, the cost is $15. Reservations are required for guided tours. The botanical garden is set in a tropical valley in the shadow of Makana Mountain that towers over the area. Limahuli Gardens gives you the opportunity to experience a living history of sorts as you view native plants, plants that were introduced by the Polynesian settlers and by westerners. You'll walk through lava rock terraces built by Limahuli's first inhabitants and see the taro that still thrives there. You'll see plants such as mango, kava, tumeric and sugar. There are benches located along the ¾-mile trail that allows you to take in the extraordinary views and scenery.

Ha`ena (Hawaiian Images)

Limahuli Garden is a part of the National Tropical Botanical Garden, which focuses on conservation and education efforts in restoring the native ecosystem.

Sightseeing Tours

If you want to take it easy and have someone do all of the driving for you, a sightseeing tour would be a good bet.

North Shore Cab, ☎ 808-639-7829, www.northshorecab.com, has tours originating on the North Shore. You can take a 3½- or 4½-hour tour that starts in Kilauea, then goes to the Kilauea Lighthouse and Wild Life Refuge, Hanalei and Waioli Mission House. You can choose to stop at Tunnels Beach and Ha`ena Beach Park. They'll customize the tour for you. Rates are $50 per hour per taxi. with a two-hour minimum.

Polynesian Adventure Tours, ☎ 808-246-0122, www.polyad.com, has a tour that will pick you up in Princeville and take you to various places along the Coconut Coast, including Fern Grotto. Then you'll head west to Po`ipu and Waimea Canyon as well.

Aloha Discovery Island Tours, ☎ 808-632-0066, www.alohadiscoverykauaitours.com, will pick you up in Princeville and take you on a tour of the island. For $99 per person, you'll see Kaua`i Museum (admission included), Menehune Fishpond, Tunnel of Trees, the shops of Old Koloa Town and Spouting Horn, Waimea Valley, Menehune Ditch, Swinging Bridge, Waimea Canyon, Kaua`i Kookie Factory and Salt Pond.

■ Adventures

Hiking

Aside from the Kalalau Hiking Trail, there are a few other good hiking trails to take a look at. There are also opportunities to take a guided hike. Guided hikes are great if you want to learn more about the area and guides tend to point out plants and animals that you might otherwise miss. They're also good for safety reasons – if you're an inexperienced hiker, it helps to have someone who knows the trails well to make the experience more enjoyable.

One of the more popular trails for experienced hikers on the island is the **Powerline Trail**. This 11-mile trail starts at Kapaka Street, up the road from Princeville Stables. It follows an electric transmission line maintenance route (hence

Kalalau Hiking Trail

the name) and ends near the Keahua Forestry Arboretum in the Lihu`e-Koloa Forest Reserve on the east side of the island. This is a definitely a dry-weather hike. Even with hiking poles, it's possible to slip and stumble about in muddy conditions. It is an all-day trip, but you can hike in a few miles and thenhike back to your starting point.

If you need to pick up hiking gear, your best bet is to buy it at K-mart or Wal-Mart in Lihu`e. Both stores have gear that's cheap enough and you can always ship it home. For food, stop by Foodland in the Princeville Shopping Center or Big Save in Hanalei at the Ching Young Shopping Village.

If you want to rent your gear, **Kayak Kaua`i**, ☎ 800-437-3507, 808-826-9844, www.kayakkauai.com, in Hanalei, also offers daily and weekly rates for daypacks and backpacks

Guided Hikes

**Kayak Kaua`i**, ☎ 800-437-3507, 808-826-9844, www.kayakkauai.com, offers hiking tours that include transportation from their Hanalei or Kapa`a office, deli lunch, beverages and, of course, a guide. They offer an easy hike of Limahuli Botanical Garden and Limahuli Valley for $84. You can also take a more strenuous hike with Kayak Kaua`i to Hanakapiai Beach along the Na Pali Coast for $126 or go farther down the trails to Hanakapiai Falls for $168 per person.

Powerline Trail

Kaua`i Nature Tours, ☎ 888-233-8365 or 808-742-8305, www.kauainaturetours.com, also has a guided hike on the Kalalau Trail to Hanakapiai Beach or you can hike to Hanakapiai Falls, starting at $97 per person. Their hikes are guided by knowledgeable scientists and environmentalists, who offer detailed background information on the area.

Princeville Ranch Adventures, ☎ 888-955-7669, 808-826-7669, www.adventureskauai.com, does a four-hour hike through the private 2,500-acre Princeville Ranch. This is a good opportunity to see lands you normally wouldn't get to see since Princeville Ranch is privately owned.

If you want to hike with a group, check out the **Sierra Club** at www.hi.sierraclub.org. The Kaua`i chapter regularly schedules group hikes all over the island, including the Na Pali Coast area. There's a $5 donation for the hike. They have a list of upcoming hikes on their website.

Dr. Carl Berg of **Hawaiian Wildlife Tours**, ☎ 808-639-2968, will take you on a personalized tour to see Kaua`i's native and vanishing species, from forest birds and flora to hoary bats, monk seals, and green sea turtles. Rates are $45 per couple, per hour. Reservations one month in advance are recommended.

Horseback Riding

Princeville Ranch Stables, ☎ 808-826-6777, www.princevilleranch.com, has a number of options for horseback riding. They take leisurely rides through the 2,500-acre Princeville Ranch, one of the oldest working cattle ranches in Hawai`i. You can go on the Waterfall Tour, which takes you across the ranch, with a short but steep hike to the waterfall. There are three- and four-hour versions of the tour ($125 and $135); the longer tour gives you more time on your horse. They also offer a shorter tour without the waterfall hike and private rides as well.

If you want a real adventure, try a cattle drive. They move their cattle every five to 10 days to a new pasture and you can see what it's like to be a paniolo yourself. You'll have to call for schedule and availability. It costs $135 for 1½ hours.

Silver Falls Ranch in Kilauea, ☎ 808-828-6718, is in Kalihiwai Ridge. You'll go on a serene, peaceful ride through beautiful privately owned lands. The guides are knowledgeable and will point out plants and make sure you have great photo opportunities. It's well landscaped and you'll get the opportunity to see loads of plants, numerous types of palm trees and wild orchids. The horses are well trained and have an even temperament, so if you've never been on a horse before, they will take the time to show you what to do and make sure you're on the horse that's right for you.

They offer a few rides ranging from a 1½-hour ride through the property to a three-hour ride to a gorgeous waterfall and swimming area with lunch provided. Prices range from $80 for the 1½-hour ride to $120 for the three-hour ride. They also do private tours.

Kaua`i Polo

Kaua`i Polo Club plays a 13-match season every Sunday between July and September at Anini Beach Polo Field across from Anini Beach Park. Gates open at 1 pm and matches begin at 3 pm. Tickets are $10 for adults, $5 for children between 12 and 17. Children under 12 are free. For more information, call ☎ 808-346-2232 or visit www.kauaipolo.com.

ZIPLINE

AUTHOR'S CHOICE ★ **Princeville Ranch Adventures** has the best zipline tour on the island. In case you're not familiar with ziplining, you're basically gliding above ground attached to a series of cables between two posts. You'll wear a harness around the hip, attach yourself to a pulley around the top of the cable and zip from post to post. They emphasize safety, so you don't really have to "fear the worst." It does make for a fun adventure.

There are stops between the eight lines, including an entire hour at a great swimming and diving spot. The full tour takes about 4½ hours, with a maximum of 11 people. You must be at least 12 years old and weigh at least 80 pounds. There is a maximum weight limit of 280.

Golf

The North Shore of Kaua`i is renowned for its golf courses. The Prince and Makai Course, both at Princeville Resort, are world-class. *Golf Digest* rates the **Prince Course** as the number-one course in Hawai`i. Designed by Robert Trent Jones, Jr, it will challenge you, push you and lead you to question why you took up golf in the first place. You'll head uphill, downhill, and negotiate tradewinds. On the upside, the views are phenomenal. There are five sets of tees on every hole, and from each one you can see the ocean. This is an 18-hole par-72 course. For tee times, call ☎ 800-826-1105 or 808-826-5070. Greens fees are $175.

Princevillei Golf Course

Once you're through with your round, you can stop by the Princeville Resort Clubhouse, which houses the Princeville Restaurant and Bar and Princeville Health Club.

Makai Golf Course

The **Makai Course** was also designed by Robert Trent Jones, Jr. and consists of three separate par-36 nine-hole courses, Ocean, Woods, and Lakes, each starting and ending at the clubhouse. All three provide you with challenge and variety. Several tees at each hole allow you to shoot from the one that best suits your skill level. For tee times, call ☎ 800-826-1105 or 808-826-5070. Green fees start at $85 for nine holes and go up to $175 for 18 holes.

After your round of golf, stop by the snack shop where you can get burgers, snacks and drinks.

Tennis

There are a few options for tennis in the area, especially in Princeville. You won't find public courts in the North Shore, but courts are available at Princeville Hotel and Hanalei Bay Resort.

The **Princeville Tennis Club**, ☎ 808-826-3620, has six courts available at $15 per person ($12 for guests) for 90 minutes. They also have an extensive pro shop where you can rent equipment.

Hanalei Bay Resort, ☎ 808-826-6522, features eight hard courts and a full-service tennis program that includes group and private lessons. There's a $6 fee to use the courts.

Biking

For mountain bikers, one of the more popular options on the island is the **Powerline Trail**. This is a tough but rewarding challenge. It follows a powerline that connects the north shore with the east side of Kaua`i. The trail takes you into the middle of the island, offering views of Mount Wai`ale`ale.

If you need to rent a bike, **Pedal n Paddle**, ☎ 808-826-9069, www.pedalnpaddle.com, at Ching Young Village in Hanalei, has mountain bikes for rent at $20 a day or $80 a week.

For road riding, you can rent a cruiser bike and cruise the roads of Princeville, which are generally wide enough to accommodate cyclists. You can also ride around the side-streets of Hanalei and along the beaches. Note that the road past Hanalei toward Ha`ena is narrow, with no shoulder to ride on.

Pedal n Paddle also has tandem bikes for $10 a day and cruisers for $10 a day or $30 a week.

On the Water

Beaches

If there's anything that the north shore of Kaua`i is known for, it's the beaches. From Ke`e Beach in Ha`ena, there are miles upon miles of world-class beaches for you to enjoy. Hanalei Bay has been named one of North America's best beaches for the last two years by Dr. Beach, Stepehn Leatherman. The area has produced some of the finest surfers around today, including Andy and Bruce Irons and Bethany Hamilton.

> **Tip:** While the beaches on the north shore are beautiful, it's important to note that they can be dangerous in the winter. The winter storms can wreak havoc on the shorelines, making swimming and snorkeling very dangerous. During the summer, the water's calm and clear.

Queen's Bath

This once little known area is literally a pool formed by a lava shelf. During the summer, it is a fantastic place for swimming, snorkeling or sunbathing. Sometimes the ocean is too calm, causing the waters to be slightly murky.

Queen's Bath

To get there from Princeville take Ka Haku Road to Kapiolani and follow till you see the small parking lot and trail head. The trail to Queen's Bath is slightly muddy and heads down 120 feet to the shore. It may look intimidating at first, but on a dry day, it's actually a short and manageable hike. Make sure you wear good reef shoes or tennis shoes. The County of Kaua`i has closed the trail in the winter months.

Larsen's Beach

Larsen's is a great beach for sunbathing. Swimming isn't so good because the bottom is rather rocky and there are strong currents. In the winter, the surf pounds the beach. It's a secluded beach that's a bit of a challenge to reach. Drive on Kuhio Highway past Anahola and turn on Koolau Road. There's an access road that will take you to the beach.

Pila`a Beach

This tract of land is owned by the Mary Lucas Trust. It's been in the Lucas family since the early 1900s and is managed by co-trustee James Pfluger, one of Mary Lucas' grandsons and better known throughout the islands as the owner of the Pflueger auto dealership. You won't find direct public access to the beach. It can be reached if you follow the trail along the shore from Waiakalua Iki.

Rock Quarry Beach (Kahili Beach)

Rock Quarry Beach is located in Kilauea Bay at the mouth of Kilauea Stream. It's named after an abandoned rock quarry. You'll probably come across ironwood, naupaka and hala growing in the sand dunes. Rock Quarry is one of the more popular surfing spots on the island.When the surf is incredibly high on the north shore to the point where it can't be surfed, surfers will come to Kahili Beach for some wraparound action. This site is also good for boogie boarding.

Kauapea Beach (Secret Beach)

Secret Beach

This long, sandy beach is between Kalihiwai Bay and Kilauea Point. Most folks know it now as Secret Beach, but the secret's out. It was so secluded that it became a popular place for nudists. There aren't that many nudists around anymore because of the beach's popularity and because it's illegal to get nekkid in Hawai`i. Don't be shocked if you see a few. Regardless, it's a great place for swimming, surfing, body boarding and sunbathing during the summer. During the winter, months, it's not safe.

The best way to get there is to take Kalihiwai Road near mile marker 24 of Kuhio Highway. Then take the first right onto a dirt road and stay on the road for a few hundred yards to the parking area at the top of the trail. There's a long trail that is steep and can be very slippery and treacherous, especially if it's been raining. You'll hike for about 15 minutes and, at the end, pure paradise awaits.

Kalihiwai Beach

Kalihiwai Beach

Home to one of the North Shore's most popular surf breaks – Kalihiwai. It's best during the big winter swells of the winter and spring, but only get in the water if you know what you're doing. You don't realize how powerful the ocean is until it's too late. The surf break is really close to the cliff and it's for experts only. Closer to the beach, there's a break that's good for bodyboarding and body-surfing. Smaller rips do form near near the mouth of the stream as well. Inland, there's a large grove of ironwood trees. That's where folks tend to park. To get there, take Kuhio Hwy and turn off at Kalihiwai Road.

Anini Beach Park

Anini Beach

There's a two-mile-long reef that starts at Kalihiwai Bay and ends at the cliffs in Princeville. This is the longest fringing reef in the Hawaiian Islands. To the east you can see Mokuaeae Island; the Kilauea Lighthouse stands watch on the hill above. During calm waters, Anini Reef is great for windsurfing, snorkeling, camping and picnics. It's also a place for spearfishing, You might be able to see someone coming out of the water with an octopus in hand or a handful of fish.

Pali Ke Kua Beach (Hideaways Beach)

Pali Ke Kua Beach

This is actually two beaches separated by a rocky point. During the large winter swells, Hideaways' surf break is often compared to the famous break called Sunset Beach on O`ahu's North Shore. Like any winter swell, it is for experts only. In big swells, however, the water will envelop the beaches and hit the base of the cliffs. This is obviously not a good time to try to take a stroll along the beach. In the summer, though, the beach provides great opportunities for snorkeling and swimming. The sea bottom is somewhat rocky, but there are more pockets of sand to take advantage of the swimming and snorkeling. There are no facilities or lifeguards here.

To get here, head toward the Princeville Hotel. Just before the gate house, there's a path that leads down to the beach. The first half of the trail is paved, so it's not that bad; the second half is a dirt trail that can be tricky to navigate, especially after a rainstorm. Parking can be a challenge as there are only 10 or so stalls assigned for public beach parking.

Directly behind the Princeville Hotel is **Pu`u Poa Beach**. It named after the hill where the hotel sits. It also sits at the mouth of the Hanalei River. It's good for swimming, surfing and occasionally for snorkeling. During the winter, the beach gets dangerous.

Black Pot Beach Park

On the other side of the Hanalei River from Pu`u Poa beach is Black Pot Beach Park. It got its name from the big black pot locals used to cook fish and stew. The land was purchased by the county in the 1970s, which saved it from becoming condominiums. Today, the area is a place to come for kayaking, surfing, swimming, windsurfing, paddling and fishing. There are pavilions for picnics, restrooms and showers.

Hanalei Pavilion Beach Park

This is on Weke Road between Pilikoa and Aku Roads. There's a beach break that's great for beginning surfers and bodyboarders. Swimming is alright during the summer, but not great. There are shower and restroom facilities at the park and a lifeguard stand.

Waioli Beach Park (Pine Trees)

This is the place where the pro surfers come during the winter. It's the home break of Bruce Irons and his brother Andy, who's the three-time ASP world surfing champion. The surfing break here is popular and it's the home of several surfing contests. It's called Pine Trees because the area is lined with ironwood trees that can be mistaken for pine trees. Rest rooms and showers are available. You can get here from either Hee or Ama`ama Roads.

Waikoko Beach

It's at the western end of Hanalei Bay. There's a reef that's shallow and wide, which protects the beach for the most part. Since it's protected by the reef, the beach is popular for families throughout the year. When the water's calm, this can be a good spot for snorkeling. Surfers head out to Waikoko surf break.

Lumaha`i Beach

This is one of the most scenic beaches. It might look vaguely familiar to you if you've seen *South Pacific*. This is where

Lumaha`i Beach (*Hawaiian Images*)

Mitzi Gaynor sang about washing that man right out of her hair. While it's stunning to look at, it's not safe for swimming. The beach doesn't have a reef to protect it, creating dangerous conditions, even during the summer. The beach is seldom safe for swimmers.

Kepuhi Beach

This beach has some of the best fishing on the north shore. There are a number of reefs that are flat and shallow. It's not a good spot for swimming, but great for fishing. You can get there from Kuhio Highway and Alealea Roads.

Tunnels Beach

Tunnels Beach

Tunnels is one of the most popular beaches on the island, and for good reason. This two-mile beach gives you plenty of room. Tunnels is the best spot on the North Shore for snorkeling. It's also great for sailing, surfing and windsurfing. The beach is lined with rocks, so it's not a good spot for swimming.

Ha`ena State Park

This is the end of the road. Literally, this is where Kuhio Highway ends. It also marks the beginning of the Na Pali Coast. The area is home to **Ke`e Beach**, an incredibly scenic beach. You have the ocean in front of you and towering mountains behind you, it makes for quite a postcard picture. Ke`e is a popular swimming and snorkeling spot when the seas are calm. If you do go swimming here, be aware that strong currents do form, even in the calm summer months.

Ke`e Beach *(shorediving.com)*

TAYLOR CAMP

Right before Ke`e beach is where Taylor Camp used to be. The camp is named for Howard Taylor, who owned the land. Yes, this Howard Taylor just happened to have a very famous sister named Elizabeth. Taylor Camp was, for all intents and purposes, a hippy commune in the late 1960s and early 1970s. During this time, many of the hippies heard that you could be in paradise and live off the land and they went to Hawai`i in droves. The state eventually condemned the property in 1977. Taylor Camp is actually where the puka shell fad began.

The story goes that a girl at the camp strung together shells to make an anklet. Howard then gave one to his sister, who then wore it in public and created the puka shell craze to the point where puka shells were selling for $6 a pound in 1974.

Snorkeling

Snorkel Tours

Captain Sundown, Hanalei, ☎ 808-826-5585, www.captainsundown.com, has a few snorkel tours to choose from on their 40-ft catamaran. The tour will take you from Hanalei Bay, where you'll see Hanalei Pier, and around the Na Pali Coast to view waterfalls. They guarantee that you'll see the entire Na Pali Coast. You'll stop at Nualolo Kai A`awapuhi to snorkel. The tour includes snorkeling gear, a deli lunch and snacks. The cost is $162 per person.

Anini Fishing Charters, ☎ 808-828-1285, www.kauaifishing.com. Captain Bob Kutkowski offers a Na Pali Tour on his new 34-ft power catamaran. Anini Fishing Charters launches right from Anini Beach, and they'll take you on a half-day charter around Na Pali with all snorkeling gear and gourmet lunch included.

Na Pali Catamaran, Hanalei, ☎ 866-255-6853, 808-826-6853, www.napalicatamaran.com, takes you on their 34-ft custom Cougar catamaran from Hanalei along the Na Pali Coast, with snorkeling and lunch included. They operate regularly throughout the summer, but only weather-permitting during the winter months.

NA PALI FROM THE NORTH OR WEST?

One question that many people have when booking their boat tour is whether to leave from Waimea/Port Allen or from the north shore. It really depends on what you're looking for.

If you're staying on the North Shore, it's a much shorter drive to the tours that originate from Hanalei, as opposed to driving all the way to Port Allen. Tours starting from the North Shore reach the Na Pali coast more quickly, so you spend more time actually seeing Na Pali. If you leave from Port Allen, you'll be in the water 20-25 minutes before you get there. On the downside, the North Shore boat companies only offer catamaran tours. That's more relaxing, but, if you're looking for more adventure, you'll be better off taking one of the tours on a rigid-hull inflatable from Port Allen.

Places To Snorkel

If you want to pick up some gear and hit the beach, here are the best places to go snorkeling in the area.

Tunnels *(shorediving.com)*

Tunnels is one of the top snorkeling places on the island. It's best during the summer when the waters are calm. There is a reef relatively close to shore that makes for good snorkeling, even for beginners. Experienced snorkelers can venture out beyond this reef and see turtles, trumpetfish, butterflyfish and a whole lot more. In spite of the popularity of the beach, there is plenty of room to explore the reefs and have fun.

Ke`e Beach *(Hawaiian Images)*

Ke`e Beach offers opportunity to see bright reef fish. It is tough to snorkel during low tide because there's not much room between you and the reef. You should also watch out for the left channel, which can form a strong current and sweep you out toward Na Pali. Your best bet is to stay within the small bay area.

The two-mile-long fringing reef at **Anini Beach Park** provides excellent snorkeling. It is a good site for beginners and gives you ample opportunity to spot eels, boxfishes and humuhumunukunukuapuaa (say it three times fast!). Be aware of the channel area, for the current can be pretty strong.

Queen's Bath is excellent for snorkeling, making the hike down worthwhile. On a good day, you can see hundreds of fish. Sometimes, the water can be too calm, which leaves the lava pools somewhat murky.

Where to Get Snorkel Gear

Honu

Hanalei Surf Company in Hanalei Center, ☎ 808-826-9000, and **Hanalei Backdoor Surf Company** in the Ching Young Village, ☎ 808-826-1900, both offer snorkel gear for $5 a day or $17 for the week. The staff at both stores is knowledgeable and will steer you to the right places for snorkeling.

Pedal and Paddle in Ching Young Village, ☎ 808-826-9069 also offers snorkel gear for $5 a day or $20 a week.

Activity Wholesalers/ Snorkel Depot, Kuhio Highway next to Postcards Cafe, ☎ 808-826-9983, offers lower rates than everyone in the area for snorkel gear, sometimes as low as $2.99 a day. The quality isn't bad. If you're on a super-tight budget, it's worth it.

Threadfin butterflyfish

You should also stop at any of the rental shops listed above or at Foodland or Big Save and pick up an underwater camera for about $12-$17. In order to get the best shots, you'll need to get pretty close. If the water's clear, you can certainly pick up the different vibrant colors of reef fish.

Surfing

Surfing on the north shore is at its best in the summer. Only the pros would disagree with that statement. During the winter, the waves are large and dangerous, perfect conditions if you're an expert, but odds are, you're not. If you visit during the winter, you're better off cruising along the rolling waves on the South Shore.

Surf Instruction

Hanalei Beach Park *(Hawaiian Images)*

As a beginner, it's a good idea to get a lesson to learn the basics so you can get up on the board right away. It's also good to get in the water with people who are very familiar with the area and can tell you where the good breaks are.

Hawaiian Surfing Adventures, ☎ 808-482-0749, www.hawaiiansurfingadventures.com, has lessons from Hanalei Beach Park. The instructors will provide you with the board that's right for you and appropriate for the conditions. They'll teach you the basics before you get in the water. The lessons are 1½ hours at $55 for a group lesson; $75 for a private lesson. They also rent boards for $5 an hour or $15 per day.

Learn to Surf, ☎ 808-826-7612. At $40 per person for a 1½-hour beginner lesson, Learn to Surf is hard to beat. They give lessons to beginner, intermediate and advanced surfers at Hanalei Bay. They also rent boards for $25 a day.

Windsurf Kaua`i, ☎ 808-828-6838, doesn't just give windsurfing lessons. They also offer two-hour beginner lessons. They also have rentals available.

Kayak Kaua`i, ☎ 808-826-9844, www.kayakkauai.com, also has surf lessons for beginners. Lessons are held at Hanalei Bay, 10 am or 2 pm daily for $50. Call to reserve your spot.

If you're a surfer who's spent some time in the water, you'll want to rent a board and jump right in the water. Popular surfing spots are found at Hanalei Bay, Tunnels Beach, Kalihiwai and Cannons.

Aside from the places mentioned above, you can rent surfboards from **Hanalei Surf Company** in Hanalei Center, ☎ 808-826-9000, and **Hanalei Backdoor Surf Company** in the Ching Young Village, ☎ 808-826-1900. Both offer boards for $5 a day or $17 for the week. The staff at both stores is knowledgeable and will tell you what breaks are good for surfing.

Boogie Boarding

If you're not a big fan of surfing, you might want to try your luck at boogie boarding. Boogie boarding spots can be found throughout the area. Although the best boogie boarding spots can be found on the east and south shores, there's still decent boogie boarding at Hanalei Bay Beach Park and Kalihiwai Beach.

Pedal and Paddle in Ching Young Village, ☎ 808-826-9069, rents boogie boards with fins for $7 a day or $25 for a week. **Hanalei Surf Company** in Hanalei Center, ☎ 808-826-9000, also rents boards for $7 a day or $22 per week.

Scuba

The north shore has great scuba diving for experienced and beginning divers alike. With places like Cannons, Tunnels, Ke`e Beach and Anini Beach, the possibilities are endless. The reef along the north shore beaches offers vibrant marine life. There are lava tubes and caverns that you can explore.

North Shore Divers, ☎ 808-828-1223, has tours that are geared more for the experienced diver. One-tank shore dives start at $78 if you're already certified. Certified divers can also go on their two-tank boat dive for $135. If you're a beginner, they do offer instruction starting at $98 for a one-tank shore dive.

Bluestripe snapper

**Dive Kaua`i**, ☎ 808-822-0452, www.divekauai.com, in Kapa`a, offers shore dives along the north shore for certified divers, starting at $103 for a one-tank dive that includes all scuba gear.

Fathom Five Diving, ☎ 800-742-6991, 808-742-6991, also operates **Ocean Quest Watersports**, which is based in Hanalei. They have dives for the experienced and for beginners at Tunnels Beach Monday-Friday starting at $65 for one tank.

Kayaking

This area has a lot of options for kayaking. You can kayak along the Hanalei River or take an adventurous trek in the ocean. The Hanalei River has a pristine beauty and is a serene adventure, whether upstream into the Hanalei National Wildlife Refuge or downstream into Hanalei Bay. It's also a great way to experience the refuge up-close.

Ocean kayaking is focussed mainly on the excursion to the Na Pali coastline. There is nothing like seeing the incredible beauty of the cliffs from a kayak. That's one reason why *National Geographic Magazine* named this adventure one of the best in America. For more about kayaking Na Pali, take a look at the Na Pali section later in this chapter.

Ke`e Beach (*Hawaiian Images*)

Kayak Kaua`i, ☎ 800-437-3507, 808-826-9844, www.kayakkauai.com, offers a whole host of options for kayaking. You can rent a kayak and they will launch you from their dock along the Hanalei River. From there, you can paddle two miles upstream into the Hanalei National Wildlife Refuge or one mile downstream to Hanalei Bay. They also have car top racks available if you want to check out the Huleia, Kilauea and Kalihiwai rivers. The staff is friendly and they will help you plan your route if you have any questions. Single kayak rentals start at $28 and doubles start at $52.

Kayak Kaua`i also provides guided tours. They have a wonderful three-hour tour that takes you down the serene Hanalei River out into Hanalei Bay, where you can experience the fun and adventure of ocean kayaking. You'll land at Pu`u

Poa Beach behind the Princeville Hotel for snorkeling and snacks. It's great for folks who are absolute beginners or don't have too much confidence in the water. The cost is $60.

Kayak Hanalei, ☎ 808-826-1881, www.kayakhanalei.com, has tours that take off from an old boatyard at the mouth of the Hanalei River and generally include a lot of information about the history of the river. They have a three-hour tour of the Hanalei River and Hanalei Bay, with snorkeling. The tours offer a lot of information and history of the area.

Pedal and Paddle, ☎ 808-826-9069, www.pedalnpaddle.com, rents single kayaks starting at $20 a day or you can rent a double starting at $35 a day.

Windsurfing

Windsurfers off Ke`e Beach

Anini Beach is by far the best place to learn how to windsurf, while more advanced windsurfers will enjoy the ride at Tunnels.

Windsurf Kaua`i, ☎ 808-828-6838, has a three hour group lesson where you learn the basics of windsurfing for an hour, then spend the remaining two in the water. The cost for the beginner lesson is $85. They sail out of Anini Beach and they also rent equipment.

Windsurfing, lessons and rentals are also available from **Anini Beach Windsurfing** at ☎ 808-826-9463.

Kite Surfing

Hanalei Backdoor Surf Company in the Ching Young Village, ☎ 808-826-1900, has kiteboarding equipment. Popular places for kite surfing are Anini Beach and Tunnels.

Fishing Charters

Anini Fishing Charters & Tours, ☎ 808-828-1285, www.kauaifishing.com, offers daily charters from Anini Beach. Captain Bob Kutowski takes you on his 34-ft power catamaran. There's a maximum of only six passengers.

North Shore Charters, ☎ 808-828-1379, offers shared or private Na Pali coast tours and fishing charters leaving from Anini Beach. Fishing charters run a half-day and include light to medium tackle and Penn International Gold Reels.

You'll catch ono, ahi and mahimahi aboard Captain Gary West's 30-foot *Na Pali Wilson*.

In the Air

Helicopter Tours

Heli USA Airways, Princeville Airport, Princeville, www.heliusahawaii.com, ☎ 808-826-6591, is good if you're staying on the North Shore and you really don't want to drive down to Lihu`e. All of their tours start you off with a video presentation. Then you'll climb aboard their A Star Helicopter and fly around the island.

They offer a 30-minute tour for $109 per person. You will see Hanalei, Waimea Canyon, Na Pali and Alakai Swamp – a general overview of the island, but you'll miss out on much, much more. The deluxe tour, at $169, also includes more of Hanapepe Valley and more of Waimea Canyon. They also do tours out of Lihu`e Airport.

Nawiliwili Bay from a helicopter tour (*Hawaiian Images*)

■ Spas & Heath Clubs

Hanalei Day Spa at Hanalei Colony Resort, ☎ 808-826-6621, www.hanaleisayspa.com, has four treatment rooms, including two couples' massage rooms. They also offer private and group yoga classes, yoga retreats and beachside massage.

Northshore Healing Massage, ☎ 808-651-4299 or 808-651-7928, is an outcall service that specializes in couples and tandem massage. They offer a variety of modalities, from lomilomi massage to Swedish massage. Beachside massages are also available.

The **Princeville Health Club and Spa**, ☎ 800-826-1105, 808-826-5030, features a state-of-the-art exercise facility with magnificent mountain and ocean views. They have fitness classes, a 25-yard swimming pool, Jacuzzi, steam room and sauna. Daily admission is $20, or $15 if you're a Princeville Hotel Guest. They offer an array of massages, facials, and body treatments based the Aveda philosophy.

■ Shopping

There are plenty of opportunities for shopping on the North Shore, anchored by the area's four shopping centers – Ching Young Village and Hanalei Center in Hanalei, Princeville Shopping Center in Princeville and Kong Lung Center in Kilauea. Each offers different stores for gifts and food and the buildings are immersed in history as well.

■ *Kong Lung Center*

This has been the home of Kong Lung Company since 1902. The company was originally established in 1881 by a Chinese mmigrant to provide household items for plantation workers. Today **Kong Lung Company**, ☎ 808-828-1822, anchors the Kong Lung Center and still offers higher-end housewares, books, clothing and Asian antiques. The building has been restored to its plantation-era design and is listed on the National Register of Historic Places.

Other stores worth checking out at Kong Lung Center include **Island Soap and Candleworks**, ☎ 808-828-1955, www.kauaisoap.com. You can see how they use local ingredients like macadamia nut and kukui nut oils to make soaps, lotions and other health & beauty products. Open from 9 am-9 pm daily.

Lotus Gallery

Banana Patch Studio, ☎ 808-828-6522, www.bananapatchstudio.com, has hand-painted ceramic tiles and pottery, photography and t-shirts, among many other items.

The Lotus Gallery, ☎ 808-828-9898, www.jewelofthelotus.com, specializes in Asian and Hawaiian art and sculptures. They're open from 10 am-6 pm. The Kong Lung Center is also home to the **Kaua`i Arts & Cultural Center**, ☎ 808-828-0438, where you can catch movies and live entertainment.

■ *Princeville Shopping Center & Hanalei*

Traveling farther down Kuhio Highway is Princeville Shopping Center. Here, you'll find mostly vacation rental agencies and real estate offices. There's a **Foodland** for grocery shopping, **Island Ace Hardware** and a few restaurants. Don't forget to fill up at the **Chevron Gas Station**. It's the last gas station between Hanalei and Ha`ena. One really fun store that I enjoyed was **Magic Dragon Toy & Art Supply**, ☎ 808-826-9144. They have lots of toys, games and other tchotchkes for the kids.

Upon entering Hanalei, you'll see the **Hanalei Dolphin Fish Market**, which is home to a few galleries and shops. It also has the **Hanalei Dolphin Restaurant** and **Hanalei Dolphin Fish Market**. Be sure to stop by **Kai Kane**, ☎ 808-826-5594, a surf shop with a sizable selection of surf apparel.

Ola's, ☎ 808-826-6937, is a neat gallery that displays the works of over 100 artists from Kaua`i and the mainland. The media range from glass to pottery, leather to ceramics. **Overboard Clothing**, ☎ 808-826-8999, has a great selection of swimwear and aloha shirts, for both men and women. **Black Pearl Hanalei**, ☎ 800-588-3448, www.theblackpearl.com. offers South Sea black pearl jewelry and designs. Within the store is **Kim McDonald Art Gallery**, which display's the artist's oil paintings inspired by the Hawaiian Islands.

From the Black Pearl

The **Mark Daniells Gallery**, ☎ 808-826-6867 features watercolors and oil paintings. Mark currently works in watercolor, oils, wood, etched glass and stained glass.

Also in Hanalei are two shopping centers directly across from one another: The **Ching Young Village**, www.chingyoungvillage.com, and **Hanalei Center**, both of which are in historic buildings and have quite a number of shops and restaurants. Some of the notable stores are in the Ching Young Village include **Hanalei Surf Backdoor**, ☎ 808-826-1900, www.hanaleisurf.com, which has surf apparel and aloha shirts, surfboards, kitesurfing and skating equipment.

Pedal & Paddle

Pedal and Paddle, ☎ 808-826-9069, www.pedalnpaddle.com, rents and sells everything you'll need for your day at the beach, from beach chairs to snorkel equipment. They also rent camping gear and bicycles, too. **Hot Rocket**, ☎ 808-826-7776, has modern and vintage aloha shirts along with tiki-themed items. **Blue Kaua`i Tattoos**, ☎ 808-826-0114, is a good place to get that permanent reminder of your vacation. **Hanalei Video and Music**, ☎ 808-826-9633, is a great place to pick up local music, beautiful koa `ukuleles and hula implements.

Evolve Love, ☎ 808-826-4755, is a gallery with a wide selection of art, some of which has a very funky style. You can buy Hawaiian-style clothing for your kids at **Kokonut Kids**, ☎ 808-826-0353.

Robin Savage Gifts & Gourmet, ☎ 808-826-7500, www.robinsavagegifts.com, is a must for fine dining ware, and kitchen equipment. They also have local art and fine linens from Tommy Bahama, as well as funky jewelry. Don't forget to pick up something sweet from the bakery. This is the best place to find a unique wedding gift.

Across the street from Ching Young Center is **Hanalei Center**. Its stores are housed in six restored historic buildings, including the old Hanalei School. Worthwhile shops are **Hanalei Surf Company**, ☎ 808-826-9000, which has everything you'll need for surfing. **Sand People**, ☎ 808-826-1008 offers upscale resortwear, health & beauty items and gifts. For retro and even borderline tacky memorabilia, you have to go to **Yellowfish Trading Company**, ☎ 808-826-1227. They have a diverse collection of vintage prints, Hawaiian antiques and aloha lamps. **Kahn Galleries**, ☎ 808-826-6677, offers high-end art and **Tropical Tantrum**, ☎ 808-826-6944, is a boutique with colorful and tasteful dresses, casual attire and menswear.

Other stores that are more side-of-the-road places are **Hanalei Book Store**, 4489 Aku Rd, ☎ 808-826-2568, which is a tiny, tiny bookstore with a large number of books. If you're looking for a book to take to the beach or just about every Kaua`i-related book in print, this place is for you. You'll find maps and teen novels here as well.

Every Thursday from 9:30 am to 4:30 pm, **The Christ Memorial Church**, 2518 Kolo Road, ☎ 808-821-8814, holds its **Craft Fair**. Vendors bring handmade jewelry and gifts. The proceeds help raise funds for the church.

For groceries, you have a wealth of options to choose from. In Princeville Shopping Center, there's **Foodland**, which has good quality and selection, but it can be expensive. **Big Save** is located in Ching Young Village. For fresh, quality fish and seafood, definitely go to **Hanalei Dolphin Fish Market** in the back of Hanalei Dolphin Restaurant.

For healthy and organic foods, **Hanalei Health & Natural Foods**, ☎ 808-826-6990, in Ching Young Village, and **Papaya's**, ☎ 808-826-0089, www.papayasnaturalfoods.com, at Hanalei Center, both have a good selection of organic goods and health goods. Papaya's tends to have a better selection and is a little cheaper.

Finally, the **Farmer's Markets** on the north shore are not to be missed. On Thursdays at 4:30 pm, the **Kilauea Neighborhood Town Center** hosts the farmer's market sponsored by the County of Kaua`i.

On Saturdays, there are also farmer's markets at 11:30 am on **Keneke Street** in Kilauea and at 9:30 am in Hanalei at the **Hanalei Neighborhood Center & Ballpark**.

■ Nightlife/Entertainment

Even though the North Shore seems quiet and secluded, there's still some nightlife happening here. Most of it consists of cocktails and live music. If you're looking for a club or you want to do some late-night partying, stay in Po`ipu.

Starting off in Kilauea, there's the **Kaua`i Arts and Cultural Center** in the Kong Lung Center, ☎ 808-828-0438. You'll be able to catch movies and small concerts here. It's the only theater in the state with a BYOB policy.

Happy Talk

In Princeville, there are a few places to go to. **Happy Talk Lounge**, 5380 Honoiki St, ☎ 808-826-6522, at the Hanalei Bay Resort. Enjoy the open-air atmosphere while you have drink and pupus.

The Living Room

It's a bit more casual than **The Living Room** in the Princeville Hotel – an open-air bar that has pleasant music, great views, and friendly people. You get great views of Hanalei Bay. It has a Sunday Jazz Jam from 3 to 7 pm Sunday, and contemporary Hawaiian music in the same lounge Monday through Saturday from 6:30 to 9:30 pm. Al Jarreau and Quincy Jones are among those who have stopped by the Sunday Jazz Jam, and the evening crowd has had its share of well-known Hawaiian jammers. On Saturday evening, Kenny Emerson, a fabulous guitar and steel guitar player, performs with Michelle Edwards.

Sushi Blues, 5-5190 Kuhio Highway, Ching Young Village, Hanalei, ☎ 808-826-9701, www.sushiand blues.com, has an eclectic mix of music every night starting at 8:30. It ranges from blues to reggae to Hawaiian.

Hanalei Gourmet is a fun place to have a beer and listen to local music. Normally, it's a couple of guys playing guitars, but they sound good. They'll play a mix of local favorites and classic tunes everyone knows. The only bad thing is that there's no room to dance.

The Landing Pad, by Princeville Airport, has Fiesta Latino on Thursday nights. If you're 21 or over, you can stop by at 8 for a salsa lesson for $10 and put what you've learned to work from 9-1:30. In the meantime, enjoy the mojitos. There's live Latin percussion most Thursdays.

The Hanalei Family Community Center hosts traditional slack key guitar and `ukulele concerts on Fridays at 4 pm and Sundays at 3 pm. Look for the sign announcing the concerts on the left just past Ching Young Shopping Center. Admission is $10 per person. For more information, contact, ☎ 808-826-1469 .

The only luau on the North Shore is the **Paina O Hanalei Luau** at Princeville Hotel. It's held poolside with great views of Hanalei Bay on Monday and Thursday at 6 pm. $99 per person. Like everything else at the Princeville Hotel, the food is excellent. The show is OK. If you really want to experience a luau, your best bet is **Smith's Tropical Paradise** is Wailua.

■ Where to Stay

Hotels

Princeville Hotel in the Princeville Resort 5520 Kahaku Road, Princeville, ☎ 800-325-3589, 808-826-9644, www.princevillehotelhawaii.com. There are two words that come to mind when describing the Princeville Hotel: "First Class." From the moment you walk in the door, you'll notice the elegance and attention to detail, from the neatly polished floors, to the Louis XIV chairs and oversized couches in the lobby area. The second thing that you'll notice is that you're pretty high up on top of a cliff and the

Princeville bedroom

views from the lobby area are amazing.

The location is incredibly convenient. So much so, you don't really need a reason to leave the property. There's a beach downstairs that great for swimming, surfing and windsurfing. The reef provides decent snorkeling (not as good if you went to a place like Tunnels). Golf and tennis are nearby. You have the best restaurants, with 24-hour room service, spa and even a movie theater. Oh yeah, there's tennis and world-class golf in the Prince and Makai golf courses, both designed by Robert Trent Jones, Jr. The hotel provides a shuttle service to both courses. What else do you really need?

They also have art classes, covering photography to painting. There's even a Keiki Aloha program, so you can ditch the kids while you run off to play elsewhere.

There are a lot of activities here at the resort for children as well as adults. There's a Hawaiian program, horseback riding, and golf. There's a health club and spa on the premises and you can rent bicycles, surfboards and kayaks.

All rooms feature bathrooms with double vanities, his and hers terry robes, slippers, and deep immersion tubs, some of which are mini-spas. Here's a neat trick – the bathroom windows are made from liquid crystal that can be controlled to change from opaque for privacy to clear so you can enjoy the view from the tub. These finely decorated rooms in beige or

Princeville Resort aerial view (*Hawaiian Images*)

green also feature king beds, refrigerators, TVs, safes, ironing boards, 24-hour room service. Suites have an extra large and plush sitting area with dining table. If it's in your budget, go for it. It's well worth it. $400+.

Condos

View from Hanalei Bay Resort

Hanalei Bay Resort, 5380 Honoiki Road, Princeville, ☎ 800-827-4427, 808-826-6522, www.hanalei-bayresort.com. Hanalei Bay Resort has undergone quite a few changes over the last few years. It used to be managed by Aston Hotels & Resorts and now it's run by Quintus. Quintus turned a number of the units into timeshares and individually owned units. A lot of owners do rent their units out. You'll probably get a better deal contacting one of the vacation rental agents listed below.

Room at Hanalei Bay Resort

Located within the Princeville Resort, it's still a fantastic location that affords beautiful views of Hanalei Bay and Bali Hai. Rooms range from a basic hotel room to a one-bedroom condo with kitchenette. The entrance is beautiful but, as soon as you walk in, you'll notice the indifferent service and staff. Don't be surprised if at some point during your stay, someone mentions buying a timeshare.

On the positive side, the resort is home to **Bali Hai restaurant** and **Happy Talk Lounge**. If you like to play tennis, then you're in luck with the eight tennis courts and a pro shop here. You can get a special rate to play golf at the Princeville Resort's Prince and Makai courses.

There's also a beautiful pool with a 15-foot lava waterfall and Jacuzzi. There have been a couple of times that I've been here when the pool wasn't too clean, which is unfortunate. You can take a path down to the beach. The bottom line is that you can do a lot better for your money. $200-$400.

**Ali`i Kai I**, 3830 Edward, Princeville, ☎ 808-826-9775, 800-826-7782. Ali`i Kai I sits on a cliff that overlooks the ocean. There are 63 units, all of which have two bedrooms and two baths. The rooms seem to be clean and well-maintained. There's a swimming pool, hot tub and barbecue area on-site. You're close to the beach, have access to incredible ocean views, and are fairly close to some of the finer restaurants in the Princeville area. Most of the units are individually owned, which means that there are a number of vacation rental agents that handle this property. There's also the Ali`i Kai Resort next door, but it doesn't offer the same views as Ali`i Kai I. $100-$200.

Ali`i Kai I

The Cliffs at Princeville, ☎ 800-367-7052, www.cliffs-princeville.com. This relatively modest place offers wonderful views of Hanalei Bay. It's situated on a cliff within Princeville Resort, overlooking the ocean. There are 220 units comprised of timeshares and individually owned vacation rentals. The units are roomy, especially the master bedroom, which is huge. Since the units are individually

The Cliffs

owned, the furnishings will vary from unit to unit, as will the overall condition of the unit. The vast surrounding grounds are somewhat unkempt, but the management staff is friendly. $100-$300.

An apartment at The Cliffs

Hanalei Bay Villas, 5451 Ka Haku Road, Princeville, www.hanaleibayvillas.com. This small, 37-unit complex is a good value for the Princeville Resort area. The units are two-story, with two bedrooms and two baths, or three bedrooms, three baths, and 1,300 square feet of living space. Everything within Princeville Resort is easily accessible. Most of the units have plenty of windows that offer mountain and some ocean views. $100-$200.

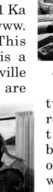

In the Hanalei Bay Villas

AUTHOR'S CHOICE ★ **Hanalei Colony Resort**, www.hcr.com, Ha`ena, ☎ 800/628-3004, 808-826-6235. An excellent choice if you really want to get away from it all. The resort is in Ha`ena, so it's secluded and isolated. You are pretty much disconnected from everything. Good luck trying to get a cell phone signal. There are no televisions in the rooms (gasp!) or phones. If you are really desperate, there is a common area that has computers and wi-fi available, so you can still at least check your e-mail. There are 48 condominium units on the property, which offers an on-site swimming pool and Jacuzzi, barbecue areas, poolside parties, continental breakfast, and children's programs. The staff is friendly and helpful and they are very willing to share their knowledge of the area. **Hanalei Day Spa** is on the property, so you can unwind with a massage or treatment.

Colony Resort

The rooms are spacious and some of them are within 50 feet of the water. You can sit out on your lana`i and enjoy the sounds of the ocean while you gaze up at the stars. The rooms are clean and comfortable. They have fully stocked kitchens, lana`i, and laundry facilities are on the property. $200-$300.

B&Bs

Hale Hoo Maha, 7083 Alamihi Road, Hanalei, ☎ 800-851-0291, 808-826-7083, www.aloha.net/~hoomaha, is a five-minute walk to Wainiha Bay and Secret Beach. It's a simple split-level home that offers four rooms at a reasonable price, with breakfast included. All rooms have hardwood floors, closet space, telephone, high-speed Internet connections, cable television and DVD player. You'll also be able to use the barbecue grill and kitchen. One room worth mentioning is The Pineapple Room, which has a king-sized round bed. $100-$200.

Princeville B&B

Princeville B&B at the Princeville Resort, 3875 Kamehameha Road, Princeville, ☎ 800-826-6733, 808-826-6733, www.kauai-bandb.com. Rooms range from the Royal Hawaiian Honeymoon Suite, which has everything you could want, even a washer and dryer, to the Bali Hai Room, which is just that – a room. Regardless, all of the rooms are spacious. The Princeville B&B is right on the Makai Golf Course, which makes it very convenient for golfers. It's a nice place to stay if you're looking for a place to rest in between activities or if you plan on playing a lot of golf. There's a three-night minimum stay and children under age 14 are not permitted. $100-$300.

Hale Luana, 4680 Kapuna Road, Kilauea, ☎ 808-828-6784, www.haleluana.com, has two rooms available, both of which offer a private bath and private entrance. The Allemanda Room and the Awapuhi Room also have color TV, VCR, microwave, coffeemaker, not to mention mountain views on one end and a pool/ocean view on the other end. Breakfast is provided every morning. $100-$200.

Hale Luana

They also offer a full guesthouse at Hale Luana for $2,300 a week. The **guesthouse** has five bedrooms and five bathrooms. The home also has a full kitchen, and a spacious living room with television, VCR and stereo. The home accommodates up to 10 people. There is a one-week minimum stay.

Garden Cottage terrace

North Country Farms, Kilauea, ☎ 808-828-1513, www.northcountryfarms.com, bills itself as an eco-tourism destination. The four-acre property is really a family farm, where organic fruits and flowers are grown. There are two cottages on the property, both of which offer a great deal of privacy. At the North Country Farms, you're within a stone's throw of the beach and the interior of the cottages is very cozy. Both are hand-built wooden homes. The smaller one, called **The Gar-**

den Cottage, is spacious and clean. It has a queen-sized bed, couch, table, bathroom and a fully stocked kitchenette with a toaster oven and microwave oven. The lana`i area is also spacious and has a gas grill. There's a huge porch with a nice gas grill. You can enjoy the quiet beauty of the area with a view of the garden and the mountains. **The Orchard Cottage** sleeps six and it has all of the amenities of the Garden Cottage. It has a huge lana`i, complete with a hammock. The view from the cottage is of the orchard.

Orchard Cottage

They don't serve breakfast here but they do greet you with a breakfast basket of coffee, teas, juice, fresh fruit and muffins upon your arrival. You're encouraged to pick from the gardens and orchards on the property during your stay. The orchard grows avocados, limes, grapefruit, oranges, mangos, lychees, and papayas. $100-$200.

Aloha Sunrise Inn

Aloha Sunrise Inn, 4899-A Waiakalua St, ☎ 888 828 1008, 808-828-1100, www.kauai-sunrise.com. Located in a quiet area of Kilauea, this is a quaint, two-story cottage attached to the owner's residence. It's small, at only 700 square feet, but the layout makes the most of the space. Upstairs is a bedroom with a queen-sized bed. The room is brightly lit with help from a skylight. There's a bathroom and full kitchen and dining area downstairs. Five-night minimum stay. $100-$200. The owners also run the Aloha Sunset Inn, which is a separate cottage on the seven-acre property.

Vacation Rentals

If you prefer not to stay at a resort or to stay a bit off of the beaten path, a vacation rental is a good way to go. There are tons of options for vacation rentals on the North Shore. Also, they tend to be less expensive than staying at a resort or hotel. Here are a few properties worth a look that are rented out directly by the owners.

Secret Beach Hideaway, 2884 Kauapea Rd Princeville, ☎ 800-820-2862, 808-635-6184. This is the ultimate hideaway that's not really a big secret anymore. Beautifully decorated cottages do reflect Asian influences, which further adds to the charm. All cottages are equipped with fully stocked state-of-the-art kitchens and cookware. Three feature luxurious furnishings including marble and granite baths and kitchens. The beauty of the location is that you're close enough to everything, but so far removed from civilization that you can just enjoy the beautifully manicured landscape, which is incredibly lush and green. Three night minimum stay. $300-$400.

Mana Yoga Vacation Rental, 3812 Ahonui Place, ☎ 808-826-9230, www.manayoga.com. For a more tranquil experience, you can stay at Mana Yoga in Princeville. Located on a five-acre property, Mana Yoga rents out the downstairs and also created a two-bedroom rental and a separate studio. The two-bedroom Kaua`i vacation rental features king- and queen-size beds, bath, fully equipped kitchen, living room, TV, VCR/DVD, water purifier, and a large gas grill on the lana`i. The studio has a king-size bed, efficiency kitchen, TV, VCR/DVD and Hawaiian-style private outdoor shower. All linens, beach towels, snorkel gear, a kayak, surf and body boards are included with the rental. The owner also runs the

Terrace at the Mana Yoga rental

Mana Yoga rental living room

Mana Yoga studio in Hanalei. Minimum three-night stay. Studio under $100; two-bedroom $100-$200.

Anini Beach Hale, ☎ 877-262-6688, 808-828-6808, www.yourbeach.com. This two-bedroom house is affordable and has a fabulous location. The house sits on a huge lot, which gives you a tremendous amount of privacy. The location is steps away from Anini Beach, which puts you near some of the island's best water sports. The accommodations are roomy. $200-$300.

View from the Anini Beach Hale

Kilauea Lakeside Estate, Kilauea, ☎ 310-379-7842, www.kauaihoneymoon.com. Two words describe this estate: private and luxurious. The land consists of a five-acre peninsula surrounded by a private 20-acre freshwater lake. There is a private beach on the property for honeymoons or family enjoyment. There's plenty to do, including swimming, windsurfing, kayaking and boating; snorkeling and surfing are near the estate. If that's not enough, you can sharpen your golf game on the par-three hole and putting

Aerial view of Kilauea Lakeside Estate

green on the property. The interior offers 3,000 square feet of living space. $300-$400.

Kaua`i Vacation Rentals List, www.kauaivacationresorts.com, is a directory that lists hundreds of condominiums, secluded honeymoon cottages, oceanfront luxury homes and beachfront bungalows throughout the island. They have listings to fit all budgets, from $400 to $21,000 per week.

Rental Agencies

Garden Island Properties, ☎ 800-801-0378, 808-822-4871, www.kauaiproperties.com, handles vacation properties across the island. They have vacation rental homes, cottages and beach condos starting from $500 a week.

**Kaua`i Vacation Rentals**, ☎ 808-367-5025, 808-245-8841, www.kauaivacationrentals.com, has a large selection of vacation rental homes. They offer Kaua`i's largest selection of vacation rental homes. Whether it's a cottage, bungalow, ocean-view condo, beachfront villa or luxurious oceanfront home, they'll probably have it in their inventory.

Bali Hai Realty, ☎ 866-400-7368, 808-826-6000, www.balihai.com, deals mostly with luxury vacation homes, although they do have plenty of condo rentals throughout the North Shore. They have a limited selection of properties for those on a tight budget as well.

Harrington's Paradise Properties, ☎ 888-826-7168 , % 808-826-9655, www.oceanfrontkauai.com, Handles vacation homes throughout the North Shore.

Hanalei North Shore Properties Sales & Vacation Rentals, ☎ 800-488-3336, 808-826-9622, www.hanaleinorthshoreproperties.com, works with economy to deluxe condos, homes, estates and tropical hideaways. They also have activities and special guest services. As a side note, they also handle Charo's Bali Hai Villa, the famous "cuchi cuchi" entertainer's home. The gorgeous estate is on Tunnels Beach and will set you back a cool $7,700 a week – in the off-season.

Re/Max Kaua`i, at Princeville Shopping Center, ☎ 877-838-8149, 808-826-9675, www.remaxkauai.com, specializes in condos and vacation rentals in the Princeville area. They have properties that suit all budgets, from inexpensive to luxury. You can make your reservations through their online reservation system.

Hostel

The beach at Camp Naue

Camp Naue, ☎ 808-246-9090, is a good way to go if you want to meet other folks or if you're traveling on the cheap. It's run by the YMCA of Kaua`i and tends to cater to large groups. It is open to the public, but on a space-available basis. At the very least, you might be able to get a camping spot on the beach to pitch your tent.

Accommodations are very simple. They're pretty much like a dorm room with electricity, running water and hot showers. You do have to bring your own bedding and cooking supplies. The cost is around $12 per night for the bunkhouse, $10 per night for a campsite.

You can't beat the location – right on the beach in Ha`ena. During the summer, it becomes a prime location because of the easy access to snorkeling, swimming and surfing. You're also near the Kalalau Trail trailhead. Under $100.

Camping

To camp on Kaua`i, you need to get a permit. Depending on where you plan on camping, you'll either have to go through the state or county to get a permit.

If you plan on camping at Anini Beach Park, Hanalei Beach Park or Ha`ena Beach Park, you'll have to go though the Kaua`i County Division of Parks & Recreation. To obtain a county permit, contact the **Kaua`i County Parks Permit Section** by calling ☎ 808-241-4463. Their hours are 8:15 am to 4 pm Monday through Friday. You can also get a permit at the **Kilauea Neighborhood Center**, ☎ 808-828-1421. However, they're only open between 8:30 am and 12:30 pm. Camping permit fees are $3 per adult, per night for non-residents and free for Hawai`i residents.

Camping fees for Hawai`i State Parks are $5 per campsite per night. If you're camping in Na Pali Coast State Park (Hanakapai, Hanakoa, Kalalau and Miloli`i), the fee is $10 per person per night. You can download an application fom the Hawai`i State Division of Land and Natural Resources at www.hawaii.gov/dlnr/dsp/fees.html or call ☎ 808-274-3444. There are a limited number of permits, so it's advisable to send in your application months (yes, months) in advance.

If you need to pick up camping gear, your best bet is to buy it at **K-mart** or **Wal-Mart** in Lihu`e. Both stores have gear that's inexpensive and you can always ship it home. For food, stop by **Foodland** in the Princeville Shopping Center or **Big Save** in Hanalei at the Ching Young Shopping Village.

If you want to rent your gear, **Pedal N Paddle** in the Ching Young Shopping Village in Hanalei, ☎ 808-826-9069, has daily and weekly rates for two-person tents, single burner stoves and sleeping bags.

Kayak Kaua`i also offers daily and weekly rates for day packs, backpacks, two-person tents, stoves and seeping bags.

■ Where To Eat

The North Shore offers quite a number of dining opportunities. If you're looking for a quick bite or a five-star meal, you can be sure to find it on the north shore.

Bali Hai at the Hanalei Bay Resort, Princeville, ☎ 808-826-6522, is an excellent choice for a romantic dinner. If you can, get there just before sunset and get a table outside to watch the sunset. It's unforgettable. The menu is mostly Pacific Rim cuisine. The

The view from Bali Hai

food and the service are well worth the money. $35-$50+.

Banana Joe's, 5-2719 Kuhio Highway, Kilauea, between mile markers 23 and 24 heading north, on the mountain side of the street, ☎ 808-828-1092. Open 9 am-6 pm daily. This little yellow stand has fresh fruit, smoothies and other drinks, packaged fruit baskets, baked goods with fruit and locally produced honey. Be sure to pick up some Anahola Granola and banana bread. Simply awesome! You can't miss it driving along the road.

Bar Acuda Hanelei Center, Hanalei, ☎ 808-826-7081, is a relatively new, yet hip and sophisticated, tapas establishment. The lunch menu is limited to pizzas, panini sandwiches and salads, all of which are good. The paninis are fabulous. The dinner menu consists of a variety of tapas-size pupus, entrées, and desserts. The portions are small considering the price. They also have live music during the weekend. $15-$35.

Bubba Burgers, Hanalei Center, Hanalei, ☎ 808-826-7839 Open daily from 10:30 am to 8 pm. Plenty of folks might tell you that this is supposed to be "The Place" to get a burger, but I was pretty disappointed. They're decent burgers, but not out of this world. All things considered, it's a quick, easy and inexpensive option when you're going to or coming from the beach. Under $15.

Bubba Burgers

AUTHOR'S CHOICE ★ **Café Hanalei**, in the Princeville Hotel, ☎ 808-826-2760. Breakfast is served starting at 6:30 am; lunch at 11 am to 2:30 pm; dinner at 5:30 pm to 9:30 pm. Be sure to make your reservations early and request an outside table. Café Hanalei is well-known for its beautiful setting and spectacular view. You'll be treated to a fine meal in an exquisite atmosphere that will create an unforgettable dining experience. Everything on the menu may seem a bit pricey, but it's well worth it.

The breakfast menu has traditional fare as well as a couple of Japanese items. They also have a breakfast buffet where you can get eggs benedict or made-to-order waffles and pancakes. The lunch menu features salads and sandwiches. The dinner menu is mostly fusion cuisine, with items such as Beef Tenderloin Tataki or Kaua`i Greens with Lilikoi Vinaigrette for starters and Macadamia Nut Crusted Swordfish for an entrée.

Café Hanalei

On Friday night, Café Hanalei offers a seafood buffet. There are five or so different food stations raging from salad to pupus to entrées, so you certainly have a lot of options. If you're not a seafood eater, you can get prime rib or chicken and beef teriyaki kabobs. And of course, don't forget the dessert. There's a rather large dessert station, so be sure to bring your sweet tooth. My personal favorite was the flourless chocolate cake.

Don't forget about the fabulous Sunday Brunch. The brunch offers traditional breakfast items as well as pancakes, omelets and crêpes. In addition, there are loads of peel-and-eat shrimp and Dungeness crab legs. Don't forget to try the sushi and poke.

Breakfast under $15-$35, lunch $35-$50, dinner $50+, Friday seafood buffet $50+, Sunday brunch $50+.

CJs Steak & Seafood, Princeville Shopping Center, ☎ 808-826-6211. Lunch served weekdays from 11:30 am-2:30 pm; dinner from 6 pm-9:30 pm. The food is good, but a bit overpriced. The menu is pretty much steak and seafood, including prime rib, lobster and crab. Entrées include the salad bar. Lunch $15-$35, dinner $50+.

Papaya's Natural Foods, 5-5161 Kuhio Hwy, ☎ 808-826-0089, www.papayasnaturalfoods.com, 9 am-8 pm every day, café closes at 7 pm. For vegetarians, Papaya's is a health food store and a vegetarian café. The store offers organic produce, beer, wine, bulk foods and health and beauty products. The café serves breakfast, lunch and dinner. You can get smoothies there as well. The food is good and priced right. There's also a Papaya's in Kapa`a. $15-$35.

Hanalei Dolphin Restaurant

Hanalei Dolphin Restaurant & Fish Market, 5-5016 Kuhio Hwy, Hanalei, ☎ 808-826-6113, www.hanaleidolphin.com. Drinks and pupus are served all day from 11 am-10 pm. Open for lunch from 11 am-3:30 pm; dinner is served from 5:30 pm-10 pm. This north shore institution is the place to go for seafood. It's the first building on the right as you enter Hanalei town, situated on the Hanalei River. The menu consists of a wide variety of items. For lunch, you can get a fresh fish sandwich or salad. The dinner menu is a nice mix of steak, seafood and salads. The melt-in-your mouth filet mignon is excellent and the Haole Chicken has a nice mix of flavors. Or you can opt for a light entrée. Lunch $15-$35, dinner $35-$50.

AUTHOR'S CHOICE ★ **Hanalei Gourmet**, 5-5161 Kuhio Hwy, Hanalei Center, ☎ 808-826-2524, www.hanaleigourmet.com. Open daily 8 am-10 pm. The restaurant is actually housed in an old school house, which was built in 1926. The style is very local and laid-back. The food is very good and the prices are reasonable. The lunch menu consists of hot and cold sandwiches and excellent burgers. For dinner, you have your pick from pastas to burgers, to salads. I recommend the Mac Nut Fried Chicken, which is fantastic. The service is attentive and friendly. The prices are reasonable. The beer is cold with a nice selection of microbrews. They have live music in the evenings. Lunch $15-$35, dinner $35-$50.

Hanalei Wake-Up Café, Aku Road, Hanalei, ☎ 808-826-5551, open from 6.30-11:30 am. This is a fun little place right across from the Hanalei Center. It's kind of hidden on the side street, and it does have a hole-in-the-wall feel to it. Once you step inside, you'll be transported to a surfer's paradise. Surfboards and photos adorn the walls, and surf videos are playing on the television. The walls are covered with photos – surfing, sport fishing, diving. They're only open for breakfast (it's safe to assume that the owners and staff spend the rest of the day in the water). The food is decent and reasonably priced. Cash only. Under $15-$35.

Java Kai, 5-5183 Kuhio Hwy in the Hanalei Center, Hanalei, ☎ 808-826-6717, www.javakai.com. Open daily from 6:30 am-6 pm. This is a charming café, quick and easy in the morning if you're anxious to get to the beach, or you can sit on the lana`i and enjoy your coffee while reading the newspaper. It's also a fun place to people-watch as well. There's a wide selection of coffee drinks, and baked goods. Their specialty is the Aloha Bar, which is a delectable treat made with toasted coconut, macadamia nuts and chocolate chips on a shortbread cookie crust. It's very, very tasty and fulfills that sweet tooth craving. They also serve waffles and breakfast items. Under $15.

AUTHOR'S CHOICE ★ **Kilauea Bakery & Pau Hana Pizza**, in the Kong Lung Center, Kilauea Rd. The Bakery is open from 6:30 am-9 pm daily. Pizza is served from 11 am to 9 pm daily. ☎ 808-828-2020. Here's another place where you can start off your day. They serve fresh bagels and spreads, unbelievable sweetbread (buy some for later!) and rolls and muffins in the morning. Pick up a bagel with smoked salmon cream cheese. As the day progresses, they serve creative pizzas such as the "Billie Holliday," made with smoked ono, spinach, onions, mozzarella and a gorgonzola-rosemary sauce.Cash only. Breakfast under $15, pizza under $15-$35.

Kilauea Bakery

AUTHOR'S CHOICE ★ **La Cascata**, at the Princeville Hotel, Princeville, ☎ 808-826-2761. Open for dinner 6-10 pm. Reservations are recommended, especially if you want a perfect view of the sunset. Classic Mediterranean décor backed by stunning scenery makes La Cascata one of the more romantic places to have dinner. The menu is mostly Italian, but also has some standard cuisine as well, such as beef tenderloin and rack of lamb. The food is excellent and artfully presented with great care. The service is top-notch. $50+.

La Cascata

Lappert's Ice Cream, Princeville Shopping Center, Princeville, ☎ 808-826-7393. Here's another location for Lappert's ice cream. It's locally made, but that really doesn't justify the price. I never did understand what the fuss is about. It's mediocre, not great. Menu items include a variety of Hawai`i-themed ice creams, coffee, cookies and brownies. Other locations are in Coconut Marketplace in Kapa`a and in Hanapepe. Open 10 am-9 pm in all locations.

Lighthouse Bistro, Kong Lung Center, Kilauea, ☎ 808-828-0480, www.lighthouse-bistro.com. Open for lunch 11 m-2 pm daily except Sundays. Dinner nightly 5:30-9 pm. The atmosphere here is open, very plantation-style and casual. The lunch menu offers mostly burgers and sandwiches, which are OK and reasonably priced. There's a wide variety of foods to choose from. The coconut-crusted pork is very tasty, but like most items on the dinner menu, somewhat overpriced. On the upside, they do have an all-you-can-eat pasta bar for $13.95, which is a good value. This is *the* fine dining establishment in Kilauea. If you're really looking for fine dining, it's probably worth the drive to Princeville. Lunch $15-$35, dinner $35-$50.

Mango Mama's Café, 4460 Hookui Road, Kilauea, ☎ 808-828-1020. Open Monday-Saturday 7 am-6 pm. You can't miss the hot pink exterior of Mango Mama's Café. The interior is just as funky with zebra print furniture and colorful walls. The healthful menu offers organic coffee, about 20 or so fresh fruit smoothies, excellent sandwiches and veggie burgers. The service is fast and friendly.

Neide's Salsa & Samba, 5-5161 Kuhio Highway, Hanalei, ☎ 808-826-1851. Lunch from 11:30 am-2:30 pm, dinner 5:30-9 pm. This small establishment boasts a wonderful Mexican and Brazilian menu. The ingredients are fresh, the food is fantastic. The chips and salsa are fresh and homemade, and the fish tacos are excellent. The portions are more than generous; the service was fast and attentive. $15-$35.

Paradise Bar & Grill, Princeville Shopping Center, Princeville, ☎ 808-826-1775. This goes with the surfer's motif. You can dine outside on the lana`i area, inside or grab a quick bite to eat in the bar area, which has a surfboard for a table. Fish, steak and seafood for lunch and dinner. The food is decent and priced right for lunch, but the same menu gets a price hike for dinner, which makes it less worthwhile. Lunch under $15, dinner $15-$35.

Pizza Hanalei, Ching Young Center, Hanalei, ☎ 808-826-9494. Pretty much your typical pizza place. There are nice people working there who give friendly service. You can order by the slice, or get a whole pie to take home. The pizza's pretty good, although the sauce is perhaps a little too sweet. They have a very affordable lunch special – slice of pizza, salad and soda for $6. Cash only. Under $15-$35.

Polynesia Café, Ching Young Village, Hanalei, ☎ 808-826-1999, www.polynesiacafe.com. Their claim to fame is serving gourmet food on paper plates. I know that a lot of people rave about the place, but I could never figure out why. Except for the French fries, the food seems just OK. Yes, the prices are reasonable. The staff seems rather indifferent. They offer a full bakery and ice cream. BYOB. Since it's right next to the Big Save, you can pick up a bottle of wine there. $15-$35.

Postcards Café

Postcards Café, Kuhio Highway, Hanalei, ☎ 808-826-1191, www.postcards-cafe.com. Dinner is served from 6 to 9 pm every night. Reservations are highly recommended. The café is located in an old, quaint plantation house as you enter Hanalei. The food is excellent. Plain and simple. They serve gourmet vegetarian seafood and everything on the menu is worth ordering. You can start out with Samurai Salmon, (like salmon spring rolls), and, for an entrée, Thai coconut curry. The sweet and spicy flavors blend just right. Be sure to top dinner off with coconut sorbet. Dinner $15-$50.

Sabella's, at Princeville, 5300 Ka Haku Rd in the Pali Ke Kua Condominium Complex, ☎ 808-826-6225. Dinner is Tuesday through Sunday from 5 to 9 pm. Open for cocktails until 10. The Italian menu is good. The food is not incredible, but not bad. It turned out to be a pleasant dining experience, but not memorable. Thursday and Sunday evenings bring live music, either classical or Hawaiian. $35-$50.

Sushi Blues, Ching Young Village, upstairs, Hanalei, ☎ 808-826-9701, www.sushiandblues.com. Sushi Blues is another hip and very happening place in Hanalei. The interior is industrial-chic, lined with copper tables and a copper bar. The pipes and brick are exposed. They have reasonably priced seafood and, of course, sushi. You'll feel like you've hit the jackpot with the tasty Las Vegas Roll – Ahi, yellowtail, avocado, tempura fried. Even if you aren't into sushi, there are still other options that make it worth coming here, such as pasta and stir fry. Live music starts every night at about 8:30. There is a $5 cover charge after 8pm. $15-$50.

Spinners Coffee Shop, Princeville Shopping Center – Have a nice cup of Peet's Coffee. They have a covered outdoor café, serving breakfast and lunch. The menu is very simple with mainly soups, sandwiches and pastries. They also have free Internet access. Open Monday-Friday 7 am-4 pm; Saturday and Sunday 7 am-2 pm.

Tahiti Nui Restaurant , ☎ 808-826-6277. This is the place to go if you want to get a real feel for the local people and their music. The food is OK, but the mai tais are better. Come here in the evening for a drink or two. The service and the patrons are friendly, so you should have no trouble chatting up the locals. $15-$35

The Beach Restaurant & Pool Bar, ☎ 808-826-2762. Located poolside, at Princeville Hotel. Open daily 11 am-5:30 pm. The bar is open from 10:30 am to sunset. A great place for lunch if you're already in Princeville or, better yet, already in the swimming pool. It's elegant outdoor dining, right by the pool. You'll get spectacular views of Hanalei Bay. The menu is pretty simple, with salads and sandwiches, or you could opt for a nice fat Kobe steak burger if you're really hungry. The food is good, but that alone really isn't worth the trip to Princeville. There's a bar you can swim up to right in the pool. If you like to drink, it is a pretty neat experience. $35-$50.

Zelo's Beach House, 5-5156 Kuhio Hwy, ☎ 808-826-9700, www.zelos-beachhouse.com. Definitely the coolest place on the North Shore, Zelo's is a great hang-out spot. The food's pretty good for the most part, and while lunch is reasonably priced, dinner is not. You're better off coming here for pupus and drinks. They have an extensive beer and wine list and very interesting martinis. I recommend having an order of nachos and wash it down with a beer or two. They go very well together. Try to get there early to get a table on the deck. Lunch under $15-$35, dinner $35-$50.

Zelos Beach House

■ Na Pali Coast State Park

You've probably read or heard every adjective possible to describe the Na Pali Coast: majestic, beautiful, rugged, immense, isolated. I could go on and on. But the Na Pali Coast is something that you really have to experience for yourself.

The Na Pali cliffs

The Na Pali cliffs offer once-in-a lifetime views you won't see anywhere else. Seeing the cliffs is at the top of most visitors' lists when they come to Kaua`i. The cliffs rise up to 4,000 feet above the shore. This 15-mile stretch of land between Ke`e Beach and Polihale beach is amazing to view.

Perhaps the most famous view of the area is of Kalalau Valley. The series of sharp peaks prompted Mark Twain to call them a cathedral. The area was inhabited by ancient Hawaiians and is revered in Hawaiian culture today. It rains often in the area, and streams and waterfalls run through the green valley.

Offshore, reefs along the coast provide plentiful fishing, and there are lots of honu and spinner dolphins. During the winter, humpback whales come to Hawaiian waters to birth, nurse and raise their calves.

What makes the Na Pali Coast so special is not only the beauty, but the fact that it's not accessible by road. You can get there by boat, by air or take a challenging 11-mile hike along the Kalalau Trail.

There are plenty of helicopter tours that will take you to see the Na Pali Coast. You'll get to see the cliffs and valleys up-close, which puts their grandeur into perspective. The

The Kalalau Lookout

helicopters do not land in the area, but from the air you get a feeling for how immense the cliffs really are.

Boat tours will also take you along the coast. Most tours originate in Port Allen or Waimea on the west side of the island, and there are two that port in Hanalei. The boat tours range from a relaxing catamaran to the more intimate and adventurous Zodiac rigid-hull inflatable boats. Most tours give you the opportunity to snorkel around the coastline.

AUTHOR'S TIP

There are a few options to consider before you book your ride. Do you want an all-out adventure? If so, book a Zodiac boat. They're smaller boats with a capacity for approximately 20 people. They're the type of boats used by Navy Seals and the Coast Guard. They're faster, with a bumpier ride. If you want to maximize your adventure, sit up toward the front of the boat. You'll really be able to feel it when the boat is jumping over the waves. If you're looking for a more relaxed ride or you're prone to sea sickness, then take a catamaran. These boats are larger, hold more people and are much slower. You won't feel the rocking and jumping as much as would on a zodiac ride.

If you want the challenge and the triumph of going at it on your own, pilot your own kayak to the cliffs. Most companies do not rent kayaks if you plan to use them in the ocean, so your best bet for kayaking Na Pali is to go with a guided tour. You really do need to be in excellent physical condition and not be prone to seasickness, as you're going to be paddling in the ocean a good five or six hours. Since the winter waves can be dangerous for kayaking Na Pali, the companies that operate guided tours of the area take off only during the summer months.

- **Outfitters Kaua`i**, ☎ 888-742-9887, 808-742-9667, www.outfitterskauai.com, meets at their offices in Po`ipu and drives you the the launch site in Ha`ena. From there, you'll paddle to Polihale State Beach Park, where a van will meet and drive you back to Po`ipu. Yes, you still stop along the way at Miloli`i beach. The cost for the full day's journey is $185 plus tax and state landing fees.
- **Kayak Kaua`i**, ☎ 800-437-3507, 808-826-9844, www.kayakkauai.com, meets at their office in Hanalei. You'll paddle to Polihale, stopping along the way at Miloli`i Beach. There's a van that will meet you in Polihale and take you back to Hanalei. This costs $185 per person, plus tax and fees.
- **Na Pali Kayak**, ☎ 866-977-6900, 808-826-6900, www.napalikayak.com, will take you along the same route from Hanalei for $180 plus tax and fees. Na Pali Kayak also offers custom private and honeymoons tours.

Another physically demanding experience is to traverse the 11 mile **Kalalau Trail**. The trailhead is at Ha`ena State Beach Park, the end of the road on the North Shore. The trail was first built in the late 1800s, and portions were rebuilt in the 1930s. A similar foot trail linked Hawaiian villages along the coastline.

The trail travels through five valleys before ending at Kalalau Beach. You can choose to hike the entire 11 miles and camp along the way or you can take a two-mile hike to Hanakapiai Beach, which makes a nice day-trip. The hike to Hanakapiai is fairly moderate, leaving the remaining nine miles to Kalalau Beach for experienced hikers.

Opposite: Kalalau Valley

The trail from Ke`e Beach to Hanakapiai Beach is a popular day-hike, especially during the summer. It'll take about 90 minutes to get there from the trail head if you're a fast hiker. As inviting as the beach may seem after a hard hike, it's not advised. The beach at Hanakapiai is not protected by a reef, making surf conditions potentially dangerous. In the winter, it's not uncommon for the beach to erode in heavy winter surf.

Along the Kalalau Trail (Matt Wright)

Ho`olulu Beach, below the Kalalau Trail (Matt Wright)

From Hanakapiai Beach, there's a difficult two-mile trail that follows a stream into Hanakapiai Valley and leads to Hanakapiai Falls. Only hike this trail in good weather. The stream is prone to flash floods and falling rocks. There was a coffee mill in the area in the late 1800s and you can still see the ruins of the mills and coffee trees.

A camping area here allows travelers to stop overnight on the way in or out of Kalalau Valley.

CAMPING PERMITS

Since the Na Pali Coast State Park is run by the State of Hawai`i Division of Land and Natural Resources, that's who you must contact to obtain a camping permit.

The camping fee for Na Pali Coast State Park (Hanakapai, Hanakoa, Kalalau and Miloli`i) is $10 per person per night. You can download an application from the Hawai`i State Division of Land and Natural Resources at www.hawaii.gov/dlnr/dsp/fees.html or you can call ☎ 808-274-3444. There are a limited number of permits, so it's advisable to send in your application months (yes, months) in advance. There is a maximum of five nights.

Once you leave the Hankapiai area, get ready for some challenging hiking. The trail makes a steep 800-foot climb out of the valley and goes through the Hono o Na Pali Natural Area Reserve, Ho`olulu Valley and Waiahuakua Valley before reaching Hanakoa Valley.

There's a place to rest near Hanakoa Stream. You'll probably need it after the four-mile hike from Hanakapiai. A rather hazardous trail also goes a half-mile up to Hanakoa Falls. There's no beach access here at Hanakoa.

The final five miles from Hanakoa leads to Kalalau Beach. The trail is more open and drier since it's exposed to the sun. Here's where you'll get to see some amazing views of the valley and coastline. The trail crosses Kalalau Stream near the valley mouth before ending at Kalalau Beach and a small waterfall. The camping area is behind the beach, beneath the trees. The beach here is not protected by a reef so, once again, use caution. Strong currents can form faster than you think.

There's a two mile trail that ends at a pool in the stream. Along the way, you'll see agricultural terraces where Hawaiians grew taro, until about 1920. These terraces are now grown guava, mango and Java Plum.

HUNTING

Goat hunting in the area is permitted on weekends in August and September. Most hunting occurs in Kalalau Valley or above the trail between Hanakoa and Kalalau. Safety zone signs are posted during hunting season. For that reason alone, you should stay on the main trails.

Hunting licenses are mandatory in order to hunt on public, private or military land anywhere in Hawai`i. You can register for a hunting license online at hunting.ehawaii.gov/hunting/license.html. If you're a Hawai`i resident, a license is $20 and that's good for the fiscal year (July 1-June 30).

The main requirement for a hunting license in Hawai`i is a hunter education card. If you're a visitor and plan on hunting, make sure that you have your hunter education card. Once you get that, you can fill out a letter of exemption, which you can get online at www.hawaii.gov/dlnr/dcre/know.htm. You mail that in, your form will be processed and you'll be able to purchase a hunting license.

To find out the hunting periods, restrictions, and areas, your best bet is to contact Division of Forestry and Wildlife Kaua`i District Office at ☎ 808-274-3438.

Beyond the Kalalau Trail, heading toward Polihale State Park, lie a few other beaches that are certainly worth a look. About a half-mile west of Kalalau, is **Honopu Beach**. It's actually a pair of beaches separated by a thick wall of lava. Beyond the beach is **Honopu Valley** or the **Valley of the Lost Tribe**. It was considered to be the last home of the Menehune.

Nualolo Kai Beach is where commercial tour boats land. There's a reef about 600 feet out from the beach that provides excellent snorkeling and diving opportunities. In the winter, the seas are rough, which precludes any possible boat landings. Nualolo Kai is also an archeological site. It's believed that the area was settled over 1,000 years ago and was a village with a natural water well, plentiful fishing and taro was grown. It's estimated that 100 people lived here and it was inhabited as late as 1919, when people left for the towns of Hanalei and Waimea.

Honopu Beach

Finally, **Miloli`i Beach** is about four miles from the western end of Polihale State Park. This area also has fantastic snorkeling and diving opportunities. It's common for local fishermen to come here for spearfishing and diving. This was also the site of an ancient Hawaiian village. There are some facilities here – a toilet and a picnic area.

The Na Pali Coast

West Shore
N
HUNTER PUBLISHING
Kalalau Valley
Honopu Valley
Awawapuhi Trail
Kalalau Lookout
Pihea
Nu`alolo Trail
Koke`e Museum
Pu`u kita Lookout
Berry Flat Tr
Koke`e
Makaha Ridge Rd.
Pu`u Hinahina Lookout.
Kumuwela Trail
Kauhao Ridge Rd.
Waipo`o Falls
Awini Falls
Polihale Ridge Rd.
Koke`e Ditch
Polihale State Park
Waimea Canyon Lookout
Nohili Dunes
Kukui Trail
Iliau Nature Loop
Pacific Missile Range Facility
MANA
Kawaiele Sand Mine Bird Sanctuary
Waimea Canyon Tra
NONOPAHU
Waiokapua (Major's) Bay
Kekaha Ditch
50
552
POKI`I
Kekaha Ditch
Kokeo`e Rd.
550
Mana Drag Strip
Kekaha
Waimea Canyon Rd
Kekaha Beach Park
Waimea
6 Miles
10 Kilometers
Kikiaola Harbor
Capt. Cook Memorial
KA`AWANUI
Lucy Wright Park
50
© 2007 HUNTER PUBLISHING, INC
Russian Fort Elizabeth State Park
Kapalawai Beach

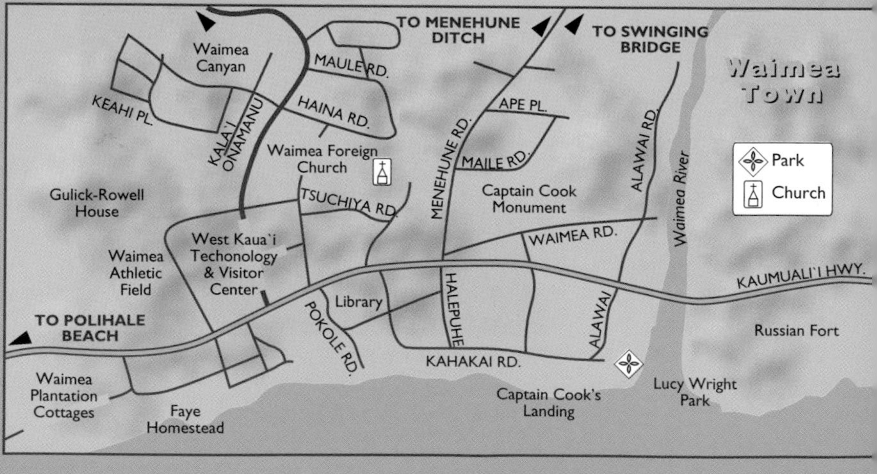
TO MENEHUNE DITCH
TO SWINGING BRIDGE
Waimea Town
Waimea Canyan
MAULE RD.
KEAHI PL.
HAINA RD.
APE PL.
KALA`I
ONAMANU
MENEHUNE RD.
ALAWAI RD.
Waimea Foreign Church
MAILE RD.
Park
Church
Gulick-Rowell House
Captain Cook Monument
Waimea River
TSUCHIYA RD.
West Kaua`i Techonology & Visitor Center
WAIMEA RD.
Waimea Athletic Field
KAUMUALI`I HWY.
Library
HALEPUHE
ALAWAI
TO POLIHALE BEACH
POKOLE RD.
Russian Fort
KAHAKAI RD.
Waimea Plantation Cottages
Captain Cook's Landing
Lucy Wright Park
Faye Homestead

The West Shore

What to See

As you wind through Highway 50 (Kaumuali`i Hwy) heading west toward a glorious sunset over Waimea Canyon and Polihale State Park, you'll drive through Port Allen, now the island's second major port of call and the historic towns of Ele`ele, Hanapepe, and Waimea. You'll also pass the Pacific Missile Range Facility and Waimea Canyon, before the road ends in Mana, near Polihale State Park.

IN THIS CHAPTER

**Ele`ele** is so small – blink and you might miss it. It's mostly residential, so there's not too much to see. You will notice the Ele`ele Shopping Center. It's a small strip mall with a few restaurants and grocery store. Turn at the shopping center and the road will take you to Port Allen.

Port Allen is the second major port on the island. You'll see the occasional cruise ship, Coast Guard boats, and there is a shopping center that's geared toward tourists with a few pleasant surprises. This is where quite a number of boat tours originate and there's an airport with a couple of places to fly as well.

Just past the Ele`ele Shopping Center you'll see a sign on the right that says "Biggest Little Town on Kaua`i." This sign is referring to the historic town of **Hanapepe**. Follow the road bearing right onto Hanapepe Road and you'll suddenly feel as if you've been transported into a small western town. The old buildings built by Asian immigrants for the most part are intact. Hanapepe means crushed bay. It's said that the town

Hanapepe Valley & Makawele River

earned its name from the landslides in the valley or from the cliffs surrounding the bay area.

Early on, the native Hawaiians settle in Hanapepe Valley and grew taro, banana, sugar cane, and sweet potato. The Hawaiians created ditches to provide water to the agricultural areas. Captain Cook arrived in Waimea in 1778, which had an impact on nearby Hanapepe. By this time, the Hawaiians had already started to cultivate salt. They then started to trade salt with the sailors. This was the earliest form of business for Hanapepe.

In Hanapepe Town

Kaua`i also had a flourishing sugar industry, which brought with it thousands of laborers from China, Japan and Korea, among many other places. The Hanapepe that remains today really began when these immigrants fulfilled their contracts with the plantations and settled there to open their own small businesses or become taro farmers.

Port Allen

Hanapepe was not immune to the arrival of the missionaries. They established the Hanapepe First United Church (now Hanapepe Hawaiian Congregational Church) in 1890 as a mission station. By the turn of the 20th century, there were almost a dozen churches of numerous denominations in town. Today Hanapepe's churches and temples include: Church of the Nazarene, Hanapepe Hawaiian Congregational Church, Hanapepe Hongwanji Mission, Hanapepe United Church of Christ, Kaua`i Soto Zen Temple Zenshuji, and Missionary Baptist Church.

By the early 1900s, the area was primarily populated by second- or third-generation immigrants and eventually became Kaua`i's commerce center. Hanapepe boasted more than 60 stores, movie theaters, roller-skating rinks, Kaua`i's first airstrip and Port Allen, the island's second-largest harbor. To support this growing area, schools, clinics, pool halls, bars, restaurants, bowling alleys, hotels and homes were also built.

In the 1930s through World War II, Hanapepe was a happening military town. The Hanapepe airfield area was a source of soldiers who came to town for rest and relaxation. A USO club was built, as were pool halls, bars, restaurants and bowling alleys.

The business hub of Kaua`i started to shift to Lihu`e in the late 1930s and the hustle and bustle of the town started to slow considerably. Over the years, it's kept a quaint, small-town charm. Recently, with the influx of artists and galleries in the area, there has been a slight resurgence in activity, as evidenced by the Hanapepe Friday Art Night, which happens every Friday night.

DID YOU KNOW?

A dark period in Hanapepe's history emerged in the early 20th century, when there was unrest betwwn plantation owners and laborers. It culminated in the Hanapepe Massacre, which was the result of a long-standing strike that ended the lives of 16 Filipino workers and four policemen. There were hundres of others that were injured.

From the time that the immigrants arrived on Kaua`i in the late 1800s to work on the plantations, they were treated like indentured servants. They were barely paid, forced to live in unsanitary conditions, disciplined with whips and contracts that dictated when they got up, when they worked, when they ate, when they slept.

American law eventually made the plantation contracts illegal, and laborers walked away from plantation life as soon as they could. Up until this time, there had already been over 50 labor strikes. In the early 1900s, labor union organizers arrived in Hanapepe. They organized strikes fighting for better conditions and better wages at sugar and pineapple plantations.

Plantations recruited more and more workers, going to the Philippines for a labor source. As they continued to recruit new labor, unrest increased throughout the first quarter-century. Most strike attempts ended in defeat for the laborers.

In April 1924, a strike began on Kaua`i that eventually grew to include over 3,000 workers across four islands, demanding better pay and an eight-hour workday.

That September, workers on Kaua`i captured two strikebreakers in Hanapepe. A riot resulted and turned deadly.

Going farther down the road, from Hanapepe, you'll pass through a number of sugar towns before you make it to Waimea. **Kauakami** is a tiny town where plantation life is still a reality. You can see a few homes where the sugar plantation workers live. You'll know you're in Kauakami when you go past a small plaza with a post office, bakery and the Ni`ihau Helicopter office.

Waimea (Hawaiian Images)

Past Kauakami, you'll be treated to another historic town – **Waimea**. This is where the westernization of the islands began when Captain Cook landed here in 1778. Even though Captain Cook was killed in 1779 off of Kealakekua on the Big Island, his journals, which included maps, opened the doors for other westerners such as fur traders and whalers, who sought to anchor in Waimea. It was used as a ship landing until Nawiliwili and Port Allen harbors were built.

Today, Waimea is a favorite destination for those who truly want to get away from it all. It's quiet. It's not geared toward tourists. You won't see franchises, strip malls or people constantly trying to sell you something. It's a place to relax, unwind and enjoy Kaua`i's natural beauty in nearby **Waimea Canyon**, **Koke`e State Park** and **Polihale State Park**.

The town was recently placed on the 2006 list of America's Dozen Distinctive Destinations by the National Trust for Historic Preservation.

Waimea Canyon

Just past Waimea is the planned plantation town of **Kekaha**. This once-thriving town was built by and depended on the Kekaha Sugar Company, which closed in 2000. Although not the vibrant community it once was, it still is pretty active thanks to the the Pacific Missile Range Facility and Pioneer Hi-Bred International, Syngenta and Monsanto. These three companies produce seed crops such as soybeans and hybrid corn for corn oil, corn syrup, cornstarch and animal feed.

You'll be able to turn off the road and make the trek up to Waimea Canyon and Koke`e Park.

The **Pacific Missile Range Facility** (PMRF), which is run by the US Navy, is the only range in the world where submarines, surface ships, aircraft and space vehicles can operate and be tracked simultaneously. There are over 1,100 square miles of instrumented underwater range and 42,000 square miles of controlled airspace.

Pacific Missile Range Facility

PMRF also played a vital role in NASA's *Pathfinder* missions. The Pathfinder is a solar-powered aircraft that is controlled remotely. The program originated in the early 1980s in California. In 1997, NASA opted to move the *Pathfinder's* operations to PMRF to take advantage of Kaua`i's location relative to the sun. In 1998, *Pathfinder* set a new altitude record of 80,201 feet for a solar-powered aircraft.

Military personnel visit Kaua`i every summer for war games at the facility. You might even see missile launches, either from Polihale State Park or from the highway. PMRF does maintain a few beaches on their base such as Major's Bay and Barking Sands, which are further described in the beaches section of this chapter. However, be aware that access to PMRF has been restricted solely to military personnel since September 11, 2001. If you want to get on the base and you're a resident, you'll have to go through an extensive background check. If you're a visitor, it would be virtually impossible to do so. But these things do change pretty frequently. You can call ☎ 808-335-4229 for information regarding visitor access and offshore boating.

WAIMEA SUGAR MILL COMPANY

Hans Peter Faye

Waimea Sugar Mill Company was originally established in 1884. The sugar mill struggled to survive financially and in 1902, the company almost folded altogether. In an unsuccessful effort to save the company, a ditch bringing water from Waimea River was constructed between 1901 and 1905. Hans Peter Faye, the manager of neighboring Kekaha Sugar Company, became interested in securing the Rowell dairy lands for free railroad right of way to the Waimea wharf and the cane land for consolidation with Kekaha Sugar to make a single operating unit. Fayé purchased the Rowell dairy lands in 1904 and gained controlling interest in Waimea Sugar Mill Company in 1905. The company's debts were paid in full by 1909. Kekaha Sugar stockholders declined to purchase the Waimea lands so eventually Faye became the sole owner of Waimea Sugar Mill Company.

Expansion of sugar on the dry west side plantations of Kekaha, Waimea and Makaweli was not successful until extensive development of irrigation water was completed. Between 1911 and 1912, George Ewart, then Waimea Sugar manager, reconfigured the Waimea Ditch, replacing the iron flumes with tunnels and increasing its flow capacity. Over the years the mill and ditch systems were renovated, which resulted in an increase of sugar production.

The US Army Corps of Engineers used the plantation shop yard as headquarters in World War II, forcing the plantation to mill its crop at Kekaha Sugar throughout the war.

In 1969, the company ceased operations, leasing its cane lands to Kekaha Sugar. Today the old sugar mill, still a landmark, is the site of the annual Waimea Town Celebration. These are the lands that are used by Gay & Robinson and Pioneer Hi-Bred International, Syngenta and Monsanto.

Ele`ele

Kaua`i Coffee Company Museum

**Kaua`i Coffee Company Museum**, ☎ 808-335-0813. Open daily 9 am-5 pm, www.kauaicoffee.com. Free admission. Kaua`i Coffee Company began in 1987 as part of an effort by McBryde Sugar Company to diversify. After almost closing its doors in the aftermath of Hurricane Iniki in 1992, Kaua`i Coffee has rebounded and now has a 3,400-acre plantation of Arabica coffee that creates five million pounds of coffee each year. This is the single largest coffee estate in Hawai`i and has about 60% of the Hawaiian coffee market. You can taste free samples of several types of coffee and there's also a snack stand where you can get sandwiches and see a video on how coffee is grown, harvested and roasted. Don't forget to buy some coffee for yourself to take home in the gift shop.

Hanapepe

Hanapepe Walking Tour. Hanapepe has a very rich history that you can explore on your own. What's great about going on your own is that you can either get through the tour in an hour or you can make a full day of it.

Quite a number of buildings (43 to be exact) in Hanapepe qualify to be listed on State and National Registers of Historic Places, assuming they are at least 50 years old, have a tie with significant historical events or people and have high artistic values or display the distinctive characteristics of a type, period or method of construction.

You can purchase the **Historic Hanapepe Walking Tour Map** for $2 at most shops in town, including Banana Patch Studio, Talk Story Bookstore, Dawn Traina Gallery and Arius Hopman Gallery. You can pick up a Historic Hanapepe Walking Tour rack card (you should be able to locate them on the racks next to baggage claim). These cards contain information about the tour and entitle you to a free map at shops in Hanapepe that sell them.

If you're going to spend the day here, the best time would be Fridays, while business are open and setting up shop for the Friday Art Night. Sunday is the worst day to go as most of the shops are closed. It's like being in an abandoned Western ghost town.

For more information about the walking tour, call the Hanapepe Economic Alliance at ☎ 808-335-5944 or visit their website www.kauai.net/hanapepe.

Hanapepe Valley Lookout, suspended bridge. Walk over this bridge for a great view of the river. You can't help but feel you're in an Indiana Jones movie when you cross this bridge. It's pretty narrow, and yes it does swing when you're walking across it. There are fantastic views of the Hanapepe River and Hanapepe Valley. Don't wander off when you get to the other side of the bridge. You're actually entering residential backyards, so it's best that you make your way back to town.

Hanapepe suspended bridge

Soto Zen Temple Zenshuji, 1-3500 Kaumauli'i Highway Hanapepe, ☎ 808-335-3521. Open to the public. This Buddhist Temple is quite exotic, with intricate statues and altars in and around the temple. Buddhism was brought to the Hawaiian islands when Japanese immigrants came to work in the sugar fields. They brought their beliefs and built many temples throughout the island.

Robinson Family Adventures Visitor Center and Museum, ☎ 335-2824, Highway 50 at Kaumakani, mile marker 19, half-way between Hanapepe and Waimea. Monday-Friday from 8 am-4 pm and Saturday 11 am-3 pm. Free admission. wwwgandrtours-kauai.com.

Along the way to Waimea, be sure to stop by **Gay & Robinson's Sugar Plantation Visitor Center**. This is Kaua`i's only remaining working sugar plantation. There are lots of photo albums and other artifacts on display that depict plantation life. Check out all facets of a working plantation, from cultivation, irrigation, harvesting, to laboratory analysis and factory operations. Daily guided tours are held at 8:45am and 12:45 pm.

Waimea

The Faye Museum is named in honor of Hans Peter Faye, a Norwegian immigrant who started a small plantation in Mana and went on to help found Kekaha Sugar and was its first general manager. The museum can be found a Waimea Plantation Cottages. The single-room museum contains exhibits and photographs tracking the journey of Faye and the sugar industry in West Kaua`i. Free admission.

Waimea Sugar Museum, ☎ 808-335-2824. Tours start in the lobby of Waimea Plantation Cottages. $10 admissions fee. Reservations are required.

You can also take the Plantation Lifestyles Tour through the ruins of the Waimea Sugar Mill and camp, which dates back to around 1900. You'll learn how the immigrants came to Hawai`i and the conditions in which they lived while working for the plantations. The tour is offered several times a week. Call Gay & Robinson Tours to make your reservations. Tours start in the lobby of Waimea Plantation Cottages.

Russian Fort Elizabeth State Historical Park. Who would have thought that the Russians would try to occupy Kaua`i well before the words "cold war" even entered our vernacular? In 1815, a ship that belonged to the Russian-American Company ran aground off Waimea. King Kaumuali`i took control of the ship and its cargo. The Russian American Company sent Georg Scheffer to regain the company's possessions. At that time in Kaua`i's history, King Kamehameha was in the process of uniting all of the Hawaiian Islands. King Kaumuali`i was against this, though he eventually relented and ceded control of Kaua`i to Kamehameha. Scheffer and Kaumuali`i eventually formed an alliance, with Scheffer promising manpower and weapons to help Kaumuali`i take control of the Hawaiian Islands. In return, Scheffer would get the right to construct factories throughout all of the Hawaiian Islands and half of O`ahu.

Scheffer then went to work. In 1816, he began to build the foundation of Fort Elizabeth (named after Czarina Elizabeth), as well as Fort Alexander and Fort Barclay near the Hanalei River. This went on for about a year, when King Kamehameha learned of the alliance and abruptly forced all Russians from Hawai`i. Scheffer left Hawai`i, leaving the unfinished fort behind. Hawaiian soldiers took over the fort and remained there until 1864, when the Hawaiian government ordered it to be dismantled. It has been in that condition ever since. In 1966, the remains were declared a National Historic Landmark. It is the only remaining Russian fort in Hawai`i.

The 17-acre site itself is somewhat disappointing because it has not been well maintained. There are a lot of weeds, some remnants of the original structure, and a few signs detailing the history of the fort. A sign indicates the foot path going around the walls of the fort. Currently, the West Kaua`i Technology and Visitor Center is leading efforts to improve and clean up the area. It's a very interesting piece of Hawaiian history to explore nonetheless.

Waimea State Recreation Pier is situated on the beach fronting the town of Waimea. It's at the end of Moana Road, a short residential street that intersects Kaumuali`i Hwy. The pier, an abandoned boat landing, attracts many local fishing enthusiasts. DLNR regulates that you can't use a spear or net within 50 yards of the pier. The water is usually dirty from

Waimea Pier

soil carried into the ocean by the Waimea River, so it isn't used for swimming.

Captain Cook's Monument

Captain Cook's Monument. Right in the middle of Waimea Town, you'll find the statue that honors Captain James Cook. This is the man that is credited with changing the course of Hawaiian history by sailing the *Resolution* and *Discovery* into Waimea. The statue that stands in the middle of Waimea is actually a replica of one in Cook's hometown of Whitby, England.

Captain Cook's Landing. At the point marking the landing site in Waimea, there is a marker that was placed in 1928 by the Kaua`i Historical Society to commemorate the 150th anniversary of the landing. The marker is a nationally registered site in Lucy Wright County Park. The landing fronts the Waimea Pier State Park. You can get there from Highway 50, turning right on Pokole Road. Waimea became an important port with Cook's visit in 1778. The original wharf was built in 1865 to compete with Koloa landing as a port of call for whaling ships. Products exported from west Kaua'i at the time were raw sugar, cattle, goats, oranges, taro, sweet potatoes, yams and rice. Small businesses catering to the port trade were built along the shore. There are parking and restroom facilities available

The **Menehune Ditch** was built to provide water to the lower Waimea Valley. This was done at the request of Chief Ola. Like the Menehune Fishpond, this was also built in one night. The Menehune were paid in shrimp for their efforts. Originally about 24 feet high, you can still see about two feet of the original stone wall near the swinging bridge on Menehune Road. The road covers most of the original wall. You can get to this nationally registered landmark by taking Menehune Road between the Fire State and Big Save Market. The road goes uphill and does get narrow. so drive with caution. You'll see the footbridge crossing the Waimea River. If there are heavy rains, stay out of the valley because of potential flash floods.

**West Kaua`i Technology & Visitors Center** (9565 Kaumuali`i Highway, Waimea, ☎ 808-338-1332, www.kedb.com/visitorcenter/index.html; open Monday-Friday 9 am-4 pm, Saturdays from 9 am-1 pm. Free admission). This museum pays homage to, well, you guessed it – technology. Starting with the ancient Hawaiians' use of stone to create poi pounders, the exhibits follow the Hawaiians' navigational techniques. The technology tour continues with the advent of the sugar mills and takes you all the way through the Pathfinder missions at the Pacific Missile Range Facility. There are also plenty of ancient artifacts on display. You can also participate in demonstrations such as lei making, salt making and poi pounding. The Visitors Center also sponsors a guided walking tour of Historic Waimea on Mondays at 9:30 am. The walking tour is free of charge, but you do need to call for reservations. There is also Internet access available at the center, free of charge.

Waimea Canyon/Koke`e State Park

**Koke`e Natural History Museum**, ☎ 808-335-9975, www.koke`e.org. Open daily from 10 am-4 pm; 10-2 on holidays. Free admission; donations are accepted. This small museum has displays on the natural history of the area. It's a great opportunity to learn about the flora, fauna and early Hawaiian culture and history. During the summer, the museum sponsors guided hikes. The museum also sponsors workshops and conservation efforts in the area. The gift shop sells books about Hawaiian history and culture. There are also detailed hiking maps that can be picked up for a few dollars.

Waimea Canyon State Park. Traveling up the road from Kekaha is Waimea Canyon. The canyon is 10 miles long, two miles wide and over 3,600 feet deep. Stop and take in the beauty of this place, the array of colors, with different shades of red, greens, purples and blues. The canyon is a result of numerous floods and rivers coming from Mt. Wai`ale`ale over thousands of years. The colors lining the canyon walls indicate different volcanic eruptions and lava flows that have occurred over the years.

There are a few places to stop and take in the view of the canyon as you travel up toward Koke`e State Park. Each overlook offers a different view and they're all spectacular. You can witness the vast empty space of the canyon and contemplate the obscene beauty of it all. I'd recommend coming here early in the morning for two reasons: 1) You beat all of the other tourists, even the tours that bike down the canyon. If you're really lucky, you might have the views all to yourself. 2) As the day progresses, clouds begin to form, which could obstruct your view.

The first stop on your way up is between mile markers eight and nine. There's a small parking area for the Kukui and Iliau Loop Trails. There you can take a quick jaunt around the quarter-mile loop that offers a great view looking up at the canyon. It has a covered picnic area as well.

At mile marker 10, you'll come to the **Waimea Canyon Overlook**. Stop, get out of the car and enjoy the view. From here, you'll look out through the canyon. You'll be able to see how deep the canyon really is and appreciate how far it stretches.

At mile marker 13, there's the **Pu`u Hinahina Lookout**, with a view of the island of Ni`ihau and the Pacific Ocean. You can see the island about 17 miles out. Here, you're at about 3,500 feet elevation.

To see one of the more brilliant views the area has to offer, keep heading up hill past Koke`e State Park. Right at about mile marker 18, you'll come to the **Kalalau Valley Lookout**. You can see the "cathedrals" that Mark Twain was referring to when he wrote about the Kalalau Valley.

**Pu`u O Kila Lookout** features wonderful views into the Kalalau Valley and across the Alakai Swamp to Mt. Wai`ale`ale – the wettest spot on earth. The Pu'u o Kila Lookout and the nearby Kalalau Valley Lookout offer some of the greatest views in Hawai`i. Pu`u O Kila Lookout is the end of the road, just past the Kalalau Valley Lookout.

Koke`e State Park** and **Koke`e Natural History Museum, at a crisp 4,000 feet, have displays of plants and animals. The staff can advise you on the park's many seasonal activities such as plum picking and summer wonder walks. Behind the museum is a nature trail with 35 marked plants.

Koke`e was said to be the last place of refuge of the Menehune. Average temperatures are 60°. "The events of WWII emphasized Hawai`i's strategic mid-Pacific location and led to the building of three tracking stations in Koke`e State Park; the Navy runs another at the end of nearby Makaha Ridge and the Air Force constructed one near Kalakau Lookout.

Don't forget to stop in the museum to pick up hiking maps and check out trail conditions. The staff of the museum is very knowledgeable and can give advice on what trails might be appropriate for your fitness condition. It's also a good idea to register at the museum for safety precautions.

There's a very easy nature trail behind Koke`e Museum, with 35 marked plants. It's very short and easy. It should take about 20 minutes to complete – a good warm up if you plan on doing more intense hiking.

Sightseeing Tours

If you want to have a relaxing experience and not worry about driving and parking, a guided tour might be for you.

Roberts Hawai`i Tours (☎ 866-898-2519, www.robertshawaii.com) offers bus tours, including Waimea Canyon, from your hotel. You'll stop at Spouting Horn and Hanapepe Valley along the way. Tours operate Sunday, Tuesday, Thursday and Saturday. The cost is $44 per person.

Polynesian Adventure Tours (☎ 808-246-0122, www.polyad.com) has two tours that will take you to Waimea Canyon as well. Their Waimea Canyon Experience Tour operates on Monday, Wednesday, Friday, Sunday. You'll stop at Spouting Horn, Hanapepe and Fort Elizabeth before reaching Waimea Canyon. The cost for this tour is $47 per person.

Gay & Robinson Sugar Plantation Tours (www.gandrtours-kauai.com/gnrtor.html) offers the Olokele Canyon Overlook Tour through the Gay & Robinson sugar plantation and Makaweli Ranch. The ranch was established in 1865 and still has its original breed of Durham Shorthorns. A picnic lunch is included.

Adventures

On Land

Hiking

The best hiking on the island is here in the area around Koke`e State Park and Waimea Canyon. There are about 45 miles of trails, with 20 paths to choose from. They range from dry canyon trails to wet and muddy swamps, while other trails take you to places that overlook the Na Pali Coast. Those that take you to the Na Pali Overlook start on the left side of the road that heads up toward Koke`e. The other trails start on the right side of the road. Be aware that some of these trails descend over 1,000 feet. It's easy to go down, but very tough climbing back up.

The **Awa`awapuhi Trail** is just about 6½ miles long. It is graded as difficult. It starts near the 17 mile marker. You'll come across a variety of native dryland plants. The trail ends on top of the ridge, 2,500 feet in elevation. There are spectacular cliff-to-ocean views into Awa'awapuhi and Nualolo Valleys overlooking the Pacific Ocean. At the end of the trail, you can enjoy the picnic area.

On the Awa`awapuhi Trail

Nu'alolo Cliffs Trail is 4.2 miles and graded as moderate. It starts along the Awa`awapuhi Trail and also connects to the Nualolo Trail. If you're an experienced hiker and in good shape, you can hike the A`awapuhi, Nualolo and Nualolo Cliff Trails for an all-day excursion. Make sure you bring plenty of water, for this is a very strenuous hike.

The **Canyon Trail** is 3.6 miles and is the most popular trail. It's very scenic as it follows the northern rim of Waimea Canyon and takes you to a spectacular waterfall in Waipoo Falls. The trail ends at Kumuwela Lookout with a beautiful view that cuts across Waimea Canyon to the ocean.

The **Kukui Trail** is a difficult five miles, with a steep drop of 2,000 feet into Waimea Canyon, ending at the Wiliwili campsite on the canyon floor. Remember, if you go down, you must somehow climb back up.

Cliff Trail is a short easy trail that leads to a Waimea Canyon overlook. Feral goats can be seen along the cliffs. You can start at the **Halemanu Trail** off of Koke`e Road. For a more adventurous journey, hop on the **Canyon Trail**.

Another short and easy trail is the **Iliau Nature Loop**. You can pick up the trail on your right between mile markers eight and nine. It's a quick 20-minute loop with markers identifying plants along the way. There are also views of Waimea Canyon.

The long (11.5 miles one-way) but moderate **Waimea Canyon Trail** starts at the end of the Kukui Trail and leads to Waimea Town. The trail travels along the Waimea River. Note that camping is not allowed south of Waialae Stream due to private ownership agreements.

Waimea Falls rainbow seen from the trail

The forest trails around Koke`e State Park are wonderful for observing the different plants, ranging from native mokihana and maile to invasive species such as banana poke.

Berry Flat Loop is an easy trail that leads through a variety of trees, including the redwood and sugi groves, eucalyptus and koa.

**Halemanu-Koke`e Trail** offers easy hiking through the Halemanu forest. You'll catch a glimpse of quite a number of plants, such as koa and o`hia trees, mokihana, maile, invasive species like blackberry and banana poka. This trail is also good for birdwatching.

The Kawaikoi Stream

Kawaikoi Stream Loop is a pretty easy trail and incredibly scenic. You'll need a 4WD vehicle and should drive to the Mohihi-Camp 10 Road. The trailhead is three-quarters of a mile past the Forest Reserve entrance sign. The area is good for trout fishing and camping.

**Alaka`i Swamp trails** are the wettest in Koke`e and thigh-deep mud is not uncommon here. It can slow a hiker's pace to one mile per hour through the swamp. Wear old, tightly laced sneakers that you don't mind getting muddy.

Alaka`i Swamp is a seven mile trail that starts at a parking area by the past the entrance sign to the Na Pali-Kona Forest Reserve sign. This difficult trail offers incredible birdwatching opportunities as it winds across the Alakai Swamp through native rain forests and bogs. It ends at the edge of Wainiha Pali and, on a clear day, you are treated to views of Wainiha and Hanalei Valleys.

At Pu`u O Kila Lookout (at the end of the road past Koke`e State Park), you can pick up the **Pihea Trail**. It's a 7½-mile trail perfect for viewing native birds and vegetation. The trail ends at Kawaikoi Camp and the **Pihea Overlook**, the highest rim point of Kalalau Valley. Do not venture beyond the Pihea Overlook because the terrain get very steep.

If you need to rent hiking gear, your best options are **Kayak Kaua`i** in Wailua or **Peddle n Paddle** in Hanalei. Good places to buy gear are **K-Mart** and **Wal-Mart** in Lihu`e.

Division of State Parks can be found online at www.hawaii.gov/dlnr/dsp/dsp.html. You can download maps and brochures of different parks, including Koke`e State Park.

If you want to hike with a group, check out the Sierra Club at **www.hi.sierraclub.org**. The Kaua`i chapter regularly schedules group hikes all over the island, including the Waimea/Koke`e areas. There's a $5 donation for the hike.

Another option for a guided hike is through **Koke`e Museum**. The museum sponsors "Wonder Walks" throughout the summer. Call the museum at ☎ 808-335-9975 for a schedule.

Hunting

Yes, there really is something for everyone on Kaua`i.

If you want to pay for your hunting expenience, you might want to consider going hunting on Ni`ihau through **Ni`ihau Safaris**, ☎ 808-335-3500, homepages.hawaiian.net/niihauisland/safaris.htmlThe price will set you back an easy $1650, not including licensing fees, and rifle rental. What is included is a round-trip helicopter flight to Ni`ihau, a hunting guide, and a bag limit of one sheep and one wild boar, which, if caught, are skinned, packed and readied for mounting. The game is plentiful, but the guides do know where to go for the game, which kind of takes the fun out of the whole process. You also won't see or come into contact with the island's residents.

Hunting licenses are mandatory in order to hunt on public, private or military land anywhere in Hawai`i. You can register for a license online at hunting.ehawaii.gov/hunting/license.html. If you're a Hawai`i resident, a license is $20 and that's good for the fiscal year (July 1-June 30).

The main requirement for a hunting license in Hawai`i is a Hunter Education Card. If you're a visitor and plan on hunting while you're in Hawai`i, make sure that you have your hunter education card. Once you get that, you can fill out a letter of exemption, which you can get online at www.hawaii.gov/dlnr/dcre/know.htm. You mail that in, your form will be processed and you'll be able to purchase a license.

There are hunting sites along Waimea Canyon. You can hunt deer, wild boar and sheep. To find out the hunting periods, restrictions, and areas, your best bet is to contact **Division of Forestry and Wildlife Kaua`i District Office** at ☎ 808-274-3438.

Tennis

There are a few places you can go for tennis, even out here, seemingly in the middle of nowhere. There are public courts in Kekaha, Hanapepe, and Waimea. Since these are public courts, they are first-come, first-served.

Kekaha Park has two lighted courts. You can find the courts on Elepaio Road. Drive west on Highway 50; once you hit Kekaha, turn right on Alae Road, heading up to Waimea Canyon. You'll find the courts just left on Elepaio Road.

Hanapepe Park has four lighted courts. Going west on Highway 50, you'll pass Hanapepe Bridge and turn left on Puolo Road. The courts are near the ocean on the right side.

Waimea High School has four courts total – two with lights, two without. Driving west from Waimea Town, you pass Waimea High School and make a right on Makeke Road. Pass the Neighborhood Center and make a right onto Haina Road. The courts are on the school grounds.

Biking

The area does offer some great mountain biking opportunities.

There aren't any places to rent a bike in Waimea so your best bet is to stop by **Outfitters Kaua`i**, 2827A Po`ipu Rd, Po`ipu, ☎ 808-742-9667, www.outfitterskauai.com, to rent a bike and a car rack, throw the bikes on it and go. They also offer bike maps to make it easier for you to find your way around.

Waimea Canyon offers several options for mountain biking. For those wanting a very serious road workout, try climbing **Waimea Canyon Road** (Route 550). You go up a hard and steep 3,000 feet for 12 miles, but the views will be amazing. It's paved the whole way, but can be dangerous, since the road winds and curves and there's not much of a shoulder.

For a fun and easy bike adventure, **Outfitters Kaua`i**, ☎ 808-742-9667, www.outfitterskauai.com, will take you on a tour down Waimea Canyon. It's pretty easy. All you have to do is hop in their van. They'll take you to the canyon, provide the bikes and helmets, give you some safety instruction and off you go. You're heading 12 miles downhill. How easy can it get? You meet at The Outfitters Kaua`i offices in Koloa and they'll transport you to Waimea Canyon and bring you back to Po`ipu. The cost is $94 per person, $74 for kids between 12 and 14 years of age.

On ATVs

Gay & Robinson Tours, www.gandrtours-kauai.com/gnrtor.html, ☎ 808-335-2824, offers an ATV Tour. You'll be taken 13 miles through the 18,000-acre cattle ranch, along the Olokele Ditch, and up to an elevation of 1,500 feet. There are incredible views of the ranch, sugar fields and the Pacific Ocean. You are given instructions on how to use an ATV and are provided with safety equipment such as helmets, gloves and glasses.

On the Water

Beaches

Westside Sporting Goods at 9681 Highway 50, ☎ 808-338-1411, Waimea, rents everything you'll need for your day at the beach. Beach umbrella ($2.50 a day), beach chair ($2.50 a day), cooler ($2.50 a day), body-boards, surfboards ($15 a day), snorkel gear ($5 a day), fishing gear such as crab nets ($7.50 a day), even a rod and reel for fishing ($7.50 a day). They're open Monday-Friday 9 am-6 pm. The store is open from 9-5 on Saturdays.

Beaches on the west side are spectacular. They're gorgeous to look at but, as far as swimming goes, they're not as gentle as those on the North Shore or in Po`ipu.

Port Allen is the island's second major commercial port after Nawiliwili. It's also where cruise ships generally dock on the island. Port Allen Boat Harbor is used by commercial boat tours, recreational boaters and the

Port Allen (Hawaiian Images)

Coast Guard. There are slips, a launch ramp and plenty of parking. This isn't a great place for swimming because the waters are murky from all of the boat activity. Just past the Chevron station there is a little beach where the sand is covered in glass. In fact, this beach is known as **Glass Beach**. Some locals believe that the ocean currents transport the glass from the shoreline nearby.

Hanapepe Beach Park is on the western end of Hanapepe Bay. The Hanapepe stream deposits sediment into the waters, causing the water to be murky. Surfers ride a small break near the beach. The bay is a breeding site for hammerhead sharks and the fishermen net younger hammerheads. Facilities include pavilions, restrooms, showers, parking.

Salt Pond Beach

Salt Pond Beach Park is the only place in Hawai`i where people still practice the ancient methods of salt making. The process of creating rock salt involves evaporating sea water in pans and large ponds. It's not too hard to figure out how this place got its name. The shore is protected from the pummeling surf by offshore rocks. The beach is generally safe for swimming and you can feel pretty comfortable bringing the whole family here. Of course, it's advisable to stay out of the water during large swells, as strong rip currents form. It's also popular with windsurfers and surfers, who can take on the breaks offshore. There is a lifeguard stand, picnic pavilions, restrooms, showers, parking and a camping area.

Pakala Beach is the surf spot on the west side of the island. It's known as **Infinities** because you can ride a wave forever. The reason is that the reef is perfectly shaped and has a slope that creates the wave that just won't end. You'll find Infinities two miles east of the Waimea River. There are a number of other breaks along the beach, but the ride's not as long. The area's not a good swim spot, but it is fantastic for sunbathing.

Lucy Wright Beach Park is just outside of Waimea. The park is where Captain Cook first came ashore in 1778. The park is named after the first native Hawaiian schoolteacher at Waimea, Lucy Kapahu Aukai Wright. The beach isn't great for swimming due to river runoff, but it is good for kayaking up the Waimea River and there are a couple of off-shore surf breaks. There are planty of facilities, including bathrooms, showers, and campsites.

It's on the western side of the mouth of the Waimea River, across from Ft. Elizabeth. To get to the park, head west on Highway 50, cross the Waimea River Bridge and take the first left onto Ala Wai Road. You'll find the parking lot on the makai side of the camp ground.

Kikiaola Harbor

Kikiaola Small Boat Harbor is notable because this is where the longest stretch of beach in the state begins (or ends, depending on how you look at it). The 15-mile stretch of beach goes on and on. The beach adjoining the harbor is shallow and sandy. It's not used for swimming because of the amount of silt in the sand, but it is used by local boaters, fishermen, beachcombers and picnickers.

Kekaha Beach

Kekaha Beach Park has a number of surf spots for experts only. The beach is totally exposed to the ocean, bringing strong currents that aren't suitable for swimming. It's a great place to catch the sunset. To get there, drive west on Highway 50 past Waimea and it's between mile markers 26 and 27. There are bathrooms at the park and sometimes there are lifeguards on duty.

Pacific Missile Range Facility does have two well known beaches and surf spots that are worth mentioning, but they're not readily accessible. **Barking Sands** is used for swimming ans surfing, while **Major's Bay** was used primarily for surfing. However, be aware that access to PMRF has been restricted solely to military personnel since September 11, 2001. If you want to get on the base and you're a resident, you'll have to go through an extensive background check. If you're a visitor, it would be virtually impossible to get on the base. As these things do change pretty frequently, you can call ☎ 808-335-4229 for information regarding visitor access and offshore boating.

Polihale Beach (Hawaiian Images)

Polihale State Park is by far my favorite beach on the island. It's vast, wide and long. Even if there are a lot of people there, it sure doesn't feel like it. The beach begins in the shadow of the Na Pali Cliffs, which create majestic scenery. In the summertime, the beach is about 300 feet wide but, once the winter swells hit the area, the beach erodes a great deal. It is the westernmost point of the US, with the exception of Ni`ihau, and it's the end of the 15-mile stretch of beach that begins in Kekaha. It is a highly recommended place to watch a sunset, where you can see the various shades of pink, purple and red as they fade into the horizon.

The best swimming here is at **Queen's Pond** about halfway down the beach. Not to be confused with Queen's Bath on the north shore, Queen's Pond is considered to be the safest swimming area around. To get there, turn south on the mainpark access road at the fork marked by two monkeypod trees and proceed 2/10th of a mile. An access road leads up on to the dunes and overlooks the pond.

You can get to the beach, follow Highway 50 until you reach the end of the road past the Pacific Missile Range Facility. Turn off onto a dirt road that goes on for about five miles.

Facilities include restrooms, showers, picnic pavilions and camping areas. There are no lifeguards here.

Tip: Driving at Polihale can be treacherous. You're in the middle of nowhere, so the last thing you want to do is get stuck. On a dry day, most cars can handle the dirt road leading to the beach. Once you get past the beach parking, the sand gets very soft and it's deep enough to get your car stuck. Someone may be around to pull you out, but that's only if you're lucky. When in doubt, stay on harder ground.

HOUSE OF THE DEAD

Polihale also has strong roots in Hawaiian mythology. The Hawaiians built a heiau in the area, believing that the souls of the dead left the island and went toward the setting sun. Polihale translates into "house of the dead." Po, is the Hawaiian afterlife and Hale means house. The belief was so strong that the homes built in the vicinity of Polihale were built with no east-facing doors, so that dead spirits could not enter.

Snorkeling

There are a number of tour companies that leave from Port Allen and Kikiaola Harbor in Waimea, taking you on excursions along the Na Pali Coast and to Ni`ihau. They stop to snorkel off of Nuaolo Kai along the Na Pali Coast. Please note that the tours may vary depending on marine conditions.

Catamaran Kahanu, ☎ 808-335-3577, 888-213-7711, 808-645-6176, Port Allen, www.catamarankahanu.com. They pride themselves on being Hawaiian-owned and -operated. It shows as they describe Hawaiian culture and history during their tours. You'll go on a snor-

Catamaran Kahanu

keling tour along the Na Pali Coast, and they show you caves, waterfalls and dolphins along the way. Prices start at $101.

Holo Holo Charters

Holo Holo Charters, ☎ 800-848-6130, 808-335-0815, www.holo-holocharters.com, Port Allen Marina Center. Holo Holo is an extremely popular tour and for good reason. They provide the chance to snorkel in the pristine waters to Lehua, the small uninhabited crater off the north coast of Ni`ihau. They leave from Port Allen bright and early, but they do provide a full continental breakfast on their 65-foot catamaran. The boat heads west and north past Barking Sands and Polihale. You'll then cruise past the Na Pali Cliffs and stop to see spinner dolphins and, during the winter, you'll probably see a couple of humpback whales.

You then head over to Lehua, where the snorkeling is excellent. If you've been to Maui, it's very similar to snorkeling at Molokini, but better, since it's not as crowded and the marine life is more abundant. Holo Holo provides snorkel equipment, various flotation devices and a deli-style lunch, drinks and snacks. Since you're in a large catamaran, the trip tends to be a smooth one. The tour to Ni`ihau costs $175 per person. If you opt for the tour that takes you along the Na Pali Coast, the cost is $135 per person.

Blue Dolphin Charters

Blue Dolphin Charters, ☎ 808-335-5553, 877-511-1311, Port Allen, www.kauaiboats.com, also offers a trip to the Na Pali coast where you stop and snorkel for a short period, then get back on the boat and head over to Ni`ihau for some snorkeling around Lehua. Cost is $196 per person. They also have a shorter tour that includes the Na Pali Coast for $148 per person.

Kauai Sea Tours' Lucky Lady

Kaua`i Sea Tours, ☎ 800-733-7997 or 808-826-7254, Aka Ula St., Port Allen, www.kauaiseatours.com, offers several options. You can go in the rigid-hull inflatable boat, holding about 15 people, or in their catamaran, which holds 50 people. You depart Port Allen and head along the coast along past PMRF and Polihale, then you stop to see honu and dolphins. If you're in the rigid-hull inflatable, you'll be able to cruise through caves and see the cliffs up-close. You pass the beaches of Na Pali, and head back to Nualolo Kai for snorkeling and a deli-style lunch. The reef is about 15 feet deep and there's plenty of room and lots of fish to see. The rigid-hull inflatable boat is a lot of fun, especially if you sit up front. However, if you're not comfortable with bouncing about, you might want to take the catamaran, the *Lucky Lady*. Prices range from $135 to $165, depending on the tour you choose.

Na Pali Explorer

Na Pali Explorer, ☎ 808-338-9999, 877-335-9909, www.napaliexplorer.com, Highway 50 in Waimea. Their offices are right next to the gas station just as you enter Waimea Town. Na Pali Explorer provides a very enjoyable experience. They take the same route as Kaua`i Sea Tours up the coast, past PMRF and Polihale, along the Na Pali coast and back to snorkel and have lunch at Nualolo Kai. The tour guides are very friendly and knowledgeable. They know their stuff when it came to Hawaiian history and aren't afraid to share it. They have two boats that you can go on, the *Explorer I* and the *Explorer II*. The *Explorer I* is a rigid-hull inflatable that holds about 20 people. It will take you through caves and, conditions permitting, can make a beach landing at Nualolo Kai. They'll also take you on a short hike around the archaeological ruins of Nualolo Kai. *Explorer II* is a larger rigid-hull inflatable (about 48 feet) that holds more people and provides a more comfortable, shaded ride.

Capt. Zodiac Raft Adventures, ☎ 808-335-2719, www.napali.com, Port Allen Marina Center. Captain Zodiac gives you the choice of a five- or six-hour tour. You take the same route as the other tours but, on the six hour tour, you land at Nualolo Kai (weather permitting), have lunch and hike through the ruins of Nualolo Kai. And, of course, don't forget the snorkeling. $159 per person.

Captain Andy's catamaran

Captain Andy's, ☎ 800-535-0830, 808-335-6833, www.napali.com, takes you on their 55-foot catamaran. They pretty much take the same route along the coast, past Polihale and Na Pali. What makes these guys special is the food. Out of all the tour companies, Captain Andy's serves the best lunch. Beyond the usual deli sandwiches and snacks, it's a catered hot lunch that is quite tasty. $129 per person.

Liko Kaua`i Cruises, ☎ 888-732-5456 or 808-338-0333, www.liko-kauai.com. Check in at Obsessions Café in Waimea, next to the Big Save Market. What makes this tour special is that the captains share Hawaiian history and mythology with you, as well as their own family experiences over the generations. It gives the tour a very intimate feel. Enjoy an hour of snorkeling and a deli lunch. $120 per person.

Where to Rent Gear

Westside Sporting Goods, at 9681 Highway 50, ☎ 808-338-1411 in Waimea, offers snorkeling gear (mask, fins and snorkel) for $5 day.

You can also stop at the **Big Save** to pick up an underwater camera for about $12-$17, so you can capture and save your underwater adventures. To get the best shots, you'll need to be pretty close.

Places to Snorkel

Salt Pond Beach Park is a great place for snorkeling if you want don't want to go on a tour. There's an outside reef and a lava wall that keep the beach virtually protected, especially on the ends. You don't have to go far to catch a glimpse of the marine life here. The smorkeling is best toward the lava wall on either end of the beach. It's a great place for beginners. Highly recommended, since parking is plentiful and there and there are plenty of showers, restrooms, and picnic areas.

Salt Pond Beach Park (shorediving.com)

Pakala Beach. I really can't recommend this beach for snorkeling for a couple of reasons. First of all, it's a surfing spot, so you're going to have to avoiding surfers. Even though there is a shallow reef inside (closer to shore), where you can see some marine life, it's not the safest spot in the world. If you must snorkel here, you should be experienced. Otherwise, head over to Salt Pond Beach Park.

Surfing

Westside Sporting Goods, at 9681 Highway 50, ☎ 808-338-1411, Waimea, rents surfboards and bodyboards for $15 a day. They're open Monday-Friday 9 am-6 pm. The store is open from 9-5 on Saturdays.

If you're an experienced surfer, you might want to try your hand at **Infinities**. Remember you're the guest here so act accordingly. No dropping in on other people's waves or cutting people off. Show respect for the local surfers. If you don't know what I mean by this, you shouldn't go to Infinities. You can find it by driving west on Kaumuali`i Hwy. You'll see the surfboards and the trucks parked along the road. Follow the path to the beach.

Other than that, there are very limited opportunities around Salt Pond Beach Park, but that's more appropriate for boogie boarding.

Boogie Boarding

Salt Pond Beach Park is the safest beach for boogie boarding on the west side. The waves tend to break on shore just a bit. Good for beginning swimmers. The water is clear; there are lifeguards.

Whale-Watching

Whale-watching season occurs in the winter months from November through April. Just about all of the snorkeling tours mentioned above will stop and incorporate whale-watching in their tours during the season. Some companies do provide tours that are specifically for whale-watching.

Na Pali Explorer, ☎ 808-338-9999, 877-335-9909, www.napaliexplorer.com, Highway 50 in Waimea. Their offices are right next to the gas station, as you enter Waimea Town. Na Pali Explorer will take you aboard the *Explorer II* boat for a 3½-hour tour for whale-watching and education. The boat is equipped with hydrophones so you can hear the whales underwater. $79 per person.

Captain Zodiac Raft Adventures, ☎ 808-335-2719, www.napali.com, Port Allen Marina offers a two hour whale-watching tour starting in January that focuses on whale observation and education. All boats are equipped with hydrophones so you can hear the whales underwater. During whale season, you also have the option to take five- or six-hour whale-watching tours. The two-hour tour is $59 per person.

Scuba

Mana Divers, ☎ 877- 348-3669, 808-335-0881, www.manadivers.com, offers a number of opportunities for diving, even if you're a beginner. They have introductory dive courses all the way through PADI (Professional Association of Diving Instructors) certification and specialty classes. Beginner classes meet in Po`ipu at the Hyatt Regency or at the Kaua`i Marriott. They charge beginners $120 for a

one-tank dive. If you're already certified, go to the offices in Port Allen. A one-tank dive for certified divers is $65 per person.

Bubbles Below Scuba Charters Port Allen, ☎ 808-332-7333, www.bubblesbelowkauai.com, offers a number of ways to get in the water and they even conduct a dive trip off the coast of Ni`ihau during the summer. They have introductory, certification and refresher classes. They also do dives off the Na Pali Coast. Rates vary by tour starting at $120.

If you want to forgo the instruction and just need to rent gear, Bubbles Below can accommodate you. They rent just about everything you might need.

Sunset Cruises

There is nothing like being out on the water, enjoying a cocktail or two and watching the sun melt into the horizon. Sunsets on Kaua`i are really special and being on a sunset cruise is a fantastic way to end your day.

Captain Andy's, ☎ 800-535-0830, 808-335-6833, www.napali.com, Port Allen, takes you on their 55-foot catamaran for sunset cruises either along the Na Pali Coast or the south shore off Po`ipu. The ride around Na Pali includes a buffet dinner, with cocktails provided throughout the tour. Cost is $105 per person. The ride around Po`ipu is a bit more basic and, at two hours, much shorter. It includes cocktails, but the choices are limited. They do have musicians playing Hawaiian music throughout the cruise. $69 per person.

Holoholo Charters, ☎ 808-335-0815, www.holoholocharters.com, Port Allen. They take their 65-foot catamaran out to the Na Pali coast to catch a glorious view of the sunset. You can have heavy pupus, soft drinks and a decent selection of drinks, including a champagne toast at sunset. And, of course, don't forget the mai tais. $95 per person.

Kaua`i Sea Tours, ☎ 800-733-7997 or 808-826-7254, Aka Ula St., Port Allen, www.kauaiseatours.com. For an excellent sunset dinner cruise, this is the tour to go on. You'll hop on the *Lucky Lady* for a dinner buffet, which isn't great but is better than a number of places in town. The staff is friendly and helpful. Cost is $109 per person. During the summer, they also offer a dinner cruise with snorkeling. $139 per person.

Blue Dolphin Charters, ☎ 808-335-5553, 877-511-1311, Port Allen, www.kauaiboats.com, has a sunset cruise that sails around the Po`ipu area. This two-hour cruise includes dinner, drinks and live music; it's available only in the summer. $95 per person. They also have a year-round cruise that goes around Na Pali for $116 per person.

Fishing

There are some options for freshwater and saltwater fishing on the west side of Kaua`i. Before, you get started, you need to make sure that you have the proper licenses and requirements fulfilled.

You can go online to get a **freshwater fishing license** at www.ehawaii.gov/dlnr/fish/exe/fresh_main_page.cgi. You fill out the information, print and sign and you're all set.

If you don't get a chance to do this before you leave for your trip, **Westside Sporting Goods**, at 9681 Highway 50, ☎ 808-338-1411, or **Salt Pond Country Store** in Hanapepe, ☎ 808-335-5966, provide licenses. Fees are $25 for a non-resident license, which is good for one year. You can purchase a seven-day tourist license for $10 or a 30-day tourist license for $20.

At **Koke`e State Park**, you can go freshwater fishing in the **Pu`u Lua Reservoir** in Koke`e State Park. It's stocked with rainbow trout. You should have a 4-wheel-drive vehicle to get to the reservoir. The season is very restricted. You can fish in the area from the first Saturday in August and then the next 16 consecutive days. After that, you can only fish on Saturdays, Sundays and state holidays. There is also a bag limit per licensed angler. At press time, the bag limit was seven. Check with the Department of Land and Natural Resources, Division of Aquatic Resources office, at ☎ 808-274-3344, before you head out. You can also find them online at www.hawaii.gov/dlnr/dar/index.html.

For deep-sea fishing, there are plenty of charters that sail out of Nawiliwili Harbor, and a few sail out of Po`ipu and the north shore. Check the *Fishing* sections in the North Shore and Lihu`e chapters.

In the Air

Helicopter Tours

**Ni`ihau Helicopter**, ☎ 808-338-1234, 877-441-3500, www.niihau.us, which is owned by the Robinson family, takes you on a three-hour tour of Ni`ihau, which the family owns. You'll fly on an Agusta 109A twin-engine helicopter over and around the island. You then land on the beach where you spend some time snorkeling, swimming, and having a picnic lunch. $325 per person.

Inter-Island Helicopters, ☎ 808-335-5009, www.interislandhelicopters.com. Here's an adventure that you won't forget. Hop in Interisland's Hughes 500. They fly with the doors off, which makes for excellent photo opportunities. They also offer a two-way communications system in the plane so you can ask the pilot questions during your flight. There are two tours. The first is 50 minutes around Waimea Canyon, Na Pali, and the north shore. This tour is $189. There's another tour where they also do a waterfall landing, weather permitting, and give you time to swim in a freshwater pool, so bring your swimsuit. This tour is two hours long and costs $280 per person.

Other Air Adventures

**Sky Dive Kaua`i**, ☎ 808-335-5859, www.skydivekauai.com. For those of you with an urge to jump out of a plane, here's your chance. Sky Dive Kaua`i takes off from Port Allen Airfield and you'll fly for about 20-30 minutes to 10,000 feet, then jump. You freefall at speeds up to 120 miles per hour. The cost is $229 for a tandem skydive, including your own DVD or VHS video. Call for reservations. You do have to be 18 or older in order to jump.

Spas & Health Clubs

Ka Hui Hoolu, ☎ 808-332-6363, is an outcall spa service that comes right to you. They'll come to your hotel, bed & breakfast, or even your campsite. They offer massages, wraps, facials and spa packages.

Waimea Plantation Cottages has a spa on its premises. **Hart-Felt Massage and Day Spa**, ☎ 808-338-2240, www.hartfeltmassage.com, offers facials, body wraps, salt scrubs, as well as a number of different types of massages, including Hawaiian Hot Stone Massage and Hawaiian Lomi Lomi.

Kaua`i Xtreme Fitness, ☎ 808-335-0049, on Waialo Road in Hanapepe, has gym equipment if you need to get to the gym.

Shopping

Head toward Port Allen off of Highway 50 just before the Ele`ele Shopping Center and you'll find a few shops such as the **Red Dirt Shirt Factory Outlet**, 4352 Waialo Road, ☎ 808-335-5670, www.dirtshirt.com. The warehouse sells T-shirts dyed with, well, red dirt from Kaua`i. It was originally called Paradise Sportswear, but was slammed when Hurricane Iniki struck in 1992. The hurricane blew the roof off of the warehouse and after the storm, the shirts were covered in mud and red dirt. Just like that, a new business was born.

You'll also find **Nite Owl T-Shirts**, ☎ 808-335-6110, www.niteowlt-shirts.com. They're located on the other side of Red Dirt shirts. They do custom printing for companies around the island and have their own unique designs for sale.

Port Allen Marina Center

Across the street from the Red Dirt Shirt Warehouse is the **Port Allen Marina Center**. It houses mostly boat tour companies and offices, but there are a few places here that are worth a look. First off, stop by **Kaua`i Chocolate Company**, ☎ 808-335-0448 for your choc-

AUTHOR'S CHOICE ★ olate fix. Everything is handmade in the store and incredibly tasty. You must try the Chocolate Opihi, a treat so good it should be outlawed. It's made from a shortbread cookie, caramel and a whole macadamia nut, then covered in chocolate.

There's also **Happy Honu Gifts**, which has typical tourist gifts to take home. Aloha shirts, trinkets, pretty much what you've seen everywhere else on the island. **Ehukai Ni`ihau Shell Lei** is also at Port Allen Marina Center. They offer Ni`ihau shell leis.

Ele`ele Shopping Center. Stop in here for restaurants, a Big Save Supermarket, 24-hour laundromat, post office and a First Hawaiian Bank branch.

Kaua`i Coffee Company, ☎ 808-335-0813, has a small gift shop where you can get a nice caffeine fix to take home. They sell gift boxes and also ship to the mainland.

As you head into Hanapepe, you'll find lots of unique works of art and gifts. Turn off at the sign that says, "The Biggest Little Town on Kaua`i," park the car, and walk around. There are a number of interesting galleries and shops that make Hanapepe a worthwhile shopping spot.

A great place to get your sweet tooth fill is the **Kaua`i Kookie Kompany**, 1-3529 Kaumuali`i Highway (Highway 50), www.kauaikookie.com, ☎ 800-361-1126. They've been around since 1965 and are well known for their macadamia shortbread, guava macadamia, and Kona coffee. You can also pick up some Hawaiian Hula salad dressing (try the Papaya Seed flavor). The Kaua`i Kookie store is open Monday-Friday from 8 am to 4 pm, and Saturday and Sunday from 9 am to 4 pm.

Of course, the biggest draw in Hanapepe are the art galleries that line Hanapepe Road.

Kaua`i Village Gallery, 3890 Hanapepe Road, Hanapepe, ☎ 808-335-0343, shows the work 25 local artists including sculptors, photographers and artists.

If you want a work of art that's a little more practical, stop by **Kama`aina Cabinets/Koa Wood Gallery**, ☎ 808-335-5483, with its koa furniture, koa photo albums, and Norfolk pine bowls on display.

Dawn Traina Gallery has paintings, drawings and prints of Native Hawaiians. 3840-B Hanapepe Road, Hanapepe, ☎ 808-335-0381.

Arius Hopman photograph

At **Arius Hopman Studio Gallery** locally renowned watercolor painter and photographer Arius Hopman showcases his work. 3840-C Hanapepe Road, Hanapepe, ☎ 808-335-0550.

8-Bells Gallery displays sculpture, oil paintings, watercolors and limited edition prints. They're well known for their Koa wood framing. 4510 Hana Road Hanapepe, ☎ 808-335-0227.

Giorgio's Gallery, 3871 Hanapepe Road, Hanapepe, ☎ 808-335-3949, www.giorgiosart.com, displays stunning tropical landscapes and abstract paintings.

Banana Patch Studio, ☎ 808-335-5944, 3865 Hanapepe Road, www.bananapatchstudio.com, has hand-painted ceramic tiles and pottery, photography, T-shirts and many other items.

Art lovers will want to check out Hanapepe's **Friday Art Night**, which is held from 6 to 9 pm every week. Sixteen galleries participate, offering pupus, demonstrations and special exhibits. Artists are there and available to answer questions about their work. There's also live music playing on the street.

In Waimea, there are a couple of places to stop by. First off, make the trip to **Aunty Lilikoi** and take home a little sweetness from your trip. Aunty Lilikoi features syrups, jellies, mustards, all made with that uniquely island flavor, lilikoi (passion fruit, sweet and sour at the same time). This little shop is filled with passion for these concoctions. Don't miss the new body care and aromatherapy products. ☎ 866-Lilikoi, 9875 Waimea Road, Waimea.

Na Pali Arch, *by Emily Miller, at Aloha-N-Paradise*

Aloha-N-Paradise, 9905 Waimea Road, ☎ 808-338-1522, www.aloha-n-paradise.com, in Waimea, is an art gallery showing the works of local artists. The works are "Kaua`i-Inspired."

**Forever Kaua`i**, 8171 Kekaha Road, ☎ 808-337-2888, is right next to the Waimea Canyon General Store. At either place, you can pick up postcards, aloha shirts, and souvenirs. They carry some of the best Ni`ihau shells on the island at prices that are better than some of the larger establishments elsewhere.

There's also the **West Kaua`i Craft Fair**, right across the street from the West Kaua`i Technology and Visitors Center. The fair is held every Thursday through Sunday from 9 am to 4 pm. Some artists have their work on display and you can also find hand-sewn quilts, glass beads, photographs, many kinds of handmade jewelry, and koa wood bowls.

NI`IHAU SHELL LEIS

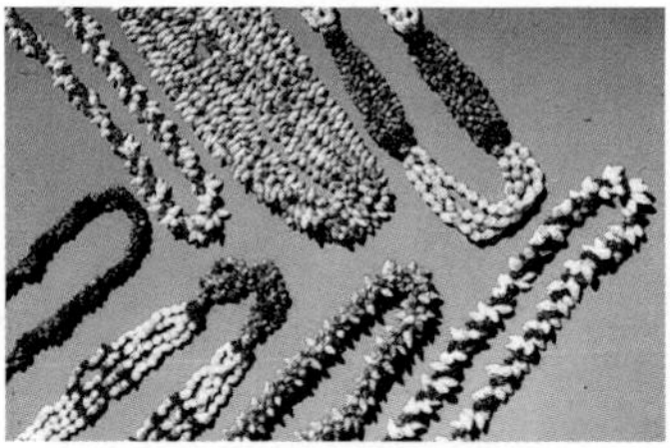

The finest shellwork made in Hawai`i comes from Ni`ihau in the form of their famous shell leis. It's a tradition passed down over generations. The shells themselves, are tiny and rare. They can be found off of the windward coast of the island.

During the winter months, it's pretty common to see the shells come up on the beaches of Ni`ihau. When that happens, typically after storms, the island's residents stop everything and rush to the beach to collect them.

They are then sorted by size and color and only the best of the best are kept. The smaller ones are the most coveted. The shells are then drilled and strung together to create intricate works of art. They are patterned after lei, chokers, or multistrand pieces.

The cost of a Ni`ihau shell lei can start at $500 for a single-strand choker and go all they way up to $10,000 or beyond. On Kaua`i, the best places to purchase authentic Ni`ihau shell leisare the **Hawaiian Trading Company** in Lawai and **Forever Kaua`i** in Kekaha, on the way to Waimea Canyon.

If you need to pick up groceries, you can go to the **Big Save Market** on Waimea Rd or **Ishihara's Market**, which is about 200 yards from Big Save. Both places carry typical grocery store items, although I do find that Ishihara's has fresher meats.

For the freshest produce, nothing can beat the local farmer's markets. On the west side, Hanapepe Town Park hosts a **farmer's market** every Thursday at 3 pm.

On your way to Waimea Canyon, there are a few places to stop for last-minute snacks or more water to get you ready for your day. You can hit the **Waimea Canyon General Store**, ☎ 808-337-9569, **Thrifty Mini Mart**, ☎ 808-337-1057 or **Menehune Food Mart**, ☎ 808-337-1335

■ Where To Stay

Resort

Resort Quest Waimea Plantation Cottages, ☎ 800-992-4632, 808-338-1625, 9400 Kaumuali`i Highway, Waimea, www.waimea-plantation.com. This is by far my favorite place to stay on the west side, if not the entire island. It allows you to be a part of a resort community but affords the privacy of having your own vacation rental home. It is quaint and maintains that old plantation charm, right down to the raised, claw-foot bathtubs. Yet it still has the modern conveniences such as television, cable, stereo and air conditioning. The only challenge here are the roosters that like to wake you

Cottage interior

One of the cottages

Waimea Plantation Cottages

up early in the morning. But I think that adds to the charm. Their units have fully stocked kitchens, so you can buy groceries at the Big Save Market or Ishihara's in town, or even at the farmer's market and cook "at home." The beachfront area of the property is lined with hammocks and benches, perfect for taking your favorite beverage and sitting outside, while you gaze at the stars and listen to the call of the ocean. During the day, you can play volleyball on the sand court or swim in the pool.

The property has an interesting history. Some of the houses date back to the 1880s and were part of the H.P. Faye company at Mana. Others were from the Kekaha Sugar Company or were Waimea Sugar camp houses, built in the early 1900s.

Rates start at $150 a night for a studio and go up to $650 for a five-bedroom cottage. There's also free wireless Internet available in the lobby area.

B & B

Inn Waimea, ☎ 808-338-0031, www.innwaimea.com, 4469 Halepule Road, Waimea, is a small bed and breakfast that is quaint and holds on to the old Hawaiian style. Rates start at $110 per night.

Vacation Rentals

Kekaha Sunset Beach Vacation Rental, ☎ 800-677-5959, www.kauai-vacationrentals.com/kekaha, has six units that range from a one-bedroom suite to a three-bedroom house.

Kaua`i Harbor House, ☎ 808-338-1625, is literally a home away from home in the middle of paradise. It's spacious, secluded and in demand, so you'll have to make your reservations well in advance. Located on the beach next to Kikiaola Small Boat Harbor, it's owned and managed by the Kikiaola Land Company, the same folks who own Waimea Plantation Cottages. Rates start at $385 for a three-bedroom, three-bath cottage.

Kaua`i Harbor House

Hostels

Camp Sloggett, ☎ 808-245-5959, www.campingkauai.com, is in Koke`e State Park, well off the beaten path. It's run by the YWCA of Kaua`i. There are a couple of dogs there protecting the property, so even though it may be a little strange and scary to be in the middle of nowhere, you are protected and safe. They have a number of options for accommodations, including your own private one-bedroom cabin for $65 a night or, if you have a large group, you can go with the **Sloggett Lodge**, which holds up to 10 people for $20 a night, based on a minimum of five people. You can pitch a tent on the property for $10 a night per person or stay in the hostel for $20 a night per person.

Koke`e State Park has cabins available. Some of the older cabins are set up like college dorms, while the newer cabins at least have separate bedrooms. Even though they both hold six people, you're better off with the newer cabins because they have newer kitchen equipment and they're just plain nicer. There are no phones or televisions in the units. The rates are

$35 for a studio, or $45 for a two-bedroom. There's also a five-night maximum stay.

Camping

To camp on Kaua`i, you need to get a permit. Depending on where you plan on camping, you'll either have to go through the state or county to get a permit.

If you plan on camping at Lucy Wright Beach County Park or Salt Pond Park, you'll have to go though the Kaua`i County Division of Parks & Recreation. To obtain a county permit, contact the **Kaua`i County Parks Permit Section** at ☎ 808-241-4463. Their hours are 8:15 am to 4 pm Monday through Friday. You can also get a permit at the **Hanapepe Recreation Center**, ☎ 808-335-3731. However, they're only open between 8:30 am and 12:30 pm. Camping permit fees are $3 per adult, per night for non-residents and free for Hawai`i residents.

State parks include the campsites at **Polihale State Park** and **Koke`e State Park**. Polihale offers tent camping and trailer camping. Koke`e offers several campsites along hiking trails, such as **Kawaikoi Camp**, **Hipalau Camp**, and **Sugi Grove Camp**.

Camping fees for Hawai`i State Parks are $5 per campsite per night. You can download an application from the Hawai`i State Division of Land and Natural Resources at www.hawaii.gov/dlnr/dsp/fees.html or you can call ☎ 808-274-3444.

If you need to pick up camping gear, your best bet is to buy it at **K-mart** or **Wal-Mart** in Lihu`e. Both stores have inexpensive gear and you can always ship it home. For food, stop by Ishihara's or Big Save in Ele`ele or Waimea.

■ Where To Eat

Barefoot Burgers, 9643 Kaumuali`i Hwy, ☎ 808-338-2082. When I got my burger after a short wait, it didn't look like much. I thought I'd been ripped off. Once I had a bite, though, I understood the big deal surrounding Barefoot Burgers. It was so ono (delicious) and the fries were done just right. Not too greasy. Perfect for a quick stop on your way to Polihale or Waimea Canyon. If you're not in the nood for a burger, they also serve smoothies and chicken sandwiches. For lunch, you can also try a plate lunch – I'd go with the teri chicken plate. Yum! Under $15.

Da Imu Hut Café, Hanapepe Rd, ☎ 808-335-0200, serves local-style foods. Their specialty is Teri Fried Chicken. Other menu items include burgers, saimin and fried chicken. The large portions will fill you up, so make sure you bring your appetite. Their food leaves visitors and locals alike saying it's ono or "Broke Da Mouth" good. They're open from 10 am to 2 pm, then 5 to 8:30 pm Monday through Friday; Saturdays from 10 am to 2 pm.

Grinds Café & Espresso, www.grindscafe.net, Ele`ele, ☎ 808-335-6027. This pleasant surprise next to the Ele`ele Shopping Center has great service and sandwiches. It's a quaint little café that serves a vast array of food. Breakfast is served all day and you can get breakfast sandwiches or omelets. The breads are fresh and baked on the premises. You can tell because they are out of this world. For lunch, they have delicious pizzas, organic salads and hot or cold sandwiches and burgers. The dinner menu includes pastas, Cajun fish and BBQ chicken. The prices are very reasonable and the service is excellent. The ambiance is that of a quaint café where surfers come to hang out. $15-$35.

Hanapepe Café, 3830 Hanapepe Road, Hanapepe, ☎ 808-335-5011. This vegetarian establishment is a great way to get started in the morning, especially if you order the sourdough French toast with bananas and syrup. For lunch, the rosemary French fries are a real treat. The ambiance is classic plantation-style. This place is packed on Friday nights for Friday Night Art; make sure you call and get a reservation. Don't forget to pick up a bottle of your favorite beverage, as it's BYOB. $15-$35.

Jo-Jo's Shave Ice, Highway 50, Waimea. The place to go on Kaua`i for the shave ice experience. Jo-Jo's

Jo-Jo's

is a colorful shack in Waimea town. It doesn't look like much, but the shave ice is awesome. There's a wide variety of flavors to choose from. Under $15.

**Koke`e Lodge**, ☎ 808-335-6061, at the Koke`e State Park, next to the museum, is perfect after a hard morning hiking. The food comes in big portions and is pretty good, though not excellent. The service is prompt and polite. Stop by for lunch, especially if you started hiking in the morning. The cornbread was killer.

Obsessions Café, Kekaha Rd, Waimea, ☎ 808-338-1110. Breakfast is served from 6 am to 10 pm, lunch from 10-2. This is a decent place to stop for a quick bite to eat. The prices are reasonable. Sandwiches and wraps are served for lunch. A pretty basic menu. They serve tasty omelets and breakfast sandwiches in the morning. Smoothies and sundaes as well.

Pacific Pizza & Deli, ☎ 808-338-1020, Kaumuali`i Hwy. Next to Wrangler's Steakhouse, this place is your typical pizza joint but with more exotic options, such as Mexican Pizza and Thai Pizza. Their service is OK, pretty much what you'd expect from a pizza joint. You can get sandwiches, ice cream and coffee drinks here as well. $15-$35.

Tois Thai Kitchen, ☎ 808-335-3111, Ele`ele Shopping Center. It's a bit hard to find, and it makes you wonder how a place can survive when it's so hidden away. That question was easily answered when I tasted their food. It was very good and you can tell that the ingredients are fresh. Specialties include various types of curries, shrimp satay and pad thai.

Waimea Brewing Co.

Waimea Brewing Co, ☎ 338-9733. On the property of Waimea Plantation Cottages, this is a great place to stop on your way back to town after a full day hiking around Waimea Canyon. If you're like me and tend to favor a dark beer, try the Porter. It's very smooth with the perfect amount of bite from the hops. They do have live music nightly. The atmosphere is fun and the food is mediocre. It does the job, but the real reason to come here is for the beer. They blend local ingredients with the right amount of hops to create a very pleasant homebrew. It bills itself as the westernmost brewery in the US. $15-$35.

Wong's Chinese Restaurant, Hanapepe, ☎ 808-335-5066. This is one of the more interesting places on this side of the island. It certainly isn't known for its service or atmosphere, but it is known for its lilikoi chiffon pies, which make the trip here worthwhile. The restaurant serves breakfast, lunch and dinner, with the menu featuring Japanese and Chinese dishes as well as local plates. The portions are tremendous and the prices are reasonable.

Wrangler's Steak House

Wrangler's Steak House, 9852 Kaumuali`i Highway, Waimea, ☎ 808-338-1218. Wrangler's pays homage to Kaua`i's paniolo (cowboy) and plantation traditions. Beautiful cuts of steak are cooked just right, with pleasant service. Their specialty is what's called a pulehu sauce, made with butter, garlic and oysters. I'd avoid that because the flavors are very light on the garlic and oyster flavors, so you wind up with a beautiful cut of meat drowned in butter. Your best bet is to leave the steak in its purest form – with nothing on it. The meal comes with a full salad bar. $35-$50.

Shrimp Station, 9652 Kaumuali`i Highway, Waimea, ☎ 808-338-1242. This place is all about shrimp. Remember that scene in *Forrest Gump* when Bubba's talking about the different kinds of shrimp dishes? It's kind of like that. Garlic shrimp, shrimp tacos, Cajun shrimp, coconut shrimp. They have all sorts of shrimp and this place does fall into the "must experience" category on the west side. Under $15.

Nightlife

There's not much nightlife on the west side. You won't find dance clubs or wild parties every night. Friday seem to be the night for partying it up.

For astronomy buffs, the west side of Kaua`i offers ample opportunity for stargazing. If its clear, the night sky can be phenomenal. There is very little light pollution, so you can see a lot of stars, even with the naked eye. There's also the **Kaua`i Educational Association for Science and Astronomy** (KEASA), which holds a monthly star watch at the Kaumakani softball fields, on Highway 50 between Hanapepe and Waimea (around mile marker 18). Starwatches begin at sunset. KEASA has a hotline you can call at ☎ 808-332-7827 for the organization's latest information. They also have a website at www.keasa.org.

Waimea Brewing Company at Waimea Plantation Cottages, ☎ 808-338-9733, www.waimeabrewing.com, has live music every Friday night. They have mostly local musicians playing island-style music. It's a fine way to wind down and enjoy a cold beer.

On **Friday Art Night** in Hanapepe, this sleepy town turns into party central. The 16 galleries and retail shops are open later, the galleries all have something to offer. 6 to 9 pm weekly. Most galleries offer pupus and drinks. There's also live music on the street.

The East Shore

What to See

IN THIS CHAPTER

Driving north on Kuhio Highway from Lihu`e will bring you to the Coconut Coast, which is basically the windward side of the island. The area got its name from the 2,000-plus coconut trees that were planted in 1896 by William Lindeman. The grove is now a part of the Coco Palms property. The area is the most populated on Kaua`i, with approximately 16,000 of the island's residents.

Starting off in Wailua, the area is steeped in ancient Hawaiian history. The remains of heiau (temples) that date back hundreds of years line the mouth of the Wailua River. The Hawaiians considered this area to be sacred. Wailua was an area for Hawaiian royalty. It was the religious center of the island. The land was so sacred that Hawaiian royals would travel here from all the islands to give birth. There were heiau built all along the river and at the river's mouth. You can still see the remains of some of them.

The area started to change dramatically in the 1950s when **Coco Palms** opened in Wailua. It was the first resort on Kaua`i. In the early 1960s, the King himself, Elvis Presley, came to Coco Palms to shoot scenes for *Blue Hawai`i*. Coconut palm trees are in abundance throughout the area.

Between Wailua and Kapa`a is a tiny town called **Waipouli**. Blink and you might miss it. It's made up of mostly condominiums and townhouses. You'll pass **Coconut Marketplace**, which has plenty of restaurants and shops.

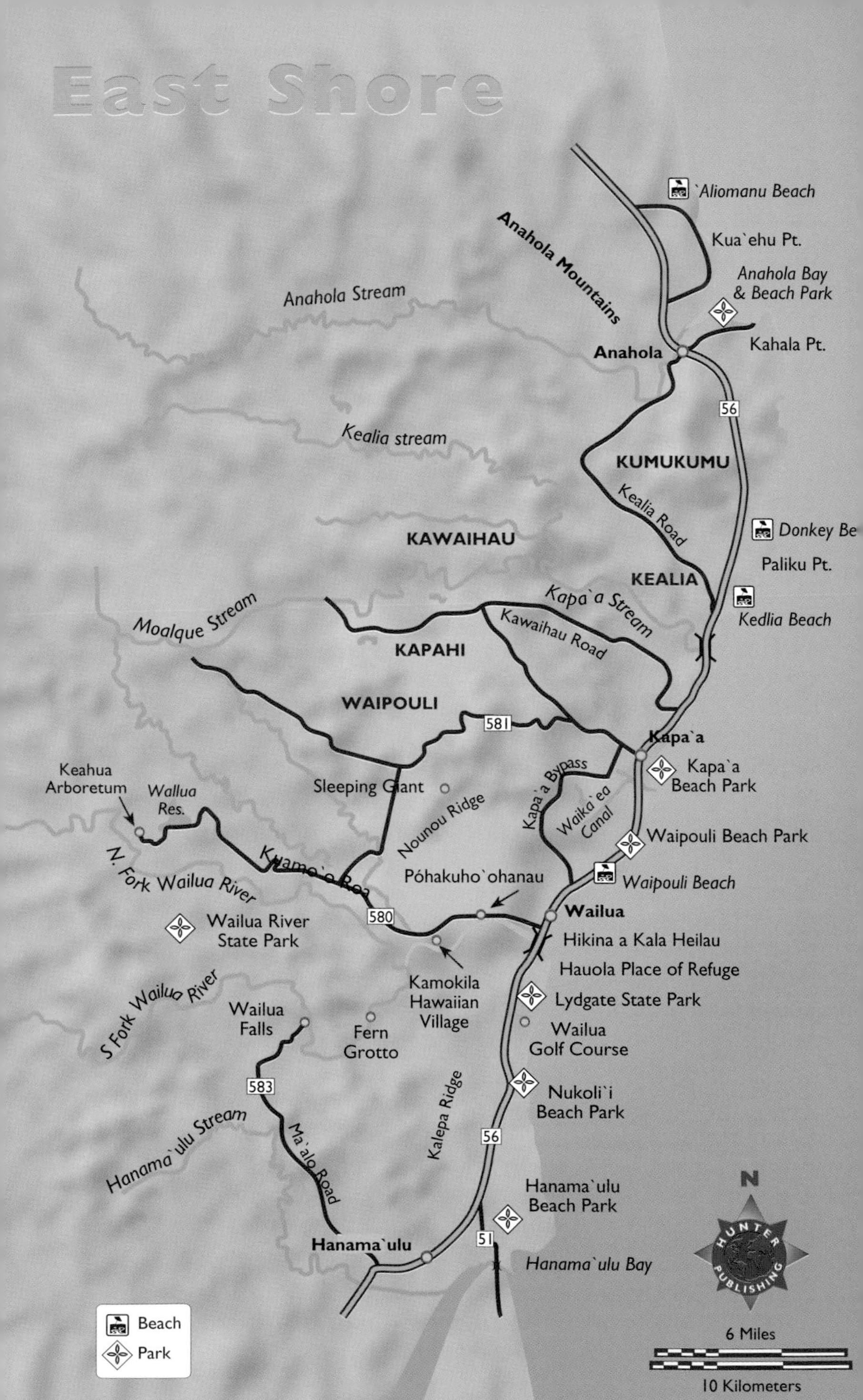

East Shore

`Aliomanu Beach
Kua`ehu Pt.
Anahola Mountains
Anahola Bay & Beach Park
Anahola
Kahala Pt.
56
Anahola Stream
KUMUKUMU
Kealia stream
Kealia Road
Donkey Be
Paliku Pt.
KAWAIHAU
KEALIA
Kapa`a Stream
Kedlia Beach
Moalque Stream
Kawaihau Road
KAPAHI
WAIPOULI
581
Kapa`a
Keahua Arboretum
Wailua Res.
Sleeping Giant
Nounou Ridge
Kuamo`o Road
Kapa`a Bypass
Waika`ea Canal
Kapa`a Beach Park
N. Fork Wailua River
Póhakuho`ohanau
Waipouli Beach Park
Waipouli Beach
Wailua
580
Wailua River State Park
Hikina a Kala Heilau
Hauola Place of Refuge
S Fork Wailua River
Kamokila Hawaiian Village
Lydgate State Park
Wailua Falls
Fern Grotto
Wailua Golf Course
583
Nukoli`i Beach Park
Kalepa Ridge
Ma`alo Road
Hanama`ulu Stream
56
Hanama`ulu Beach Park
Hanama`ulu
51
Hanama`ulu Bay

N
HUNTER PUBLISHING

Beach
Park

6 Miles
10 Kilometers

© 2007 HUNTER PUBLISHING, INC

Up the road you'll enter **Kapa`a Town**. Kapa`a was home to a sugar plantation and there was a pineapple cannery from 1913 to 1960. When the sugar and pineapple industries left Kaua`i, the area did have a new industry to turn to – tourism. Once Coco Palms was built, it helped lure people to the area. After the devastation of Hurricane Iniki in 1992, the entire east side of the island had trouble coming back to life. Kapa`a is in the middle of a renaissance as old buildings have been renovated in recent years, making way for shops, cafés and restaurants that are both fine and funky.

Traffic in Kapa`a can be atrocious most of the time, especially if you're heading toward Lihu`e in the morning or evening rush hour. You can take **Kapa`a Bypass Road**, which goes around Kapa`a and Wailua. Heading south on Kuhio Highway, you'll see a sign for the Bypass Road on the right side at Lehua Street. Take Lehua and than make a left on Kapa`a Bypass Road.

Past Kapa`a, you'll pass through the towns of Anahola and Kealia. These are largely residential areas that were once sugarcane fields. With the exception of Kealia Beach and Anahola Beach Park, there's not much reason to stop in either place.

Wailua

AUTHOR'S CHOICE

Lydgate State Park is home not only to a fantastic beach, but also to a couple of the most culturally significant heiaus on the island.

- **Hikina`akala Heiau** (Rising of the Sun) is named for the fact that the sun was first visible from here each morning. Hawaiians would chant and pray with the rising of the sun. The heiau occupied an acre of land at the mouth of the Wailua River. It's said to have been built in approximately 1300 AD. When traditional religion was abolished in the 1800s, the site was converted to secular use. All that you can see today are the boulders that formed the foundation for the walls that were up to six feet high. It is at the north end of Lydgate State Park.

- Just past Hikina`akala Heiau is **Hauola Pu`uhonua**, or City of Refuge. If you had broken kapu or the rule of law at the time, you would be punished, most likely by death. Lawbreakers could come to Hauola Pu`uhonua and receive immunity. The challenge, of course, was getting here and, once you entered, you would have to go through certain rituals with the priests. Then, you'd be free to go home.

Malae Heiau, which is in the process of restoration and is slated to become a cultural park, is on the south side of the Wailua River, across Kuhio Highway from the Aloha Beach Resort. **Kalaeokamanu Heiau** is on the north side of the river along Kuamo'o Road, just beyond the old Coco Palms Hotel. Nearby are the royal birthstones (pohaku ho' ohanau), where women who were royal or of a high rank came to give birth. Nearby is **Holoholoku Heiau**, believed to be the oldest on the island.

Ancient **petroglyphs** can be found on the rocks at the river mouth to the left of the Kaua`i resort. Today, the meaning of these petroglyphs remains a mystery.

Fern Grotto

The historic **Fern Grotto** was once one of Kaua`i's major cultural attractions. It was used by the ancient Hawaiians and is a fern-filled cavern with excellent natural acoustics. It's also known as the place where Elvis Presley sang the Hawaiian wedding song in *Blue Hawai`i*. The most amazing feature of the grotto is the 80-foot opening to a cave where a waterfall used to run from the Wailua River. The water was diverted to maintain the sugar crops and the sword fern spores in the cracks of the cave. The ferns grow upside down in the grotto at an average of three to five feet long.

During the major heavy rains of 2006, Fern Grotto was closed to the public due to rocks and boulders falling from the ceiling. Fern Grotto has been in disrepair and decline since Hurricane Iwa in 1982. Various funding issues contributed to the decline; tourism soon dropped as well. A minor closure that was expected to last only three weeks turned out to be a major renovation taking roughly six months. With the restoration, local businesses hope that the grotto returns to its former glory.

Fern Grotto is accessible only by boat. You can take **Smith's Fern Grotto Wailua River Cruise**, ☎ 808-821-6895. It makes the two-mile journey up the Wailua River to Fern Grotto. Along the way, you'll be treated to stories about the area and even learn hula. The 1½-hour cruise costs $18 for adults, $9 for children aged two-12. You can also take a canoe ride with **Kamokila Hawaiian Village**, Kuamoo Road, Wailua, ☎ 808-823-0559, www.kamokila.com. $5 per person, $3 for ages five through 12, free for kids under five. Or rent a kayak and paddle up the Wailua River on your own.

Kamokila Hawaiian Village offers cultural tours of their four-acre reconstructed Hawaiian village. King Kaumuali`i, the last reigning king of Kaua`i, was a resident of the area. The village contains 14 thatched-roof homes, including a canoe house, a birthing house, a hula house, the chief's assembly house and a doctor's house. Storyboards explain the function of each house within the village. The property is also full of gardens featuring plants that had many uses within the village, such as awa and ti. You can try your hand at Hawaiian games such as spear throwing. Kamokila also offers canoe rides to Secret Falls and Fern Grotto. The cost of canoe rides, including village admission, is $30 per person, $20 for children. The canoe rides are not recommended for kids under five.

Smith's Tropical Paradise, Wailua Marina State Park, Wailua, ☎ 808-821-6895. Open daily 8:30 am-4 pm. Admission: adults $6; children aged two-12 $3. The grounds are beautifully kept with over 20 fruit trees, including breadfruit, star fruit, jackfruit, macadamia nuts and soursop. There are replicas of Filipino and Polynesian huts, as well as a beautiful Japanese-style garden. Strolling along the grounds is a peaceful way to spend the afternoon. If you're going to Smith's Fam-

Smith's Tropical Paradise

ily Garden Luau, get there early so you have time to experience the gardens.

Coco Palms, Kuhio Highway, Wailua. Ancient Hawaiians once considered the 45-acre area to be a gathering place. In the 13th century, it was the home of Kaua`i's royalty. Kaua`i's oldest hotel opened here in 1953 with 24 rooms and four employees. Within the resort area lies a 2,000-tree coconut grove, where Elvis Presley filmed the end of *Blue Hawai`i* in 1961. Since then, the resort grew in size and stature as many celebrities of the time stayed at Coco Palms to enjoy the sunshine.

Coco Palms

Unfortunately, Coco Palms was badly damaged during Hurricane Iniki in 1992 and has been closed since then. Despite this, weddings are performed and you can see the area with **Hawai`i Movies Tours**, ☎ 800-628-8432, 808-822-1192. You can walk by and still sense the old ghosts of that period. Currently, plans are underway to rebuild Coco Palms to its former splendor. The $200 million project is slated to reopen in August of 2008 with 200 condominium units and 104 hotel rooms. While it's not planned to be an exact replica of the old Coco Palms, it will retain the 1950s feel. Even Cottage 56, which was Elvis' bungalow in *Blue Hawai`i*, will be restored and used as a memorial, with a gift shop nearby. For more information on this project, check out www.cocopalms.com.

AUTHOR'S CHOICE ★ **Saiva Siddhanta Church**, 107 Kaholalele Road, Wailua, ☎ 808-822-3012. Open to the public daily from 9 am to noon. There also is a weekly guided tour of the grounds that includes the San Marga Iraivan Temple. The weekly tour time varies, call ahead. In 1970, Satguru Sivaya Subramuniyaswami, founder of the church and monastery, selected this 458-acre site in Wailua as a place of worship. He recognized that Hawaiians also felt the spiritual power of the area. The San Marga Iraivan Temple is in the process of being built on the site and will not be completed until 2010. It's designed to last 1,000 years or more. The granite for the temple is being hand-quarried by some 70 stonemasons in India, then shipped to Kaua`i for final shaping and fitting on the site. The center of the temple will hold a 700-pound crystal, known as the Sivalingam, now displayed at the monastery's smaller temple on the grounds.

If you do decide to visit, bring an umbrella, since it can be rainy in the area. Also wear "modest dress." Shorts, short dresses or skirts, T-shirts and tank tops are off-limits.

To get there, take Kuamoo Road from Kuhio Highway for four miles. Just past the four-mile marker, turn left on Kaholalele Road. The Information Center is at the end of the road. Upon entering the pavilion, a guide will greet you and escort you through the monastery.

Keahua Forestry Arboretum, Kuamoo Road, Wailua, is a 30-acre property that offers streams, pools, forests and meadows. It's a great place to come for a picnic as there are plenty of tables available throughout the property, each with a unique view. Some have exceptional views of Mount Wai`ale`ale. You'll also see tropical plants, such as mango, eucalyptus and monkeypod trees. There are several streams and freshwater pools that feed into the Wailua River nearby, providing a cool, relaxing area to swim and frolic.

There are a number of hiking trails in the area. One is an easy trail within the confines of the arboretum; another is a more challenging four-mile trail just outside of the property. There's also the Powerline Trail just past the arboretum. The Kulilau Ridge Trail starts in this area as well.

To get here, take Kuamoo Road from Wailua for eight miles. You'll pass through Wailua Homestead, and University of Hawai`i Agricultural Station. The road gets bumpy about three quarters of the way up. You'll come to a river crossing where you can park.

Bell Stone. This piece of Hawaiian culture was used to announce royal births. If you struck the stone just right, sounds would resonate throughout Wailua Valley. To get there, drive on Kuhio Highway and turn on Kuamoo Road. Just past mile marker one is a dirt road heading back to the ocean. The bell stone is a quarter-mile down at the end of the dirt path.

**Opaeka`a Falls**. Named after the shrimp that were once abundant in the stream, Opaeka`a (rolling shrimp) Falls has parking and is a popular viewpoint that was developed for tourists. On one side, you'll see the 150-foot falls. The other side offers a magnificent view of the Wailua River Valley. To get there, take Kuamoo Road and drive approximately two miles until you reach the viewing area. You do not have to hike to see the falls.

On the way to Opaeka`a Falls, you can stop to view the remains of **Poliahu Heiau**. It is believed to have been built by Menehune in 1600s. The walls were made of stacked rock some five feet high. Poliahu Heiau was named for the snow goddess of the Island of Hawai`i, who lived on Mauna Kea.

Opaeka`a Falls

The largest heiau on Kaua`i, this site contains several terraces, idol sites, and a "god stone" five feet high.

Sleeping Giant. If you look from the right angle, Nounou Mountain looks very much like a sleeping giant. There are numerous stories about the Sleeping Giant. The first story says that there was a giant who lived on Kaua`i and was friendly with the Hawaiians. The Hawaiians would plant taro in his footsteps. One day, a village chief ordered a new heiau to be built. The villagers were too busy farming, but the giant said he would do it. Within two weeks, the giant completed the heiau. The Hawaiians threw a huge luau in appreciation for the giant's efforts. The giant ate so much, he lay down to sleep and has yet to awake.

Sleeping Giant

Kapa`a Waipouli & Wailua

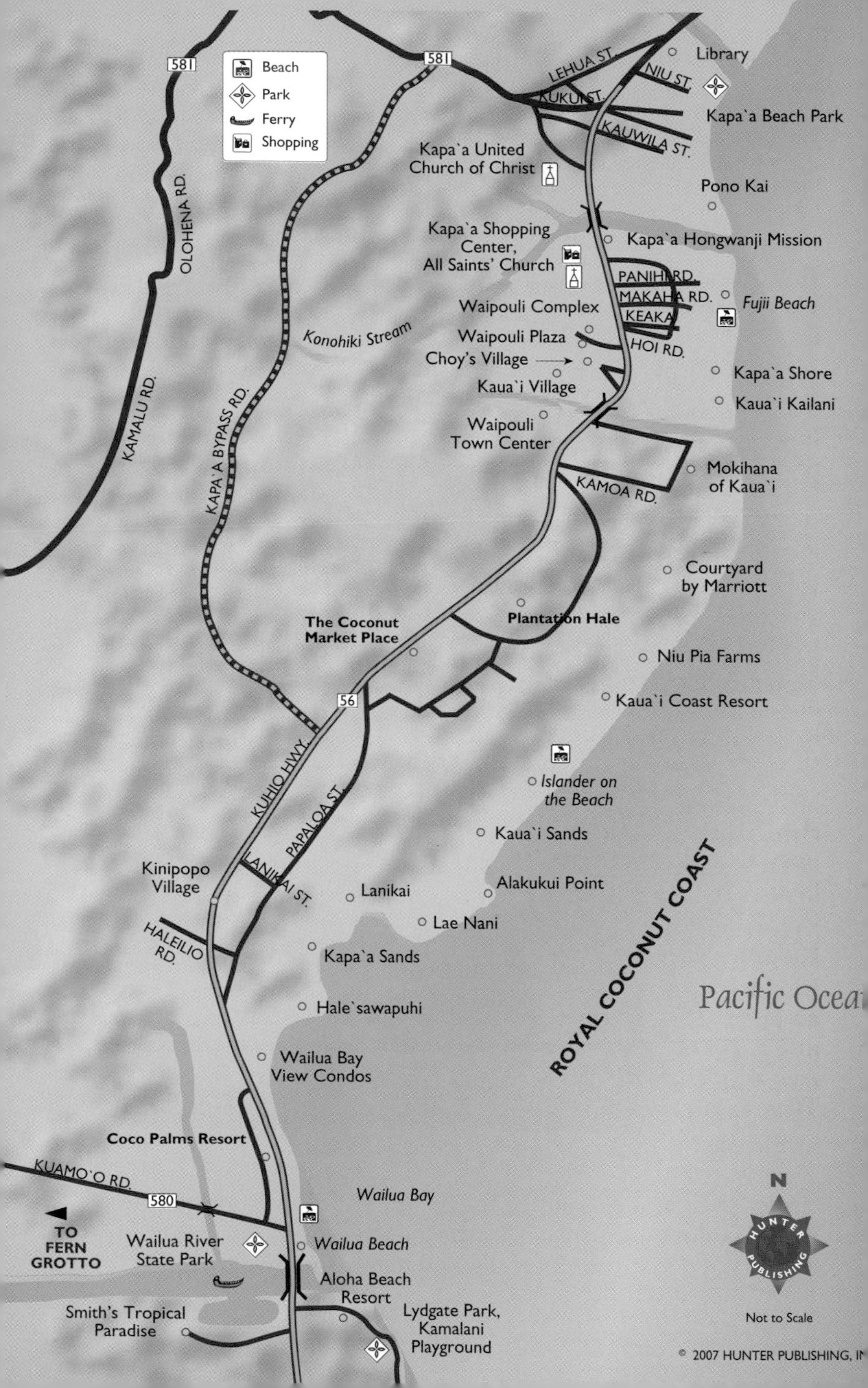

Beach
Park
Ferry
Shopping
581
581
OLOHENA RD.
KAMALU RD.
KAPA`A BYPASS RD.
Konohiki Stream
LEHUA ST.
NIU ST.
KUKUI ST.
KAUWILA ST.
Library
Kapa`a Beach Park
Kapa`a United Church of Christ
Pono Kai
Kapa`a Shopping Center, All Saints' Church
Kapa`a Hongwanji Mission
PANIHI RD.
MAKAHA RD.
KEAKA
HOI RD.
Fujii Beach
Waipouli Complex
Waipouli Plaza
Choy's Village
Kaua`i Village
Kapa`a Shore
Kaua`i Kailani
Waipouli Town Center
Mokihana of Kaua`i
KAMOA RD.
Courtyard by Marriott
Plantation Hale
The Coconut Market Place
Niu Pia Farms
56
Kaua`i Coast Resort
KUHIO HWY.
PAPALOA ST.
Islander on the Beach
Kaua`i Sands
ROYAL COCONUT COAST
Kinipopo Village
LANIKAI ST.
Lanikai
Alakukui Point
Lae Nani
HALEILIO RD.
Kapa`a Sands
Hale`sawapuhi
Pacific Ocean
Wailua Bay View Condos
Coco Palms Resort
KUAMO`O RD.
580
Wailua Bay
TO FERN GROTTO
Wailua River State Park
Wailua Beach
Aloha Beach Resort
Smith's Tropical Paradise
Lydgate Park, Kamalani Playground
N
HUNTER PUBLISHING
Not to Scale

Another story says that the people of Wailua were tired of feeding the giant, so one day they hid rocks in fish and poi. The giant ate the rocks, poi and fish, then he lay down to sleep and has yet to wake up.

Other folklore says that people used to ward off invaders by lighting fires behind the mountain, creating an impression that something big was lurking about the island.

To see Sleeping Giant, take Kuhio Highway north from Wailua to Kapa`a. There's a Chevron station on the right and a marker for the Sleeping Giant viewing area.

Kapa`a

**Kaua`i Children's Discovery Museum**, Kaua`i Village Shopping Center, Kapa`a, ☎ 808-823-8222, www.kcdm.org. Open Tuesday-Saturday 10 am-5 pm. Admission: adults $5, children $4. Everyone from keiki to adults will appreciate this non-profit museum. This is a place where you can bring the whole family. There's something for everyone here. Kids can visit the StarLab Planetarium, learn about marine life, or take part in ongoing education programs. There's an area for kids to run, climb and jump, put on costumes, bowl, pretend, and have fun. There's also a Cultural Village, which features kid-sized houses representing Japan, Polynesia, China and the Philippines. Exhibits and programs change frequently, so call the museum for the latest programs.

King Kong's Profile. Driving north along Kuhio Highway, just past mile marker 16, look back you'll see a mountain that bears a striking resemblance to King Kong. Did you know that the 1976 *King Kong* movie remake was filmed on Kaua`i?

Hawaiian Art Museum, 4504 Kukui Street, Suite 11, Kapa`a, ☎ 808-823-8381. The museum features Hawaiian artifacts from Serge Kahili King's private museum of art and artifacts, focussing on Hawai`i, Africa, Oceania, Asia and the Americas. The museum is sponsored by Aloha International. They have hula and healing classes throughout the week.

Sightseeing Tours

Roberts Hawai`i Tours, ☎ 866-898-2519, www.robertshawaii.com, offers bus tours from your hotel to Waimea Canyon. You'll stop at Spouting Horn and Hanapepe Valley along the way. Tours operate Sunday, Tuesday, Thursday and Saturday. The cost is $44 per person.

Polynesian Adventure Tours, ☎ 808-246-0122, www.polyad.com, has two tours of Waimea Canyon as well. Their Waimea Canyon Experience Tour operates on Monday, Wednesday, Friday, Sunday. You stop at Spouting Horn, Hanapepe, Fort Elizabeth, before reaching the canyon. The cost is $47 per person. They also have a second tour of sights along the Coconut Coast, such as Opaeka`a Falls and Nawiliwili Harbor, for $68 per person.

Kaua`i Movie Tours, ☎ 800-628-8432 or 808-822-1192, www.hawaiimovietours.com, offers highly popular tours that take you around the island in their mobile theater, enabling you to visit the locations while you're watching the film and TV scenes in which they appear. The shows include *Jurassic Park*, *Raiders of the Lost Ark*, *South Pacific*, *Blue Hawai`i*, *Gilligan's Island*, *Fantasy Island* and about 30 others. They have three different types of tours daily, starting at $111 per person.

**Kapa`a History Tour**, Kaua`i Historical Society, ☎ 808-245-3373, Tuesday, Thursday, Saturday, 10 am. Reservations required. Admission is $15 per person. This 90-minute walking tour led by the Kaua`i Historical Society will give you an understanding of the history and architecture of Kapa`a Town.

■ Adventures

On Land

Hiking

The **Powerline Trail** is a challenging 11-mile path that connects the north side of the island to the east side. The trail gets its name from the electric line that brings electricity to the north shore. You can start from the trailhead in Princeville or the trailhead at the Keahua Arboretum. Starting from the Princeville trailhead is a bit easier. You won't see many hikers as the trail is used more often by mountain bikers. If you're not up to doing the entire trail, you can always start at one end, hike inland for a while, and then return to your car. Be aware that hunters are known to frequent the area. Consider wearing bright colors as a precaution.

To get to the trailhead on the east side of the island, take Kuamoo Road from Kuhio Highway. You'll come to a stream crossing where the road ends. The trailhead is only a half-mile from here. If the water's low, you can drive across, but use your best judgment. You can also park your car before the crossing and walk to the trailhead from this point. Follow the dirt road and you'll see a sign marking the trailhead for the Powerline Trail.

On the Sleeping Giant Trail

AUTHOR'S CHOICE ★ **Sleeping Giant Trail** (Nounou Mountain Trail East Side). This is a moderate to difficult hike that climbs 960 feet in elevation, ending on the chest of Sleeping Giant. The trail is clearly marked, so you shouldn't have any problems finding your way. The incredible views at the top make the challenging climb worthwhile. You'll look down to the coast and, on a clear day, you'll have a great view of Mount Wai`ale`ale. Be sure to stop at the picnic tables near the top of the trail for a well-deserved rest. Beyond the tables, the trail becomes really narrow and dangerous. At about 1½ miles in, the east side of the trail joins the west side trail.

You can get to the trailhead from Haleilio Road in Wailua. Turn onto Haleilio from Kuhio Highway and drive up to the parking area adjacent to the Department of Water pump site.

Nounou Mountain Trail West Side is a very difficult climb. It's shorter than the east trail (about 1½ miles), but it's much steeper than the east side. Even though you get to only 800 feet in elevation, this is a tough way to get there. If you really want the challenge, you can reach the trailhead by driving up Kuamoo Road and then turning onto Kamalu Road (Highway 581).

Kuamoo-Nounou Trail is a pretty easy trail that connects with the Nounou Mountain Trail West Side. The trail is two miles long, starting on Kuamoo Raod about a half-mile past Opaeka`a Falls.

View from the Kuilau Ridge Trail

The **Kuilau Ridge Trail** is a two-mile trek through a heavily forested area. Along the way, you'll come across a picnic area before the trail meets with the Moalepe Trail. If the weather cooperates, you can see stunning views of Mount Wai`ale`ale. The trailhead is at the Keahua Arboretum, just before the parking area. You can choose to continue on the Moalepe Trail, which is a moderate 2½-mile path that get very sloppy when it's raining.

**Hoopi`i Falls Hike** is in the northern end of Kapa`a. This is a 1½-mile moderate trail that runs parallel to a stream and leads to Hoopi`i Falls. To get there, take Kuhio Highway toward the northern Kapa`a. Turn onto Kawaiahau Road, then onto Kapihi Road. Follow the road until you see a dirt road on the left. Get out of the car here, take that road to the stream, then follow the stream. Keep an ear out for rushing water as you'll get to a point where you walk down a staircase that leads to the falls.

Guided Hikes

**Kayak Kaua`i**, ☎ 800-437-3507, 808-826-9844, www.kayakkauai.com, offers hiking tours that include transportation from their Hanalei or Kapa`a office, a deli lunch, beverages and, of course, a guide. They have a three- or four-hour hike of Sleeping Giant on weekdays. The cost is $81 per person with a two-person minimum.

**Kaua`i Nature Tours**, ☎ 888-233-8365 or 808-742-8305, www.kauainaturetours.com, leads guided 4½-mile hikes over Sleeping Giant. The hike is rated easy to moderate. They depart from Po`ipu and the cost is $92 per person. Lunch is included. Their hikes are guided by knowledgeable scientists and environmentalists, who offer a very detailed perspective on the area.

If you want to hike with a group, check out the **Sierra Club** at www.hi.sierraclub.org. The Kaua`i chapter regularly schedules group hikes all over the island, including the Na Pali Coast area. There's a $5 donation for the hike. They have a list of upcoming hikes on their website.

Gooney bird & newborn chick on Kaua`i

Dr. Carl Berg of **Hawaiian Wildlife Tours**, ☎ 808-639-2968, will take you on a personalized tour to see Kaua`i's native and vanishing species, from forest birds and flora to hoary bats, monk seals, and green sea turtles. Rates are $45 per couple, per hour. Reservations one month in advance are recommended.

Hunting

There are hunting sites along this side of the island, primarily around the Kealia Forest Reserve.

Hunting licenses are mandatory in order to hunt on public, private or military land anywhere in Hawai`i. You can register for a hunting license online at **hunting.ehawaii.gov/hunting/license.html**. If you're a Hawai`i resident, a license is $20 and that's good for the fiscal year (July 1-June 30).

The main requirement for a hunting license in Hawai`i is a **hunter education card**. If you're a visitor and plan on hunting while you're in Hawai`i, make sure that you have your hunter education card. Once you get that, you can fill out a letter of exemption, which you can get online at www.hawaii.gov/dlnr/dcre/know.htm. You mail that in, your form will be processed and you'll be able to purchase a hunting license.

To find out the hunting periods, restrictions, and areas, your best bet is to contact **Division of Forestry and Wildlife Kaua`i District Office** at ☎ 808-274-3438.

Horseback Riding

Esprit De Corps Riding Academy, 1491 Kualapa Place, Kapa`a, ☎ 808-822-4688, www.kauaihorses.com, rides Monday-Friday, with reservations required. They offer trail rides that tend to be geared to riders with some experience. There's a three-hour ride for $120, a four-hour ride for $160 and a six-hour ride for $250. Esprit de Corps also offers a six-hour ride with meditation for $250. If you're a novice rider or you want to go at a leisurely pace and take pictures, go for the three-hour ride. For the other rides, you should at least be able to trot and canter. All rides venture through the mountains in Kapa`a and offer unique views of the coast. Lessons and private rides are available.

Keapana Horsemanship, Kawaihau Road, Kapa`a, ☎ 808-823-9303, www.keapana.com, offers private rides along public trails such as Sleeping Giant, Moalepe, Kuilau and Powerline. A two-hour ride allows you to choose your trail for $145 per person. There's a half-day trail that goes through Keahua Arboretum. You'll have a chance to swim and have lunch. This five-hour tour is $275 per person. You can also do the Powerline Trail, which is an all-day affair, for $375 per person.

Tennis

Tennis courts are abundant on the east side of the island. You'll find courts at most resorts and condominiums. There are also a few public courts that are first-come, first-served.

There are two lighted courts at **Kapa`a New Park**. They're on Olohena Road in Kapa`a. Take Kuhio Highway north to Kapa`a Town and turn left at the traffic light onto Olohena Road. The courts are a quarter-mile down on the right.

Wailua Homesteads Park has two lighted courts. You'll find them on Kamalu Road in Wailua. Heading north, just past the Wailua Bridge at the traffic signal, take a left off of Kuhio Highway onto Kuamoo Road. Travel up about three miles and turn right onto Kamalu Road. The courts are a half-mile farther on right side.

Finally, **Wailua Houselots Park** has two lighted courts, on Nonou Road, Wailua. Heading north, take a left off of Kuhio Highway onto Heleilio Road; a quarter-mile toward the mountain, take the left fork onto Nonou Road. The courts are about a half-mile farther on the right side.

Golf

Wailua Municipal Golf Course, 3-5350 Kuhio Highway, Wailua, ☎ 808-241-6666, www.kauai.gov/golf. Greens fees for non-residents $32 on weekdays, $44 Saturday and Sunday. After 2 pm, the rates are $16 weekdays, $44 weekends. 18 holes, 6,981 yards, par 72. This is the best golf deal you can get. Wailua Municipal Golf course is a superb value. It was originally built as a nine-hole course back in 1929. Local golf legend Toyo Shirai designed the other nine holes in 1961.

Wailua Municipal Golf Course

Its signature hole is the 456-yard, dogleg left #2, which runs along the ocean and is considered the most difficult on the course. The first, second, 14th and 17th holes have greens that overlook the ocean. The par-five holes average over 530 yards and the par-three holes for the most part are reachable. The par-four holes can be a bit of a challenge and require a combination of strength and skill.

Wailua has hosted three USGA Amateur Public Links Championships and has been voted one of Hawai`i's best 15 golf courses by *Golf Digest.* The course tends to be packed with local golfers and visitors alike. It's wise to book your tee time at least a week in advance.

Biking

There are plenty of trails for mountain biking on this side of the island. The **Kuamoo-Nounou Trail** is a quick singletrack that will give you a good workout. It's for intermediate to advanced riders as the climbing can be a challenge.

The **Moalepe Trail** can be a fun and potentially sloppy trail. You can get to it from Olohena Road in Kapa`a or you can ride the **Kuilau Trail** from Keahua Arboretum. If you're a beginner to intermediate rider, your best bet is to start from the trailhead at Olohena Road. Here, the trail is a doubletrack for the first 1.7 miles. After that, it becomes narrow and muddy, which should please the more advanced riders.

Speaking of challenges, don't forget about the **Powerline Trail**. If you start from this end of the island, note that you'll face some tough climbing. You'll climb almost 1,400 feet before descending into Hanalei Valley.

For road riders, you can take a leisurely ride through the back roads of the Coconut Coast on the bike path from **Anahola to**

Lydgate State Park. There's also a 2½-mile bike path that circles **Lydgate Park**. This will be a link within the 17-mile Nawiliwili to Anahola bike path, Ke ala hele makalae. The path runs along the beach to the north end of the park, then comes back around. The Kamalani Kai Bridge is located south of the camping area.

To rent a bike, you can go to **Kaua`i Cycle and Tour**, 1379 Kuhio Highway in Kapa`a, ☎ 808-821-2115. They offer rentals starting at $15 a day. They also have maps, as well as guided tours starting at $65 a day.

Stop by **Outfitters Kaua`i**, 2827A Po`ipu Rd, Po`ipu, ☎ 808-742-9667, www.outfitterskauai.com, to rent a bike and a car rack. They also offer bike maps to make it easier for you to find your way around.

Coming from Hanalei, you can also rent a bike from **Pedal n Paddle**, ☎ 808-826-9069, www.pedalnpaddle.com, at Ching Young Village. They rent mountain bikes for $20 a day or $80 a week. Pedal n Paddle also has tandem bikes for $10 a day and cruisers for $10 a day or $30 a week.

On Water

Beaches

AUTHOR'S CHOICE ★ **Lydgate State Park** is a great place to bring the entire family for the day. It's one of the safest beaches on the island. The park sits on 40 acres at the mouth of the Wailua River. The beach is safe for swimming, snorkeling, windsurfing, surfing, diving, fishing or just to hang out and catch some sun.

Lydgate State Park (shorediving.com)

What makes the beach so safe is the rock barrier that was installed in 1964. The pools are named after Alfred Morgan, who would take his family to Lydgate for a day at the beach. At the time, the beach area wasn't protected for swimming. Upon a trip to Sorrento, Italy, Morgan became inspired by the protected area within the bay. He returned to Kaua`i and worked with Senator Billy Fernandes. Together, they put the plan in motion to create the pools at Lydgate.

There's a large picnic pavilion and there's also Kamalani Playground, which was built in 1994 by a whopping 7,000 volunteers. It has a maze of caves, swings, tunnels. It's a kid's dream. Don't forget about the 2.5-mile bike path around the park. There are plenty of facilities – restrooms, showers, lifeguards.

Getting to the park is easy. Take Kuhio Highway to Leho Drive. You won't be able to miss the park on Leho Drive.

Wailua Beach is directly across from the old Coco Palms resort on Kuhio Highway. The 100-foot-wide beach runs about half a mile north of the river. It's popular with surfers and bodyboarders, as there's a surf break at the northern part of the bay called Horners. Other than that, the swimming isn't that good here and there are no facilities or lifeguards. During the spring, high surf can create dangerous conditions. You can see the ancient heiau sites at the mouth of the river.

Wailua Sunrise

Waipouli Beach runs behind the hotels and condos at Coconut Marketplace. It's a long, narrow beach that makes for a pleasant stroll in the morning or evening. The beach has a mostly rocky bottom and can have particularly strong currents, which makes swimming uninviting.

**Kapa`a Beach Park** is a 16-acre park in Kapa`a Town that's used primarily by locals. There's a community swimming pool, picnic area, restrooms, showers and barbecue grills. Here's another beach that is nice to walk around at sunrise or sunset. There is a rocky bottom. It's used for fishing more than swimming.

Kealia Beach. This half-mile beach is a popular spot for surfers and bodyboarders. It has a sandy bottom, which makes for good surfing. During periods of high surf, there are strong rip currents. The beach is easy to get to. Take Kuhio Highway about two miles north of Kapa`a and turn on the dirt road on the right side.

Kealia Beach (Hawaiian Images)

Donkey Beach is named after the donkeys Lihu`e Plantation Company kept in the area. The beach is secluded and therefore popular for nudists (although letting it all hang out is illegal). The beach is very rocky and not a good place for swimming. To get there, take Kuhio Highway north toward Anahola. Park before mile marker 12 and walk about 10 minutes to the beach. Keep in mind that this is private land, although there is usually some sort of public access available.

Anahola Beach Park (shorediving.com)

Anahola Beach Park is very popular with locals, especially in the summer. There's a narrow area with a shallow reef that protects the beach and is good for swimming. The beach has great sunbathing and good swimming conditions since board surfing isn't allowed in the area. The facilities include restrooms and showers, along with picnic and camping facilities. To get there, take Kuhio Highway to Anahola. Turn right onto Anahola Road and right on Manai Road.

Aliomanu Beach is typically secluded and you will probably see occasional nude sunbathers. The beach has an extensive offshore reef and is a popular fishing spot for locals. It is a beautiful beach fronted by one of the longest and widest fringing reefs on Kaua`i. Even though the beach is protected, the bottom is too rocky for swimming. From mile marker 15 on Kuhio Highway take Aliomanu Road toward the ocean. Take the first left to Aliomanu Estates. Continue until you see a beach access sign on the right side. Turn right and drive down to the parking lot. Follow the trail to the shore.

Snorkeling

Good snorkel spots are limited on this side of the island. The best spot by far is Lydgate State Park. The man-made lava pools can help boost the confidence of any novice snorkeler. Of the two lava pools, stay in the larger area. This is a deeper area and large enough so you don't feel too crowded.

You can rent gear from **Snorkel Bob's**, 4-734 Kuhio Hwy, Kapa`a, ☎ 808-823-9433; **Kaua`i Water-ski, Surf, and Kayak Co**, Kinipopo Shopping Center, Wailua, ☎ 808-822-3574.

Surfing

Kaua`i Water Ski and Surf Co, Kinipopo Shopping Center, Wailua, ☎ 808-822-3574, gives private surfing lessons. Call for availability. They also rent boards.

If you don't need a lesson, you can also rent a board from **The Wave Surf Co**, 1267 Ulu Street, Kapa`a, ☎ 808-821-1199. They rent long boards for $20 per day and short boards for $10 per day.

You can try out your skills at Lydgate State Park, Wailua Beach or Kealia Beach.

Boogie Boarding

You best options for boogie boarding are at Lydgate State Park, Wailua Beach or Kealia Beach.

You can rent a board from virtually anywhere in the area. **The Wave Surf Co**, **Kaua`i Water Ski and Surf Co**, **Snorkel Bob's**, **Activity Warehouse** and **Dive Kaua`i Scuba Center** are good options. Also check with your condo or hotel. Some of them might have rentals available or boards you can use at no charge.

Kitesurfing

Akamai Kiteboarding School, ☎ 808-826-9340, gives kiteboarding lessons either on the north or east shores of the island. A three-hour lesson for beginners starts at $275 per person. All gear is provided.

Waterskiing

Kaua`i Water Ski and Surf Co, Kinipopo Shopping Center, Wailua, ☎ 808-822-3574. This is the place to go if you want to ski up the Wailua River. You have the option to waterski, wake board, or hydrofoil. The rates are $120 per hour and $65 per half-hour. The rental includes ski boat, driver and equipment.

River Trips

Smith's Fern Grotto Wailua River Cruise, ☎ 808-821-6895, takes you on a two-mile journey up the Wailua River to Fern Grotto. Along the way, you'll be treated to stories about the area and even learn hula. The 1½-hour cruise costs $18 for adults, $9 for children between the ages of two and 12.

Kamokila Hawaiian Village, Kuamoo Road, Wailua, ☎ 808-823-0559, www.kamokila.com, will put you to work on an outrigger canoe up the Wailua River to explore waterfalls and swimming holes. The Wailua River offers a calm and serene setting for this activity. The Village is a short distance from hiking trails that lead to waterfalls as well as grottos and swimming holes. They provide two outriggers that come with a steersman.

Kayaking

Kayak Wailua, ☎ 808-822-3388, www.kayak-wailua.com, offers a 4½-hour guided tour that heads up to Secret Falls. You start out at the Wailua Marina and kayak approximately two miles up the Wailua River. Along the way, your guide will point out the flora and fauna. The paddle takes about 45 minutes. You'll then go for a short hike to Secret Falls, where you eat the "bring your own" lunch and swim around the falls. This is a fantastic paddle for beginners. Amazingly, this tour only costs $39 per person.

Kaua`i Water Ski and Surf Co, Kinipopo Shopping Center, Wailua, ☎ 808-822-3574, offers a the "Deluxe Discovery Tour," a guided kayak tour on the Wailua River that includes a picnic lunch, bottled water, hike to a waterfall, and swimming. The local guide shares his knowledge of Hawaiian history, culture, legends and local flora. This five- to six-hour tour costs $75 per person. They also rent kayaks.

Paradise Kayaks, Kuhio Highway, Kapa`a (across from Kaua`i Products Fair), ☎ 808-822-1112, has five- and six-hour tours that travel up the Wailua River, then hike to a waterfall and diving pool. Lunch is provided as well. This is a very child-friendly outfit and has kayaks just for kids. The five-hour tour costs $98 in a double kayak, $138 for a single kayak. The six-hour tour is $128 for a double kayak, $188 if you want to ride in a single kayak. They also rent kayaks that start at $30 a day.

**Outfitters Kaua`i**, Po`ipu Plaza, 2827A Po`ipu Road, Po`ipu, ☎ 888-742-9887, 808-742-9667, 808-742-7421, www.outfitterskauai.com. They will take you from their Po`ipu office to Wailua, where you'll paddle downstream and take a somewhat rugged one-mile hike up the valley to a dramatic 130-foot waterfall with a pool at the bottom. There you'll have lunch and then hike back down to the kayaks. Along the way back, your guides talk about the unique food and medicinal plants of the area.

**Ali`i Kayaks**, Harbor Mall, Lihu`e, ☎ 808-241-7700, offers a tour of the Wailua River. Your guide will also explain why the river is so revered in Hawaiian culture. You'll also hike up to Secret Falls, where you have lunch. Plan on four miles of kayaking, and about 1½ miles of hiking. Tour duration is approximately 4½ hours and costs $104 per person.

Wailua Kayak & Canoe, Kuhio Highway, Wailua (across from Kintaro Restaurant), ☎ 808-821-1188, offers a four-hour waterfall tour that travels up the Wailua River to a picnic lunch. The guides share Hawaiian history and legends along the way. Tours start at $39 per person. They also rent two-person kayaks and launch from their baseyard right on the river. There's no need to struggle with car racks.

Wailua River Kayak Adventures, ☎ 808-822-5795, has a couple of tours of the Wailua River area. The Jungle River Safari is a four- to five-hour trip up the Wailua River. You paddle at your own pace while your trained guide fills you in on the historical and religious significance of the area. You also stop on the edge of the river for drinks and snacks, then take a jump off a rope swing. The Jungle River Safari is $85 per person. The second tour takes you to Secret Falls. It is also four to five hours in duration and costs $85 per person. They rent singles for $25 and doubles for $50 all day.

**Kayak Kaua`i**, Kapa`a, ☎ 800-437-3507, 808-826-9844, will let you strike out on your own, renting you a double and car top for your kayak from their Kapa`a office, located minutes away from the boat launching area. You can paddle to Secret Falls or Fern Grotto. A double kayak rental starts at $75 a day.

Activity Warehouse, ☎ 808-821-9071, 788 Kuhio Highway, Kapa`a (across from McDonald's), rents kayaks starting at $50 a day.

Scuba

Dive Kaua`i Scuba Center, 1038 Kuhio Highway, ☎ 808-822-0452, www.divekauai.com, has all of the gear you need. You can rent tanks, wetsuits, weight belts and much more. They offer introductory shore dives for $105 (one-tank dive)

and $140 (two-tank dive). If you're already certified, they have shore dives and boat dives starting at $90. They also do night dives and offer PADI certification courses.

If you have your own equipment or you want to get in the water, **Lydgate State Park** offers decent diving. There are better places throughout the island, but if you're confined to the east side, this is an option.

Lydgate State Park *(shorediving.com)*

Fishing

**Hana Pa`a Charters**, 6370 Kalama Road, Kapa`a, www.fishkauai.com, ☎ 808-823-6031, has fishing excursions on their *Maka Hou II*, a 38-foot Bertram Convertible III Sport Fisher with fly bridge, full tuna tower, main cabin, two bunk rooms and full head. They catch tuna, marlin and wahoo. They offer private or shared trips off Kaua`i waters daily. A four-hour shared charter starts at $310, with a two-person minimum.

Paradise Outdoor Adventures, ☎ 808-822-1112, rents a six-person Boston Whaler, equipped with a 25 hp electric-start Yamaha. This powerboat rental comes on a trailer along with a complimentary loaner Jeep Wrangler for towing. A half-day rental costs $295 and a full-day is $590.

For fishing supplies, you can stop by **Lihu`e Fishing Supply**, ☎ 808-245-4930, or **Waipouli Variety Store** in Kapa`a, ☎ 808-822-1014.

■ Spas & Health Clubs

Pua Day Spa, ResortQuest, Kaua`i Beach at Makaiwa, ☎ 808-822-6669, offers treatments such as body wraps, hot stone massage and facials, sports massage, lomi-lomi massage, along with many other treatments.

**Kaua`i Wellness Center**, 4544 Kukui Street, Kapa`a, ☎ 808-823-6087, www.kauaiwellnesscenter.com. Call between 8 am and 5 pm to schedule an appointment. They provide on-site or outcall massages, including Lomi Lomi, couples massage, aromatherapy, hot stone, deep tissue and sports massage.

Touch Kaua`i, ☎ 808-651-9769, combines Hawaiian Lomi Lomi, Indian Ayurvedic, sports massage and Swedish modalities to create one intense massage that leaves you feeling incredibly relaxed.

**Kaua`i Gym**, 934 Kipuni Way, Kapa`a, ☎ 808-823-8210, has free weights, fitness classes, cardio and even boxing equipment. Daily and weekly passes are available for visitors. Daily passes run $10 a day, while weekly passes are $35.

■ Shopping

The east shore of Kaua`i holds plenty of shopping opportunities, from the tourist trap extravaganza of Coconut Marketplace to smaller shops on the side of the road that are true gems. Here's a rundown of what you'll find and can buy in the area.

Traveling up Kuhio Highway from Lihu`e, there are a number of places worth a stop. Your first should be **Kinipopo Shopping Center**. This nondescript place is just behind the

Shell Gas station on the right-hand side and includes the following three shops.

Pin-up from Tin Can Mailman

Tin Can Mailman, ☎ 808-822-3009, www.tincanmailman.net, is filled with vintage Hawaiiana – thousands of rare and used books about Hawai`i, old postcards, pin-ups and even menus, some of which date back to the 1940s. You'll also find classic alohawear and vintage jewelry. If you like the classic look of old Hawai`i, you'll love this store.

If you have a skateboarder in the family or you happen to be one yourself, you'll want to pay a visit to **Island Board Connection**, ☎ 808-822-4400. They have helmets, pads, short boards, long boards and mountain boards. They also carry a wide selection of apparel and accessories.

Goldsmith's Kaua`i, ☎ 808-822-4653, www.goldsmiths-kauai.com, is a jewelry store that features the fine work of its four designers. You'll find jewelry made with colored stones, diamonds and Tahitian black pearls. Most of what you see in the store is handmade right there in the studio.

Nearby, on Kuhio Highway, is **Bambulei**, ☎ 808-823-8641. The store is housed in two adorable plantation cottages, both of which are packed with everything you could think of. Bambulei carries vintage and contemporary clothing and Asian antiques. The store is fun and funky, one of my favorites on the island. There's always something that you just have to take home, like a funky vintage aloha shirt. A lot of the items go back to the 1930s and 1940s. If you are looking for vintage Hawaiiana, this is the place.

Coconut Marketplace isn't too impressive. There are plenty of shops and restaurants that are geared to tourists, but very few stores have anything unique. Here are some stores that are worth checking out, however.

- **Ship Store Gallery**, ☎ 808-822-4999, 800-877-1948, www.shipstoregalleries.com, specializes in fine art and antiques. You'll see paintings and some very rare nautical antiques.
- **Kaleidescope Galleries of the Pacific** (formerly Kahn Galleries), ☎ 808-822-3636, features the work of artists from Kaua`i and all over the globe. The gallery also has bronze sculptures and handcrafted koa pieces.

Shadows of the Past, *N. Jonas Englund, Ship Store Gallery*

- **Coffee Bean & Tea Leaf**, ☎ 808-822-4754, at the Waipouli Town Center, has a program called "Art at the Bean," which features local artists. They turn the existing wallspace into a gallery. It's worth checking out while you enjoy a cup of coffee.

Whaling Wall

You won't be able to miss **Kaua`i Village**; just look for the green, plantation-style shopping center and the Whaling Wall murals, painted by world-renowned marine life artist, Wyland. He also has a gallery in the shopping center, ☎ 808-822-9855, which features his paintings and sculpture, as well as those of other artists. Love him or hate him, the shop is always an interesting adventure.

Another funky shop full of vintage Hawaiian clothes is **Hula Girl**, 4-1340 Kuhio Highway, Kapa`a, ☎ 808-822-1950. They have alohawear for men and women, artwork and ceramics, Hawaiian books, music and DVDs. Next door to Hula Girl is **Jacques Amo Fine Jewelry**, ☎ 808-822-9977. This is a full-service, independent store specializing in unique custom designs. The work is conceived, cast and fabricated by Jacques himself.

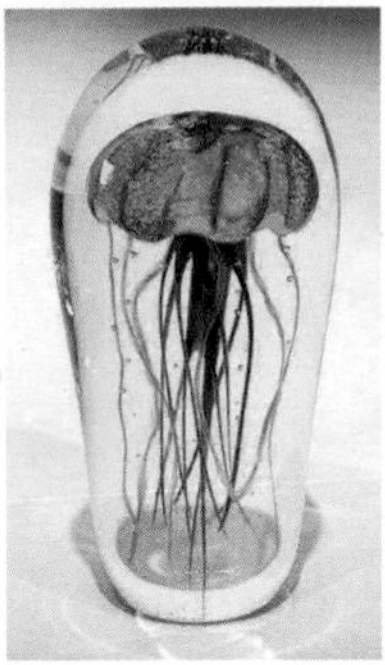

Kela's Glass Gallery, ☎ 808-822-4527, www.glass-art.com, has the best selection of glass art in the state, showing the work of more than 140 artists from all over the world. The pieces are stunning to look at. There are unique vases, sculptures, and glass fish. The styles range from functional to abstract.

Davison Arts, ☎ 808-821-8022, has koa furniture and gifts, paintings, sculpture, glass art, jewelry and rugs. You name it, they have it.

The Root, ☎ 808-823-1277, is a women's boutique that features funky and trendy clothing along with some sexy lingerie. It's on Kuhio Highway in Kapa`a right next to Bubba's Burgers.

If you want a gift that will last forever, get a tattoo. In Kapa`a, you can go to **Garden Isle Tattoo**, 4-356 Kuhio Hwy, ☎ 808-822-3314, or **Island Tattoo II**, ☎ 808-822-2588, in the Wailua Business Center.

**Kaua`i Products Fair**, ☎ 808-246-0988, www.kauaiproductsfair.com, is an outdoor market that takes place every Thursday-Sunday from 9 am to 5 pm at the north end of Kapa`a, right next to the Red Dirt Shirt Store on Kuhio Highway. It features fresh local produce, plants and flowers, alohawear, sculpture and jewelry.

Green Ti Boutique, ☎ 808-821-0225 4-1373 Kuhio Highway, www.greentiboutique.com, specializes in men and women's fine clothing, handmade textiles and silks, plus artwork from Southesast Asia and the Himalayas.

Lightwave Pottery & Ceramic Art, 961 Kipui Way, Kapa`a, ☎ 808-826-9576. This working pottery studio has works ranging from functional to abstract. You can pick up a teapot or look at larger sculptures. You can also watch new creations come to life before your eyes.

Growing Greens Nursery, 66-60B Kawaihau Road, Kapa`a, ☎ 877-856-9999, 808-822-3831, www.fungarden.com. Hawaiian "Fun Gardens" – miniature tropical foliage, and exotic flowering live plants grown in lava rock. Bring a piece of the islands of Hawai`i into your home or office. Give your friends or loved ones a slice of tropical paradise. These live plants are truly a living, breathing example of this tropical playground, and make ideal gifts & souvenirs of Kaua`i, Hawai`i.

Growing Greens Nursery

Groceries

If you're cooking at your condo and need to stock up on supplies, there are a number of places you can go to. In the Waipouli Town Center is Foodland. Kaua`i Village is home to Safeway and Papaya's for a good selection of health food and organic goods.

Kapa`a Shopping Center has a Big Save. There's also Kojima Store, ☎ 808-822-5221 in the North end of Kapa`a. Kojima's carries island meats and goods. Whalers General Store has most of your typical convenience-store items available.

The local Farmer's Markets happens every Wednesday at 3pm at the Kapa`a New Town Center.

Where to Stay

Hotels

**Aloha Beach Resort Kaua`i**, 3-5920 Kuhio Hwy, Kapa`a, ☎ 888-823-5111, 808-823-6000, www.alohabeachresortkauai.com. Formerly the Holiday Inn Sun-Spree Resort, this is in a great location – right at the mouth of the Wailua River. You're also a stone's throw from Lydgate State Beach Park. On the property, you'll find a swimming pool, shuffleboard, tennis courts and picnic tables. The resort is very family-friendly and will on occasion have family packages available. Call about those before you make your reservation. There are 216 rooms on the property, plus 26 two-room beach cottages. The rooms are pleasant and very clean, with garden or ocean views. If you want extra privacy, reserve one of the cottages, some of which are oceanfront. Rooms range from $198-$330; cottages start at $363.

**Kaua`i Sands Hotel**, 420 Papaloa Road, Kapa`a, ☎ 808-560-5553, 808-822-4951, www.kauaisands-hotel.com, is part of a Hawaiian-owned and -operated hotel chain that has accommodations throughout the state. The hotel provides simple accommodations right next to Coconut Marketplace. The two-story, 200-room hotel sits on six acres of lawns and native plants, with two large swimming pools. The rooms are clean and simple and the location is close to everything. Overall, it's a great value, especially if you don't plan to spend much time in your hotel room. Under $100-$200.

Hotel Coral Reef

Hotel Coral Reef, 1516 Kuhio Highway, Kapa`a, ☎ 800-843-4659, 808-822-4481, www.hotelcoralreef.com, is known more for its location than for anything else. There are only 24 rooms and the oceanfront location is near Kapa`a Beach Park. The hotel provides standard rooms with above-average views at very reasonable rates. This is a great alternative for budget-minded travelers who want to be close to the beach. Rooms feature color cable TV, ceiling fans, and air conditioning. Most have a partial ocean view and a private lana`i. $100-$300.

Condos

Hotel Awapuhi

Hale Awapuhi, 366 Papaloa Road, Kapa`a, ☎ 800-882-9007, www.haleawapuhi.com. The two- and three-bedroom oceanfront condos are incredibly spacious. The ocean views through the floor-to-ceiling windows in the dining room and living room are grand. If that's not relaxing enough, there are in-room spa services available. Each unit has a full kitchen and its own covered private lana`i. There's a swimming pool and barbecue area on the grounds. $200-$300.

AUTHOR'S CHOICE **Kapa`a Sands**, 80 Papaloa Road, Kapa`a, ☎ 808-822-4901, 800-222-4901, sits on what were once the grounds of a Shinto Temple, and you can still see some of the Japanese influences throughout the property. The 20 units are all oceanfront studio or two-bedrooms. With oceanfront studios starting at $110, this makes Kapa`a Sands a fantastic value. All 24 Kaua`i condo rental units include a fully stocked gourmet kitchen, dining area, cable television and a lana`i. You'll also find a swimming pool and barbecue area on the premises. There's a three- or seven-night minimum stay, depending on the time of the year. $100-$200.

Kapa`a Sands

Best Western Plantation Hale Suites, 484 Kuhio Highway, Kapa`a, ☎ 800-775-4253, 808-822-4941. The condos are spacious, with a garden lana`i, but not very private, especially if you're on the ground floor. The units are furnished with rattan furniture and pastel couches. The units were fairly clean, but could be slightly

Plantation Hale Suites

cleaner. On the positive side, the location is fantastic. You're right in Coconut Marketplace, which means that you can take a quick drive to the North Shore for the day or go for a long walk around the area. You're also about 100 yards from the beach, which is a great place for a sunrise stroll. There's free wireless Internet access in the lobby area. The staff is friendly and attentive. It's a good value, especially if you're traveling with your family. If you don't like to carry things up flights of steps, note that there is no elevator access to the upper floors.

ResortQuest Islander on the Beach

ResortQuest Islander on the Beach, 440 Aleka Place, Kapa`a, ☎ 808-822-7417, www.resortquest-hawaii.com. Islander on the Beach certainly is on the beach. The eight plantation-style buildings are located behind Coconut Marketplace on six acres facing Waipouli Beach. The complex completed a $10 million renovation in 2005. All 198 guestrooms were refurbished, and the lobby was given a fresh, open plantation-style look. All rooms have private lana`is with ocean or garden views. The rooms are air-conditioned and include mini-refrigerators, flat-screen TVs with cable, mini-stereo systems, in-room safes, and microwave ovens. High-speed Internet access is available for a fee. A swimming pool and barbecue area are on the property. Access to the second and third floors is via staircase only. $100-$200.

**ResortQuest Kaua`i Beach at Makaiwa**, 650 Aleka Loop, Kapa`a, formerly Kaua`i Coconut Beach Resort. This hotel also recently underwent a major renovation. As a result, the rooms are bright and spacious, tastefully decorated with furnishings imported from Bali and Indonesia. You'll have a view of the ocean, mountains or pool from your lana`i. The 311-room resort also includes a day spa, restaurant and lounge

ResortQuest Kaua`i Beach at Makaiwa

with live entertainment, swimming pool, and spa tub. If that's not enough, there is a tennis court, basketball hoop, swimming pool, and fitness room for the more active folks. Wireless Internet access is complimentary throughout the hotel. One problem: parking costs $7 per 24 hours. $100-$300.

ResortQuest Islander on the Beach

Castle Lanikai Resort, 390 Papaloa Road, Kapa`a, ☎ 800-367-5004, 808-822-7700, www.castle-resorts.com. There are only 18 units spread out over two three-story buildings. This gives you a bit more privacy and quiet. These pleasant beachfront two- and three-bedroom condominiums are very clean and have full kitchens and private lana`is that overlook the ocean. There's plenty of living space and this would be a good choice if you want a quiet getaway. A swimming pool, sundeck and barbecue area are on-site. Outside staircases, not elevators, provide access to upper floors; stay on the lower level if you don't like to climb stairs. Two-night minimum. $300-$400.

Wailua Bayview

Wailua Bayview, 320 Papaloa Road, Kapa`a, ☎ 800-882-9007, www.wailuabayview.com. The good news: All of the units are oceanfront with ocean view, overlooking Wailua Bay. They are moderately priced. These are very pleasant one-bedroom one-bathroom units with fully equipped kitchens. You have a swimming pool and barbecue on the property. You're centrally located in Kapa`a. The bad news: The Wailua Bayview is so close to the highway that it can be a challenge to truly unwind. You can shut all of the windows and turn on the air conditioning to drown out the traffic. If you're a light sleeper, that might not even work. There's a three-night minimum stay required. $100-$200.

AUTHOR'S CHOICE ★ **Outrigger Lae Nani**, 410 Paploa Road, Kapa`a, ☎ 808-822-4938, is one of the more expensive accommodations in the area. Despite this, you'll still find value in the service, the location and the condition of the units. Outrigger manages 58 units, while others are individually owned. The one- and two-bedroom units are very roomy and clean. The Outrigger staff is incredibly helpful and

Ourigger Lae Nani

friendly. They'll go out of their way to accommodate you. The units are individually owned, but they're well maintained. They are quiet. Even if your room is away from the ocean, you can still hear the waves coming on shore. If you do decide to stay here, try to get a room closest to the ocean. These rooms tend to be farthest from the parking lots. Tennis courts and a swimming pool are on the property. There's also an enclosed swimming area that perfect for kids. Kukui Heiau is on the premises. It's a 500-year-old Hawaiian temple and sacred site. $200-$400.

Bed & Breakfasts

Kakalina's Bed & Breakfast, 6781 Kawaihau Road, Kapa`a, ☎ 800-662-4330, 808-822-2328. Kakalina's is located on a three-acre working tropical flower farm. There are four suites available. You can get as simple as a studio, or go for a one-bedroom or two-bedroom. They're also offering Hale Eha, which is a two-bedroom suite equipped with queen-size beds, two full bathrooms, each with a bathtub/shower combination, a fully stocked kitchen, a large dining room and plenty of living room space. Each unit has a color television, VCR, coffee maker, microwave, and refrigerator. A continental breakfast is served every morning. Under $100-$200.

Mahina's Women's Bed & Breakfast, Kapa`a, ☎ 808-823-9364. This four-bedroom beach house caters to women and is a very friendly place to stay. The bedrooms are clean and named for powerful Hawaiian women (Pele, Hina, Laka and Queen Emma), each invoking aspects of the goddess. It's a great place to get in touch with your divine side. You get plenty of time to interact with other guests as you share the living room, kitchen and bathrooms. Every month, Mahina's hosts a monthly women's brunch and goddess gathering.

A Toe in Paradise, Kapa`a, ☎ 888-822-7197, 808-822-7195. There are two very spacious studios attached to the main house. Each studio has its own private entrance and bathroom. There's a king bed, shower and cable television in the rooms. Breakfast is not served here, but your room is equipped with a kitchenette. The house sits on three acres of wonderfully landscaped gardens. Depending on the season, you might be able to get fresh fruit from the orchard. Overall, this is a nice getaway for budget-minded couples. Two-night minimum stay. Under $100.

Vacation Rentals

Moloa`a Kai, Anahola, ☎ 808-247-3637, www.hibeach.com. This spacious three-story home with two bedrooms and two bathrooms is tastefully furnished and made of wood. The floors are beautiful hardwood. The house has an interesting layout that works well. It has a master bedroom on the top floor plus an open loft area complete with a separate bathroom and sleeping area for an additional three to five people. The kitchen and living room are on the third floor. You're in a private, secluded area with excellent swimming, diving, snorkeling, and surfing nearby. Five-night minimum stay. $200-$300.

Makana Crest, ☎ 808-245-6500, www.makanacrest.com. The two-bedroom cottage is a cozy 750 square feet, with rattan furniture, private bathroom with shower and a stocked kitchen. It's located behind Sleeping Giant, with a view of Mount Wai`ale`ale. The property is landscaped with orange, grapefruit, tangerine, lemon, lime, macadamia nut, guava, and coconut trees, not to mention a fishpond. Cable television is pro-

Makana Crest

vided. Wir sprechen auch Deutsch (that means they speak German). Three-night minimum stay. $100-$200.

Rainbows End, 6470 Kipapa Road, Kapa`a, ☎ 808-822-5216, www.rainbowsendkauai.com. This is a completely restored plantation one-bedroom cottage that was originally built in the 1930s. In the living area, a futon affords comfortable seating for reading or relaxing or can be opened into a full-size bed with upgraded mattress for extra guests. There is a small kitchenette with a refrigerator, microwave, and electric coffee and teapots. The bathroom retains the look of the 1930s, with its claw-foot Jacuzzi bathtub. $100-$200. Three-night minimum stay.

Rainbows End

**Rosewood Kaua`i**, Kamalu Road, Kapa`a, ☎ 808-822-5216, www.rosewoodkauai.com, handles the rental for Rainbows End as well as many other properties in the Coconut Coast area. You can rent a room in a bed and breakfast, get an oceanfront condo or rent a private home or cottage.

Kaua`i Vacation Rentals List, www.kauaivacationresorts.com, is a directory that lists hundreds of condominiums, secluded honeymoon cottages, oceanfront luxury homes and beachfront bungalows throughout the island. They have listings to fit all budgets, from $400 to $21,000 per week.

Garden Island Properties, ☎ 800-801-0378, 808-822-4871, www.kauaiproperties.com, handles vacation properties across the island. They have vacation rental homes, cottages and beach condos starting from $500 a week.

Kaua`i Vacation Rentals, ☎ 808-367-5025, 808-245-8841, www.kauaivacationrentals.com,has a large selection of vacation rental homes. Whether it's a cottage, bungalow, ocean-view condo, beachfront villa or luxurious oceanfront home, they'll probably have it in their inventory.

Paradise Vacation Rentals, 4760 Aliomanu Road, Anahola, ☎ 800-569-3063, 808-822-5754, offers three separate rentals. The Seaside Studio is in the upper level of the main house. Privacy is a little limited, but you're still close to the beach. The Beach Cabin is a hoot! It's decorated in a retro-Hawaiian style. There's a large lana`i area and, again, you're literally steps away from the beach. The Beach Cottage is an excellent choice. You're close to the beach, and there's a hammock and a large lana`i area. The cottage is nicely decorated. This a wonderful place to come for a quiet, private getaway. $100-$200.

**Re/Max Kaua`i**, at Princeville Shopping Center, ☎ 877-838-8149, 808-826-9675, www.remaxkauai.com. Even though Re/Max Kaua`i is located in Princeville and they do specialize in the Princeville area, they have some rentals along the Coconut Coast, mainly in the Waipouli Beach Resort. You can make your reservations through their online reservation system.

Hostels

**Kaua`i International Hostel**, 4532 Lehua Street, Kapa`a, ☎ 808-823-6142, provides clean and safe accommodations for very little money. Private rooms start at $60 a night for a basic room or you can spend $75 for a room equipped with a refrigerator, television and private bathroom. Dorm-style accommodations are only $25 a night. You can't beat that. There's a common television with a cable hook-up, pool table, volleyball and barbecue area. It's also in a central location, within a short walk to Kapa`a's restaurants and shops. It has a common kitchen as well and laundry facilities, all of which are surprisingly clean. Under $100.

Camping

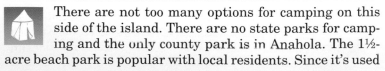

There are not too many options for camping on this side of the island. There are no state parks for camping and the only county park is in Anahola. The 1½-acre beach park is popular with local residents. Since it's used primarily by locals, it's very possible you might run into problems if you're a "haole." Also, swimming here is extremely dangerous due to the pounding waves and strong currents that form, particularly during high surf. I wouldn't recommend camping here, but if you really want to stay, you'll have to go though the Kaua`i County Division of Parks & Recreation. To obtain a county permit, contact the Kaua`i County Parks Permit Section by calling ☎ 808-241-4463. Their hours are 8:15 am to 4 pm Monday through Friday.

You can also get a permit at the Kapa'a Neighborhood Center, ☎ 808-822-1931 or 808-822-0511. However, they're only open Monday-Friday between 8:30 am and 12:30 pm. Camping permit fees are $3 per adult, per night for non-residents and free for Hawai`i residents.

■ Where To Eat

Aloha We Deliver, ☎ 808-822-4712, www.alohawedeliver.com. Delivery Monday-Saturday 5-9 pm. This restaurant delivery service is perfect if you don't want to cook, yet don't want to leave your hotel. They will deliver meals from participating restaurants. At press time, they're working with eight restaurants, including Acropoli, Blossoming Lotus, Norberto's El Cafe, Pacific Island Bistro and Wasabi's On the Reef. Check ahead as new restaurants are added regularly. They deliver only to the Kapa`a area and charge $5 delivery fee and $3 per additional stop. Under $15-$50.

Beezers Old Fashioned Ice Cream, ☎ 808-822-4411. Open daily from 11 am to 10 pm. This old-fashioned soda shop will take you back to the 1950s the moment you walk in the door. It's designed just like an old soda shop, complete with shiny red stools and memorabilia along the walls. They use Dryer's Ice Cream to create the best sundaes around. You can get anything from a single scoop of ice cream, malts and shakes, to a huge banana split. It might seem a little pricey, but it's certainly worth it. They also serve hot dogs, sandwiches and hamburgers. Under $15.

AUTHOR'S CHOICE ★ **Blossoming Lotus**, 4504 Kukui Street Kapa`a, ☎ 808-822-7678, www.blossominglotus.com. Serving dinner daily 5- 9:30 pm; Sunday Champagne Brunch

11 am-3 pm. Blossoming Lotus has a well-earned reputation as one of the best vegetarian restaurants in the state. Some items are served live, meaning that they aren't cooked above 116 degrees. It's world cuisine, so expect to see Thai, Greek and even Mexican items on the menu. The food is phenomenal. It's definitely worth the trip. Dinner $15-$35, Sunday brunch under $15.

Blossoming Lotus

Bubba Burgers, 4-1421 Kuhio Hwy, Kapa`a, ☎ 808-823-0069. Open daily 10:30 am-8 pm. Plenty of folks might tell you that this is supposed to be "The Place" to get a burger, but I was pretty disappointed. They're decent burgers, but not out of this world. All things considered, it's a quick, easy and inexpensive option when you're going to or coming from the beach. Under $15.

The Bull Shed Kapa`a, ☎ 808-822-3791, 808-822-1655. Open daily at 4:30 for cocktails; dinner is served from 5:30 to 10 pm. Locals and tourists come here for one reason – sizable portions at a reasonable price. The quality is also top-notch. It's what makes The Bull Shed such an excellent value. On the menu is prime rib, slow-cooked and tender. Be sure to try the baby back ribs, so tender they just fall off of the bone. There are also seafood selections like lobster tail and shrimp. $15-$35.

Caffe Coco, 4-369 Kuhio Highway, Wailua, ☎ 808-822-7990. Open Tuesday-Friday from 11 am to 5 pm for lunch; dinner 5-9 pm. Housed in a restored plantation-era cottage, Caffe Coco is a quaint and casual restaurant with a healthy menu selection. You'll dine in vine-covered gardens and enjoy fresh fish dishes, organic salad, vegan desserts and espresso from the full espresso bar. Vegetarians will appreciate Caffe Coco. Don't forget to pay a visit to their art gallery. Under $15-$35.

Kountry Kitchen, 1485 Kuhio Highway, Wailua, ☎ 808-822-3511. Open daily 6 am-1:30 pm. It's not much to look at, but the food is surprisingly good. Here you are in control of your own omelet. You can create it from a variety of fillings. If you're not into eggs, then order Coconut French Toast. It's fantastic. For lunch, the menu is standard, with sandwiches and burgers. Under $15.

Coconuts Island Style Grill & Bar, 4-919 Kuhio Hwy, Kapa`a, ☎ 808-823-8777. Open for dinner Monday- Saturday 4-10 pm. Coconuts is casual and affordable. The menu includes pupus, soups, salads and fabulous entrées, including fish and steak. For dinner, try the Lobster Ravioli. If you have a sweet tooth, you might want to skip dinner and go straight for the Chocolate Volcano Cake or Lilikoi Sorbet. Happy Hour is from 4 until 6 pm Monday-Saturday, with a good selection of beer and wine. $15-$35.

AUTHOR'S CHOICE ★ **Duane's Ono Char Burger Roadside Stand**, Anahola, ☎ 808-822-9181. Open Monday to Saturday from 10 am to 6 pm; Sunday from 11 am to 6 pm. This little shack in Anahola is the best stop for cheap burgers and they've been doing it for years. Come to think of it, Duane's has the best burgers on the island. It may not look like much from the outside, but the burgers rock! Definitely try the Teri Burger. They also serve Boca burgers, chicken and milkshakes. If you go at lunch, you might have to wait a while, but it's worth it. Under $15.

Duane's Ono Char Burger

Eggbert's Coconut Marketplace, ☎ 808-822-3787. Eggbert's is primarily a breakfast restaurant and is known for its convenient location in Coconut Marketplace. It's something of a tourist trap. The service and food are mediocre. They do serve lunch and dinner. There are a number of other places in the area to go for a better meal. Under $15-$35.

AUTHOR'S CHOICE ★ **Hukilau Lana`i**, Kaua`i Coast Resort at the Beachboy, Kapa`a, ☎ 808-822-0600. Open for Happy Hour from 3 pm daily; dinner Tuesday-Sunday 5-9 pm. Hukilau Lounge is a refined dining experience in a casual atmosphere. If you get there between 5 and 6 in the evening, they serve an incredible six-course food and wine tasting menu that has an emphasis on local ingredients. Each course is paired with a different wine. For instance, you can have sweet potato ravioli paired with a gewürztraminer. It makes for a gastronomical adventure. The food and wine pairing is only $40 per person, which is very reasonable. If you're the designated driver, the six course meal is only $28. They also have fresh fish specials and steaks. $35-$50.

Java Kai, 4-1384 Kuhio Hwy, Kapa`a, ☎ 808-823-6887, www.javakai.com. Open 6 am-5 pm Monday through Saturday; 7 am-1 pm on Sundays. Java Kai is a charming café. It's quick and easy in the morning if you're anxious to get to the beach, or you can sit on the lana`i and enjoy your coffee while reading the newspaper. It's a fun place to people-watch as well. There's a wide selection of coffee drinks, and baked goods. Their specialty is the Aloha Bar, which is a delectable treat made with toasted coconut, macadamia nuts and chocolate chips on a shortbread cookie crust. It's very, very tasty. They serve waffles and breakfast items as well. Under $15.

Kaua`i Hula Girl Bar & Grill, Coconut Marketplace, ☎ 808-822-4422, features everything from Hawaiian-style creations to steak and seafood. The food is hit and miss. Sometimes it's excellent; other times, it's just OK. The service is consistently indifferent and slow. They do have live entertainment every evening.

**Kaua`i Pasta**, 4-939B Kuhio Highway, Kapa`a, ☎ 808-822-7447. Open for dinner from 5 to 9 pm. This is a great little Italian place if you're looking for, well, pasta. They actually have a pretty extensive menu, with items such as salads, panini, lasagna, Italian herb grilled shrimp, and chicken parmesan. Try not to fill up on garlic bread, because it is addicting. For dessert, you must try the tiramisu cheesecake. The restaurant does get crowded for dinner; if you're the impatient type, you can order a take-out pasta dinner for four (includes salad and garlic bread for $29.95). $15-$35.

Lemon Grass Seafood & Sushi Bar, 4-885 Kuhio Highway, ☎ 808-821-2888, 826-9561. Dinner served from 5 to 10 pm daily. Reservations recommended. Delectable cuisine, mingling the flavors of Thailand and Hawai`i, awaits at this charming spot, sheltered in an old homestead. Fresh ingredients figure prominently, and fish and seafood are especially appealing, whether in sushi rolls, in sautés, or simply cooked to perfection. If you're in the mood for meat, you'll find that pork, chicken, and lamb are also skillfully prepared. Great place for sushi. Try the Kalaua Won Ton for an appetizer. $35-$50.

AUTHOR'S CHOICE ★ **La Playita Azul**, Kaua`i Village, Kapa`a, ☎ 808-821-2323. Open daily for lunch 11 am-2pm; dinner 5-9 pm. This is my favorite Mexican restaurant on the island. It doesn't look like much, and it's very easy to pass by if you're walking around Kaua`i Village. The food is awesome. It comes in huge portions and is delicious. If you're really hungry, try the seafood burrito, enough to feed an army. The service was excellent – very attentive. Ask for crayons so you can write on the walls. The only downside is that the place is so small, it can be difficult to get a table. $15-$35.

Fajitas from La Playita Azul

Lizard Lounge Bar & Grill, Waipouli Town Center, Kapa`a, ☎ 808-821-2205. Open daily from 10:30 am to 1:30 am. This is a typical bar with a typical bar menu of burgers, sandwiches, salads and steaks. The kitchen stays open until 1 am. They have 30 beers with a passable selection of imports and microbrews. It's a nice atmosphere to come and hang out, play pool or darts. Under $15-$35.

Mema Thai & Chinese Cuisine, Wailua Shopping Plaza, Wailua, ☎ 808-823-0899. Open Monday-Friday for lunch from 11 am to 2 pm; dinner is served daily from 5 pm to 9:30 pm. Mema Thai serves good Thai food at reasonable prices. The atmosphere is somewhat romantic, yet casual. The waitstaff wears bright and beautiful traditional Thai clothing. The menu is extensive, with a large variety of curries. There are a number of options for vegetarians as well. The restaurant is BYOB. You can stop at Safeway or Foodland to pick up a bottle of wine. $15-$35.

Mermaids Café, 1384 Kuhio Highway, Kapa`a, ☎ 808-821-2026. Open daily 11 am-9 pm. Located right in Kapa`a Town, Mermaids Café offers healthy options with a nice spicy kick to them. They use local ingredients to create an imaginative menu. If there's anything you must try on the menu, it has to be the ahi nori wrap. This starts with a spinach tortilla and nori (sushi wrap made from seaweed), then adds rice, seared ahi and wasabi sauce. It's large enough for two people to share and worth the trip to Kapa`a. Under $15.

Norberto's El Café, 4-1373 Kuhio Highway, Kapa`a, ☎ 808-822-3362. Open Monday-Saturday 5-9 pm. This local favorite has been serving up delicious Mexican food with a local flair for more than 25 years. The portions are huge and the food is excellent. They have unique plates such as Hawaiian Taro Enchiladas And Rellenos Tampico. They also make a mean margarita. $15-$35.

Pizzetta, ☎ 1387 Kuhio Highway, Kapa`a, ☎ 808-823-8882, www.pizzettarestaurant.com. This is the second Pizzetta on the island (the first is in Koloa) and it's just as good. The menu is pretty much the same; the pizza and service are also excellent. The meatball sub is awesome. The large doors in front open to the street, so it has an open atmosphere. Happy Hour is from 3 to 6 pm, something to consider when you're sitting in traffic in Kapa`a. You can't beat the specials on mai-tais and beers. The only downside is that, just like the Pizzetta in Koloa, it can get pretty crowded at dinner. If that's the case, they can deliver on the east side from Wailua to Anahola. $15-$35.

Olympic Café, 4-1354 Kuhio Highway, ☎ 808-822-5825. Open daily 7 am-9 pm. If you like to people-watch, this is the place to go. Olympic Cafe is right in the middle of Kapa`a

Town upstairs in the old green Hee Fat Marketplace building. If you can, grab a spot that overlooks Kuhio Highway. You'll get to see all sorts of characters wander through town. Of course, the food is another reason to come here. They serve breakfast, lunch and dinner. You could also stop by for a cocktail or coffee. Menu items include omelets, egg scrambles, vegetarian dishes, wraps, sandwiches, burgers, fish and much more. $15-$35.

Ono Family Restaurant, 4-1292 Kuhio Highway, Kapa`a, ☎ 808-822-1710. This tiny family restaurant certainly is ono (delicious). It's frequented by locals and tourists alike. This is a fantastic choice for breakfast. Whether you get a loco moco, pancakes or omelets, you're in for a treat. Everything is good. However, the service is inconsistent. At least the food isn't. They serve lunch, which is an inexpensive option. Under $15.

Pacific Island Bistro, Kaua`i Village Shopping Center, Kapa`a, ☎ 808-822-0092, www.kauaibistro.com. Open daily for lunch 10:30 am-3 pm; dinner 5-9:30 pm. Reservations recommended. This small establishment gives you the feeling of island-style dining. The lunch menu is pretty basic, with sandwiches and burgers, with a couple of twists thrown in such as curry meatballs and Huli Huli chicken. The dinner menu features a delectable selection of seafood, steaks, chicken and duck. The service is excellent and the food superb. $15-$35.

Papaya's Natural Foods, Kaua`i Village, Kapa`a, ☎ 808-823-0190, www.papayasnaturalfoods.com. Open Monday-Saturday 9 am-8 pm; Café closes at 7 pm. For vegetarians, there's Papaya's, which is a health food store and a vegetarian café. The store offers organic produce, beer, wine and bulk foods and health and beauty products. The café serves breakfast, lunch and dinner. You can also get smoothies there as well. The food is good and priced right. There's also a Papaya's in Hanalei. Under $15.

Scotty's Beachside BBQ, ☎ 808-823-8480, www.scottysbbq.com. Monday through Saturday 11 am to 9 pm for breakfast, lunch and dinner. Sunday brunch 10 am-3 pm. Sunday BBQ buffet 3-8 pm. There's a reason why this is considered the best barbecue place on the island by locals and tourists alike. They have a terrific pulled pork sandwich. For a real diet killer, try the fried cheesecake. They consistently serve the best barbecue around and the service is good. If you're not in the mood for barbecue, they also serve burgers and salads. $15-$35.

Sukhothai Restaurant, Kapa`a Shopping Center, Kapa`a, ☎ 808-821-1224. Open for lunch 10:30 am-3 pm and dinner 5-9 pm. Sukhothai serves Thai, Vietnamese, and Chinese dishes. The menu is so extensive it can be intimidating. You can choose from curries, soups, saimin or noodles. There are also plenty of options for vegetarians. $15-$35.

Tropical Burgers & More, Coconut Marketplace, ☎ 808-823-8808. The worst dining experience I've ever had on Kaua`i. Bad food, even worse service. Don't waste your time or money.

Wahoo's Seafood Grill & Bar, 4-733 Kuhio Highway, Kapa`a, ☎ 808-822-7833. Wahoo's has a reputation as one of the top seafood restaurants in the area. The food tends to be cooked just right and the presentation is impressive. The interior of the restaurant gives the impression that you're in a five-star restaurant. Despite this, you still feel like you're in a casual environment. The menu has a variety of fresh local fish along with steak and chicken. The wine list is just as good as the food. It is a little pricey, but worth it. $35-$50.

Waipouli Restaurant, Waipouli Town Center, Kapa`a, ☎ 808-822-9311. Open for breakfast and lunch 7 am-2 pm Tuesday-Sunday; dinner is served Wednesday-Saturday 5-8:30 pm. This simple local-style restaurant isn't much from the outside or inside, but the food is good and really cheap. Come on, where can you get a burger for under $4? Breakfast consists of typical options (eggs, pancakes, etc.) and it can be hard to get a seat. For lunch, you can get sandwiches, burgers, plate lunches and saimin. Under $15.

Wailua Family Restaurant, Kuhio Highway, Wailua, ☎ 808-822-3325. Open Sunday-Thursday 6:30 am-9:30 pm; Friday and Saturday 6:30 am-10 pm. I like to consider Wailua Family Restaurant to be a local version of Sizzler. That's not a bad thing. You can try the all you can eat buffet for as little as $12. You can't beat that. The food is good, considering it's done buffet-style. You have a wide array of choices at breakfast, lunch and dinner. For lunch, help yourself to eggs, fresh fruit and Portuguese sausage. Lunchtime is perfect for local flavors such as laulau. Under $15-$35.

Wailua Marina Restaurant, Wailua State Park, Wailua, ☎ 808-822-4311. Open Tuesday-Sunday 10:30 am-2 pm and 5-8:30 pm. Wailua Marina Reataurant provides stunning views of the Wailua River and Sleeping Giant. They have indoor and outdoor seating available, but outdoor seating affords the best views. The food is hearty for the most part, although there is a salad bar and sandwiches on the menu for light eaters. The portions are generous and the food is good. A wonderful dish to try is the island ahi stuffed with crab. You can also feast on steak or pork chops. Lunch $15-$35, dinner $35-$50.

Wasabi's Sushi Restaurant, 4-1388 Kuhio Highway, Kapa`a, ☎ 808-822-2700. Open daily 11 am-10 pm. Wasabi's is known for its innovative take on sushi. They do serve the standard tempura and Philly rolls, but they also have rolls that you just won't find anywhere else. My favorite was the Oxymoron Roll (OK, mostly because of the name), which is tempura shrimp, avocado, cucumber and tobiko. The atmosphere is vibrant and lively. Be sure to check out the Happy Hour sushi specials from 3 to 6 pm. $15-$35.

■ Nightlife/Culture

OK night owls, here's a rundown on what's happening where in the evening hours.

If you want to catch a movie, you're in luck. There's a **movie theater** at **Coconut Marketplace**, ☎ 808-821-2324, that has first-run films on their two screens.

Lizard Lounge Bar & Grill, ☎ 808-821-2205, in Waipouli Town Center, serves American bar food until 1 am. The menu features sandwiches and salads and a great selection of pupus. The atmosphere is casual and laid-back. They carry a surprisingly good selection of microbrews. You can come here to catch the big game or play pool and just hang out.

Also check out **Break Time Billiards & Café**, ☎ 808-821-6900, across from the Kapa`a Shores in Kapa`a. They have 10 pool tables and host a tournament on Wednesday nights.

Tradewinds - A South Seas Bar, in Coconut Marketplace, ☎ 808-822-1621, www.tradewinds-kauai.com, is the place to go if you want to drink and party it up. This is a relatively small bar with drink specials throughout the day. You can order food from a few of the restaurants in Coconut Marketplace. In the evening, you can try karaoke a couple of nights during the week. The evening entertainment consists of live music on Thursdays and Fridays and a DJ on Wednesdays. They also have a dart league throughout the week.

**Hukilau Lana`i**, Kaua`i Coast Resort at the Beachboy, Kapa`a, ☎ 808-822-0600. Open for Happy Hour 3-5 pm daily; dinner Tuesday-Sunday 5-9 pm. From 6:30 to 9:30 pm on Tuesdays, Thursdays and Sundays, Hukilau Lana`i features local entertainers playing Hawaiian and contemporary music. If you're feeling a little thirsty before 5, stop by for a mai tai or Keoki's beer (made on Kaua`i) on tap. They have a nice selection of exotic drinks like Coconut Coast Cooler and Mango Kiss, (margarita with mango purée), along with the standard Lava Flow (piña colada with strawberry swirl).

Luaus

AUTHOR'S CHOICE ★ **Smith's Family Garden Luau**, Wailua Marina State Park, Wailua, ☎ 808-821-6895. Monday, Wednesday, and Friday at 5 pm. $63 per adult, children seven-13 $27, three-six $17. Once you check in at 5, you'll be greeted with a shell lei and you can stroll the beautifully kept grounds with over 20 fruit trees including breadfruit, star fruit, jackfruit, macadamia and soursop. There are replicas of Filipino and Polynesian huts as well as a beautiful Japanese-style garden. You might even see a peacock or two. Promptly at 6, the conch shells will blow, indicating that it's time for the imu ceremony. You'll get an explanation of the imu and how the pig is cooked in the underground oven, followed by cocktails and music. The musicians entertain throughout your meal with appealing hula and Hawaiian songs. At 6:30 pm, the luau begins. Tables are dismissed one at a time to go through the line of food such as kalua pig, poi, teriyaki beef, adobo chicken and haupia (coconut custard) for dessert. The food is very good when you consider how many people they're feeding.

Even though there are hundreds of people, the staff goes out of their way to make you feel welcome and have a great time. There's an emphasis on the family part of the establishment, and that comes across from every member of the staff.

As for the show, I don't think they've changed their show in 50 years, but that's part of the charm. It's thoroughly entertaining, representing cultures throughout Polynesia. Overall, Smith's Family Garden Luau gives you an extraordinary experience.

Tihati's Hiva Pasefika Luau, ResortQuest Kaua`i Beach at Makaiwa, ☎ 808-823-0311, www.rqkauaibeach.com. Tuesday-Sunday at 5:45 pm. Adults $62, kids 12-17 $40, three-11 $30, seniors (over 60) $57. You'll start at 5:45 with a lei greeting and Hawaiian arts and crafts. You then have cocktails before the imu ceremony and dinner. The menu items include Kalua pig, fish, taro, salmon and poi. There's a pareo fashion show before the Hiva Pasefika Revue. The show is a journey that reflects the one the Tahitians made to the Hawaiian Islands. Along the way, you'll see hula dances, kahiko (ancient) hula chants and it all ends with a lengthy and always enthralling fire-knife dance.

Hula

Coconut Marketplace has a free hula show every Wednesday at 5 pm. Catch the weekly hula show every Wednesday at 5 pm in the Center Stage in the middle of the marketplace.

Hawaiian Art Museum, 4504 Kukui Street, Suite 11, Kapa`a, ☎ 808-823 8381, holds hula classes where you can learn hula, chanting and drumming. Classes are for all levels and are on Tuesdays at 7 pm. The museum also has a "Talk Story" where Serge Kahili King and Alakai of Aloha International discuss Hawaiian culture, history, legends, language, geography, healing, and the Huna philosophy. Talk Story is on Wednesdays at 7 pm. Finally, the museum conducts a Huna Healing Circle on Thursdays at 7 pm. Here you'll learn to use ancient healing techniques of Huna to heal yourself and others.

The South Shore

What to See

Driving to the southern part of the island from Lihu`e is a terrific journey. It's here in this area where the new and old worlds of Kaua`i converge to create a spectacle of beauty and fun that you won't get anywhere else on the island. If you love action, this is the place to be because there's plenty of it. First-class restaurants, accommodations, beaches and a tremendous number of activities await. The South Shore is the sunny side of the island, so you can feel free to work on your tan, cool off in the ocean or enjoy the trade winds blowing in from the ocean.

IN THIS CHAPTER

Turning on Highway 520 from Kaumuali`i Highway (Highway 50), the first thing you'll notice is the **Tunnel of Trees** towering over you. After a few minutes heading down the winding road, you'll get to **Koloa Town**, which represents the old world of Kaua`i.

The area was a prime destination for whalers who landed at Koloa Landing, as well as for sugar plantation workers, which made Po`ipu a bustling economic center. While today Lihu`e has the county seat, **Po`ipu** has the attractions and activities that are a draw for visitors from all over the world.

Koloa was the site of Hawai`i's first successful sugar plantation, called Ladd & Co that was established in 1835. That history is evident as you see renovated plantation buildings, old mom and pop shops that go back for generations. There are plenty of old churches and homes (especially down Waikomo Road) that maintain the charm of this town. The population is

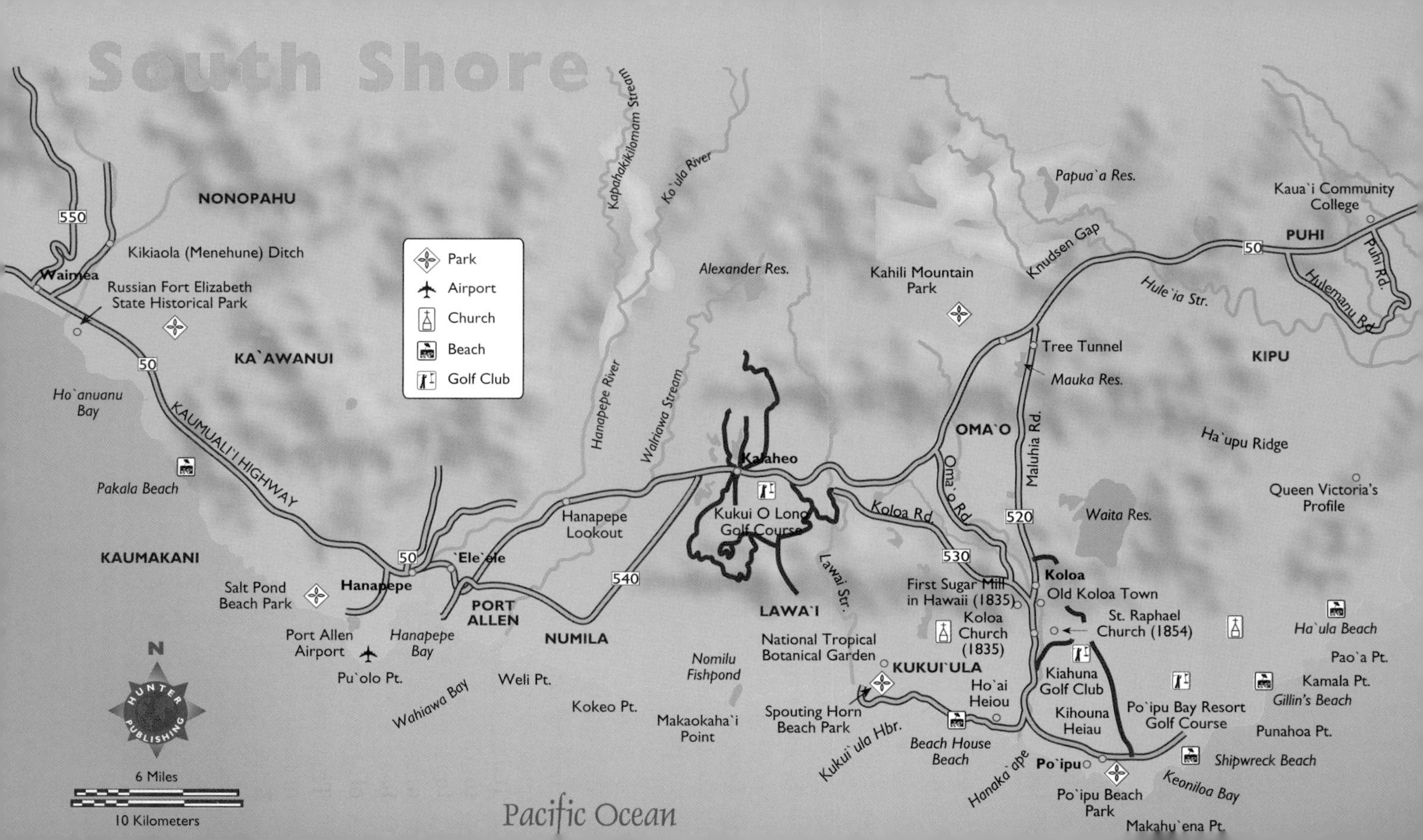
South Shore
Park
Airport
Church
Beach
Golf Club
NONOPAHU
550
Waimea
Kikiaola (Menehune) Ditch
Russian Fort Elizabeth
State Historical Park
KA`AWANUI
50
Ho`anuanu
Bay
KAUMUALI'I HIGHWAY
Pakala Beach
KAUMAKANI
Salt Pond
Beach Park
Hanapepe
`Ele`ele
PORT
ALLEN
Port Allen
Airport
Hanapepe
Bay
Pu`olo Pt.
Wahiawa Bay
Weli Pt.
NUMILA
540
Hanapepe
Lookout
Kapahakikilomam Stream
Ko`ula River
Hanapepe River
Walriawa Stream
Alexander Res.
Kalaheo
Kukui O Lono
Golf Course
Kokeo Pt.
Nomilu
Fishpond
Makaokaha`i
Point
LAWA`I
Lawai Str.
National Tropical
Botanical Garden
KUKUI`ULA
Spouting Horn
Beach Park
Kukui`ula Hbr.
Kahili Mountain
Park
Koloa Rd.
530
OMA`O
Oma`o Rd
Maluhia Rd.
520
Tree Tunnel
Mauka Res.
Knudsen Gap
Papua`a Res.
Hule`ia Str.
First Sugar Mill
in Hawaii (1835)
Koloa
Church
(1835)
Ho`ai
Heiou
Beach House
Beach
Hanaka`ape
Koloa
Old Koloa Town
St. Raphael
Church (1854)
Kiahuna
Golf Club
Kihouna
Heiau
Po`ipu
Po`ipu Beach
Park
Waita Res.
Po`ipu Bay Resort
Golf Course
Keoniloa Bay
Makahu`ena Pt.
Shipwreck Beach
Punahoa Pt.
Gillin's Beach
Kamala Pt.
Pao`a Pt.
Ha`ula Beach
Queen Victoria's
Profile
Ha`upu Ridge
KIPU
PUHI
Kaua`i Community
College
Puhi Rd.
Hulemanu Rd.
N
HUNTER PUBLISHING
6 Miles
10 Kilometers
Pacific Ocean

made up of immigrants and descendants of immigrants from Japan, Korea, the Philippines and Puerto Rico.

Koloa's residents show their appreciation for the area's history by hosting the **Koloa Plantation Days Festival** every July. It's a week-long event that celebrates the sugar plantation heritage and immigrant cultures.

Most people stay in Po`ipu when they visit Kaua`i. Here's a quick guide to help you plan your day as you drive around the island.

DRIVING TIMES FROM PO`IPU	
Kalaheo	15 minutes
Eleele/Port Allen Harbor	19 minutes
Hanapepe	22 minutes
Waimea Town	27 minutes
Waimea Canyon	42 minutes
Polihale State Beach Park	46 minutes
Lihu`e	22 minutes
Kapa`a	28 minutes
Kilauea	52 minutes
Princeville	1 hour
Hanalei	1 hour 10 minutes
Ha`ena State Beach Park	1 hour 20 minutes

Today, the region is bustling with Hawai`i's new cash crop – tourism. The one drawback here is that everything is geared to tourists. Koloa still maintains the old Hawai`i feel, but the area overall has a commercial feel to it. Despite this, the beauty of the sun's rays, the gentle breezes and the lushness of the area are hard to ignore.

The tiny hamlets of **Kalaheo**, **Lawai** and **Omao** are also part of the South Shore. These upcountry communities still have some remnants of the time when sugar was king. However, the lush upcountry area is now home to a new crop: not tourism, but coffee, which you'll see everywhere as you head west on Kaumuali`i Highway.

Koloa

Tnnnel of Trees

Driving from to Po`ipu, you'll be greeted by the **Tunnel of Trees**, an amazing one-mile stretch lined with eucalyptus trees. They were planted by Walter Duncan McBryde, a Scot who was a cattle rancher on Kaua`i.

The trees are eucalyptus robustus, a native of Australia. This is one of over 50 eucalyptus species that introduced to Hawai`i for various purposes. Although the trees were damaged by Hurricanes Iwa and Iniki, they still form a beautiful canopy to welcome you to the South Shore.

To see the Tunnel of Trees, take Kaumuali`i Highway (Highway 50) west from Lihu`e. Turn left on Maluhia Road (Highway 520). The Tunnel of Trees lines the first section of the road on the way to Po'ipu. Roll down the windows and breathe!

Knudsen's Gap is a narrow passage between the Haupu Mountain Range and Kahili Ridge. Its primary function was as a small sugar farm planted by the Knudsen family. Old stories say that crossing this area in the late 1800s was extremely dangerous as robbers hid here and ambushed travelers passing through.

The land is privately owned, but you can still see Knudsen's Gap just before you turn off of Kaumuali`i Highway to Maluhia Road.

Waita Reservoir is the largest man-made reservoir in the State of Hawai`i. It was built in 1906 and still supplies the area with its water. It's also known for very good bass fishing.

Koloa means "long sugar" in Hawaiian. Seems rather appropriate, considering the history of the region.

Cutting sugar cane on Kaua`i, 1910

Koloa Sugar Plantation. In 1833, William Hooper, Peter Brinsdale and William Ladd formed Ladd & Company in Honolulu as a trading company. In 1835, they leased over 900 acres in Koloa and started planting sugar. The plantation was successful right away and grew very rapidly. Homes for workers were built, stores were opened. Koloa soon grew into a self-sufficient town with churches (some are among the oldest on the island) and schools. Immigrants from all over the world came to Kaua`i to work at the plantations. People came from other Hawaiian islands, China, Japan, Europe and the Philippines in droves.

In 1837, these plantation workers were the first to use plantation scrip to purchase goods, which brought a new style of commerce to Hawai`i. The mill closed in 1996.

Ruins of the Sugar Mill

What remains of the plantation is very little. In an open field as you enter Koloa Town, you can see the quiet remains of the old sugar mill. There's also a memorial dedicated to the immigrants and Hawaiians who toiled the fields. You can see the Old Koloa Sugar Mill at the end of Weliweli Road.

KOLOA PLANTATION DAYS FESTIVAL

Every July, the town of Koloa gathers to celebrate the sugar heritage and immigrant cultures that converged on the area during the town's heyday in the late 1800s. Koloa Plantation Days is a week-long festival that's loaded with activities, sporting events and even a rodeo. There's also a parade through Koloa Town that's worth seeing. In 2006, the theme of the parade was Filipinos in Kaua`i, a reference to the fact that the first laborers came to work the cane fields from the Philippines 100 years ago.

There are tennis, golf, and softball tournaments, guided walks and canoe races, all making the festival a true family affair. Be sure to sample the local food – always in abundance.

For more information, call Koloa Plantation Days at ☎ 808-822-0734 or visit www.koloaplantationdays.com.

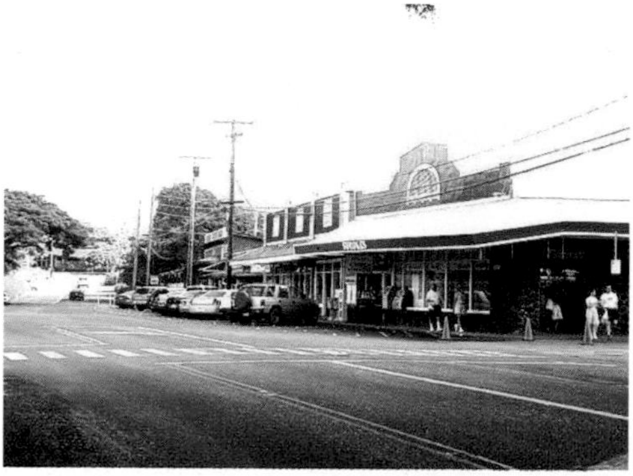

Koloa Town

Your visit to Koloa is not complete without a trip to the **Koloa History Center**. The center is small, but it's packed with old photographs and artifacts that detail the intriguing history of the area. You can also pick up a map of the Koloa Heritage Trail. To get to the Koloa History Center, drive down Maluhia Road (Highway 520) into Koloa Town. The center is in Old Koloa Town shopping center, next to the Salvation Army Church.

The **Koloa Heritage Trail** is a 10-mile walking trail that will take you through 14 historic and cultural sites in Koloa and around the South Shore. You'll learn the history and stories behind Koloa Landing, Moir Gardens, Po`ipu Beach, Keoneloa Bay,Yamamoto Store, Koloa Hotel, the Koloa Jodo Mission and Koloa Missionary Church. You can pick up a brochure at Koloa History Center and at racks and hotels throughout the island. Start out at any point on the trail. You don't have to start at Spouting Horn. If walking 10 miles seems a bit daunting, you can bike or drive the trail.

Koloa Church. This gorgeous white church was built in 1859 and was once the site of the Koloa Mission. You can't miss the white steeple, which seems somewhat out of place. Its official name is The Church at Koloa, but it's also known as Koloa Church or White Church.

Old Koloa Church

Koloa Union Church is made of black lava rock and has a very rich history dating back to the mid 1800s. In the 1920s the church underwent a major renovation and formally chartered itself as Koloa Union Church. You can see the church next to Koloa Church as you drive along Po`ipu Road.

St. Raphael's is the first Catholic church on Kaua`i. Although missionaries were allowed to practice their religion freely, the Hawaiian Kingdom did not allow Catholics to celebrate Mass until 1939. Father Arsenius Robert Walsh originally went to Honolulu in 1936 but was denied entry by the Hawaiian Kingdom. The captain of a French ship convinced the Hawaiian government to allow Father Walsh to stay and they relented. During that time, Catholics were persecuted by Congregationalists, who had good relations with Hawaiian Kingdom. In 1939, the French threatened to attack Hawai`i if Catholics couldn't practice their religion. The Hawaiian Kingdom conceded. Father Walsh went to Kaua`i in 1841 to establish the church and named it after St. Raphael the Archangel. The first Catholic Mass was celebrated on Christmas 1841. The existing church was built in 1856 and was renovated in 1936. There's also an old cemetery on the grounds of the church. St. Raphael's Catholic Church is at 3011 Hapa Road

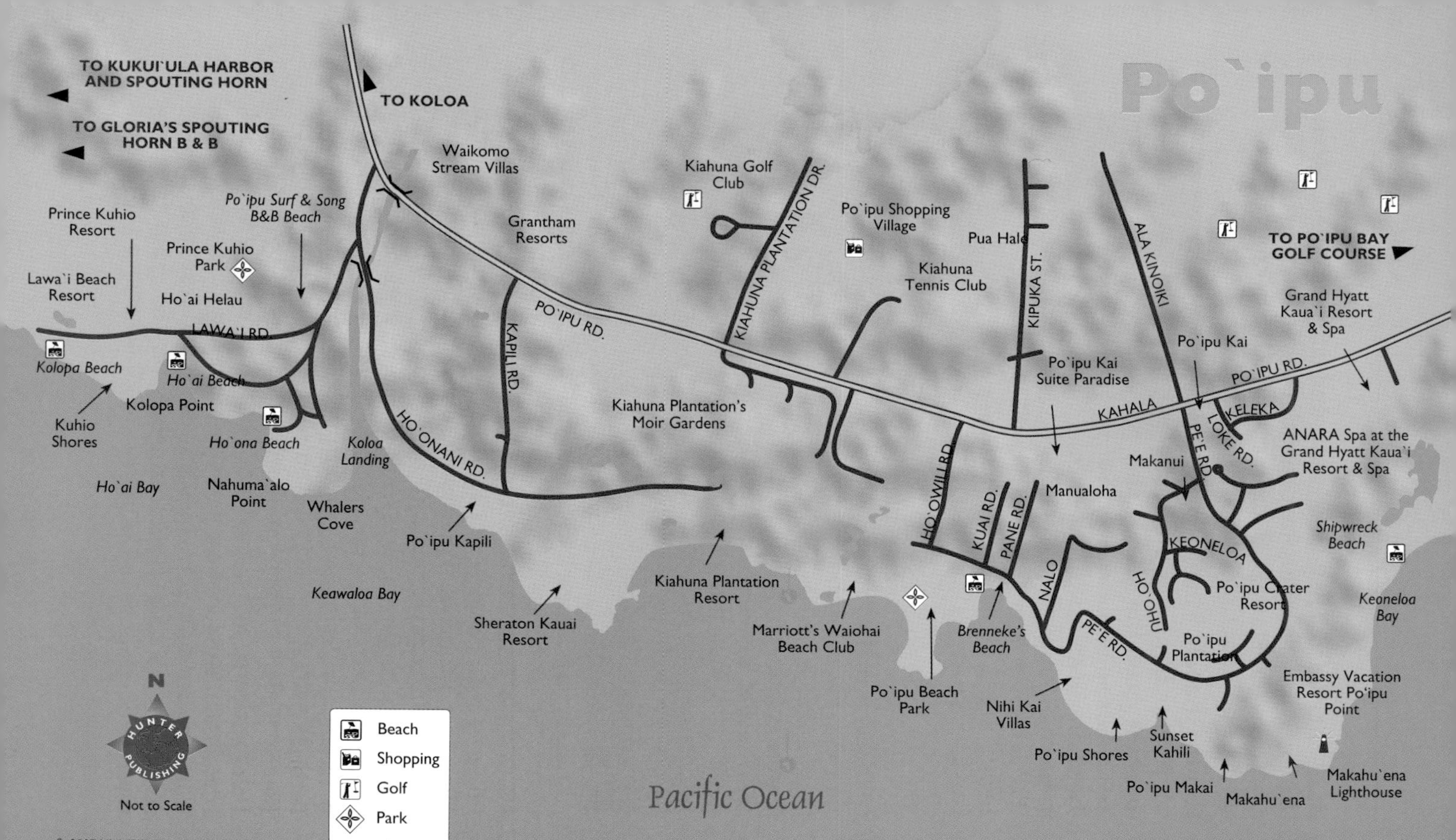
Po`ipu
TO KUKUI`ULA HARBOR AND SPOUTING HORN
TO GLORIA'S SPOUTING HORN B & B
TO KOLOA
TO PO`IPU BAY GOLF COURSE
Waikomo Stream Villas
Kiahuna Golf Club
Po`ipu Surf & Song B&B Beach
Prince Kuhio Resort
Prince Kuhio Park
Grantham Resorts
Po`ipu Shopping Village
Pua Hale
Lawa`i Beach Resort
Ho`ai Helau
Kiahuna Tennis Club
Grand Hyatt Kaua`i Resort & Spa
LAWA`I RD.
KAPILI RD.
PO`IPU RD.
KIAHUNA PLANTATION DR.
KIPUKA ST.
ALA KINOIKI
Po`ipu Kai
Kolopa Beach
Ho`ai Beach
Po`ipu Kai Suite Paradise
Kolopa Point
Kiahuna Plantation's Moir Gardens
KAHALA
KELEKA
LOKE RD.
PE`E RD.
Kuhio Shores
Ho`ona Beach
Koloa Landing
HO`ONANI RD.
ANARA Spa at the Grand Hyatt Kaua`i Resort & Spa
Makanui
Ho`ai Bay
Nahuma`alo Point
Manualoha
Whalers Cove
HO`OWILI RD.
KUAI RD.
PANE RD.
Shipwreck Beach
Po`ipu Kapili
KEONELOA
Kiahuna Plantation Resort
NALO
HO`OHU
Po`ipu Crater Resort
Keoneloa Bay
Keawaloa Bay
Sheraton Kauai Resort
Marriott's Waiohai Beach Club
Brenneke's Beach
PE`E RD.
Po`ipu Plantation
Po`ipu Beach Park
Nihi Kai Villas
Embassy Vacation Resort Po`ipu Point
Sunset Kahili
Po`ipu Shores
Makahu`ena Lighthouse
Po`ipu Makai
Makahu`ena
Pacific Ocean
N
HUNTER PUBLISHING
Not to Scale
Beach
Shopping
Golf
Park

in Koloa. To get there, take Weliweli Road and bear right on Hapa Road. The church will be at the end of the road.

Koloa Landing (shorediving.com)

Koloa Landing, In the mid-1800s, Koloa was a major center of commerce on Kaua`i. It was the third-largest whaling port in the Hawaiian Islands and was the only port used for imports. The landing was used extensively by the sugar industry until 1912.

Po`ipu

Moir Gardens

Moir Gardens is part of the Outrigger Kiahuna Plantation property. The property was once the manger's estate of Koloa Plantation. The gardens were planted by Alexandra Moir, the wife of the plantation manager during the 1930s. There were numerous cacti and orchids planted and they thrived. The garden opened to the public in 1954 and orchids and lily ponds were added. This renowned garden is worth a visit. They are open the public for free.

Prince Kuhio Park

Just west of Po`ipu, you'll see **Prince Kuhio Park**. A monument marks the birthplace of Kaua`i's favorite son, Prince Jonah Kuhio Kalanianaole. Prince Kuhio was the first royal and first Hawaiian in Congress, when he represented the Hawaiian Territory. He was so revered by

Hawaiians, his birthday (March 26) is a state holiday. On the park grounds, you can still see the foundation of the house and remains of a heiau. Kuhio Park is on Lawa`i Road just west of Po`ipu.

National Tropical Botanical Gardens, Lawa`i Road, reservations ☎ 808-742-2623. The entrance is on Lawa`i Road, right across the street from Spouting Horn. This is the only tropical botanical garden with a charter from the United States Congress and it includes McBryde Gardens and Allerton Gardens (see below). You can walk around the grounds here at no charge and browse among the bananas, pineapples and bamboo trees, among many, many other plants. Here is where you can make your reservations for tours of McBryde and Allerton Gardens as well. If you made your reservations by phone (recommended), this is where you'd meet for your tour. The gardens were once owned by Queen Emma in the late 1800s.

McBryde Gardens

- **McBryde Gardens**. Self-guided tours require a 15-minute tram ride to the gardens. Tram rides are daily at 9:30, 10:30, 11:30 am, 12:30, 1:30 and 2:30 pm. Adults $20; children six-12 $10; children five and under are free.

McBryde Gardens has a wonderful collection of Hawaiian plants. It's considered to be the largest collection of native plants in existence. There are also various species of palm trees, coffee, ginger plants and coral trees. The self-guided tour takes approximately 1½ hours.

Allerton Gardens

■ **Allerton Gardens.** Guided tours are held Monday through Saturday at 9 am, 10 am, 1 pm, and 2 pm. Adults $35; Children 10-12 years old $20. This is a stunning estate that is an absolute feast for the eyes. The land lies on 100 acres at the mouth of the Lawa`i Stream. The land belonged to architect Robert Allerton, who designed one wonder after another. You are guided by an incredibly

AUTHOR'S CHOICE ★

Path in Allerton Gardens

knowledgeable tour guide as you stroll through the "rooms." There's the Diana Fountain, which features a statue of the goddess Diana overlooking a reflection pool and fountain. There's the Thanksgiving Room, which used to host the Allterton Thanksgiving feasts. The three pools feature natural waterfalls. You'll also see the huge ficus tree that was featured in *Jurassic Park*. There's a tremendous collection of plants from all over the world that you must see to believe. The tour of Allerton Gardens lasts about 2½ hours.

Spouting Horn

Spouting Horn is part tourist spectacle, part shopping destination and part natural wonder. The phenomenon of Spouting Horn occurs when incoming waves rush through a hole in the rock, then water shoots back out through the hole and creates a crying sound. Legend has it that there's a lizard stuck in the rock who cries when there's an incoming wave. You can frequently see honu (turtles) here and whales during the winter months. People like to venture out on the rocks around the blowhole. I'm certainly not one of them. Please use common sense if you do this. Waves can come up and sweep you into a lava tube or out to sea. Do not, under any circumstances, stand between the blowhole and the ocean.

Kalaheo

Kukuiolono Park. Above the small town of Kalaheo lies this beautiful park adjacent to the Kukuilono Golf Course. Kukuilono means "light of the god Lono" in Hawaiian. There's a walking loop about one mile long that goes through a lava rock garden, a Hawaiian garden and a beautiful Japanese garden with a stone footbridge, sculptures, bonsai trees and fountains overgrown with plants. There are ironwood and eucalyptus trees around the trail. And there are those darn chickens again! You can stop and take in the beautiful scenic views. Kukuilono Park is a very romantic spot for a picnic. Park hours are daily from 7 am-6 pm. The gates close to cars promptly at 6:30. For more information, call ☎ 808-332-9151. The park is on Papalina Road in Kalaheo.

Sightseeing Tours

Hummer Safari

Kaua`i Hummer Safari, 5532 Tapa Street, Koloa ☎ 877-811-9218, 808-639-6695. Archeologist Nancy McMahon will take you on a trip through ancient Hawaiian sites in the luxury and comfort of a Hummer. You'll go through rainforests and see historic sites, waterfalls and polls that you would not be able to get to in your rental car. You'll get a wonderful history lesson from the perspective of an archeologist, which is a treat. The tours are small with a maximum of six people and tours can be customized to suit your needs. The standard tours run two hours and costs $150 per person.

Roberts Hawaii Tours, ☎ 866-898-2519, www.robertshawaii.com, offers bus tours from your hotel to Waimea Canyon. You stop at Spouting Horn and Hanapepe Valley along the way. Tours operate Sunday, Tuesday, Thursday and Saturday. The cost is $44 per person. They also offer a tour of Waimea Canyon and Fern Grotto for $64 per person.

Polynesian Adventure Tours, ☎ 808-246-0122, www.polyad.com, has two tours to Waimea Canyon as well. Their Waimea Canyon Experience Tour operates on Monday, Wednesday, Friday, Sunday. You stop at Spouting Horn, Hanapepe and Fort Elizabeth before reaching Waimea Canyon. The cost is $47 per person. They also offer a second tour that allows you to see sights along the Coconut Coast, such as Opaeka`a Falls and Nawiliwili Harbor for $68 per person.

Kaua`i Movie Tours, ☎ 800-628-8432 or 808-822-1192, www.hawaiimovietours.com, offers highly popular tours around the island in their mobile theater, so you can visit the locations while you're watching the scenes from the films in which they appear. The films and television shows include *Jurassic Park*, *Raiders of the Lost Ark*, *South Pacific*, *Blue Hawaii*, *Gilligan's Island*, *Fantasy Island* and about 30 others. They offer three different types of tours daily, starting at $111 per person.

Aloha Discovery Island Tours, ☎ 877-632-0066, 808-632-0066, has a number of tours that will pick you up in Po`ipu and whisk you off to places like Menehune Fish Pond, Kilohana Plantation, Spouting Horn, Old Koloa Town, Captain Cook's Landing, Waimea Canyon and Menehune Ditch. Aloha Discovery also offers tours of the East Shore or the North Shore and they have land tours combined with a helicopter ride or luau as well. Tour prices start at $69 per person.

■ Adventures

On Land

Hiking

Mahaulepu Trail. At the eastern end of Po`iputhis wonderful hiking trail offers spectacular views. The trail runs mostly along the coast and goes inland in some spots. It passes sand dunes that were formed over thousands of years, heading east past a Hawaiian heiau. There are also fossil remains (look, but don't touch) and archeological sites. The most amazing thing about this area is that it reflects the formation of two major volcanoes. Mahaulepu Trail is about two miles long. The trailhead is at Shipwreck Beach. Go down Ainako Street past the Hyatt Regency.

Guided Hikes

**Kaua`i Nature Tours**, ☎ 888-233-8365 or 808-742-8305, www.kauainaturetours.com, will take you on a 2½-mile walk around Mahaulepu. Led by a scientist or environmentalist, these tours show how the land has changed over thousands of years. Tours depart from Po`ipuand cost $87 per person. You'll get lunch, along with plenty of time for snorkeling and swimming.

If you want to hike with a group, check out the **Sierra Club** at www.hi.sierraclub.org. The Kaua`i chapter regularly schedules group hikes all over the island, including Mahaulepu. There's a $5 donation for the hike. They have a list of upcoming hikes on their website.

Dr. Carl Berg of **Hawaiian Wildlife Tours**, ☎ 808-639-2968, will take you on a personalized tour to see Kaua`i's native and vanishing species, from forest birds and flora to hoary bats, monk seals, and green sea turtles. Rates are $45 per couple, per hour. Reservations one month in advance are recommended.

Anara Spa, www.anaraspa.com, at the Grand Hyatt Resort & Spa, offers morning fitness walks along the grounds of the property. Call ☎ 808-742-1234 for more information.

Horseback Riding

CJM Country Stables, Po`ipu, ☎ 808-742-6096, www.cjmstables.com, takes you on a gorgeous ride along the Mahaleupu shoreline. The scenery is stunning as you ride through pastures and along beaches. They have a couple of tours available. The first is a morning ride that traverses the beach with plenty of photo opportunities. This three-hour tour is only offered on Tuesday, Thursday and Saturday and costs $105 per person. They have a shorter ride that costs $90 per person. CJM also hosts a monthly rodeo, which is free to the public. Call for more information.

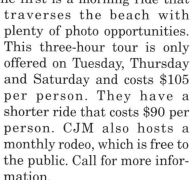

Outfitters Kaua`i zipline

Zipline

**Outfitters Kaua`i**, 2827A Po`ipu Road, Po`ipu, ☎ 888-742-9887, 808-742-9667, has a zipline trek that's good if you're a beginner or if you're afraid of heights. You meet at the Outfitters Kaua`i office in Po`ipu and they take you on a van to Kipu Ranch. There, you're be briefed on safety, you get your gear and you zip about 300 feet, returning to your starting point by going over a wicked little suspension bridge. You'll do this two more times and then take a hike over to Kipu Falls for swimming and jumping from rope swing. This zipline is fun, but I was expecting more than one zipline and more of an adventure. The three-hour tour costs $115 per person. If you want more of an adventure, try the Kipu Falls Safari Tour, which includes a two-mile kayak ride, hiking and ziplining for $155 per person.

Tennis

In the immediate Po`ipu area, most condominium and hotels have tennis courts on the premises. If you want to have a really special game, go to the **Grand Hyatt Resort and Spa**, ☎ 808-742-1234, www.kauai.hyatt.com. The resort has four courts available for $30 an hour. Reservations are required. There's also a pro shop and lessons are given.

Kiahuna Swim and Tennis Club, ☎ 808-742-9533, offers 10 courts for rent at $10 an hour. They have both hard and synthetic grass courts. The pro shop stocks tennis attire and balls, also providing racquet rentals, racquet re-stringing, and lessons with the tennis pro.

If you don't want to pay for tennis there are two options at no charge.

Koloa Park has two lighted courts. You can find them on Maluhia Road. If you're heading west on Kaumualii Highway, turn left onto Maluhia Road to Koloa Town. You'll find the courts on the left almost at the end of road before Koloa Town.

Kalawai Park in Kalaheo also has two lighted courts. To find the courts, drive west on Kaumualii Highway, turn right on Puuwai Road and then right again almost immediately, staying on Puuwai Road. The courts are in Kalawai Park on the left side.

Golf

Po`ipu Bay Golf Course, 2250 Ainako Street, Koloa (across from Grand Hyatt Resort & Spa), ☎ 800-858-6300, 808-742-8711, www.poipubaygolf.

Po`ipu Bay Golf Course

com. 18 holes, 7,123 yards, par 72; greens fees $185 (includes cart), after 12 pm $125, after 2:30 $72. Po`ipu Bay Golf Course offers the best in championship golf. It has numerous awards from golf and travel magazines and has hosted the PGA Grand Slam of Golf every year since 1994. Designed by Robert Trent Jones, the course is a real treat. The setting is beautiful. You have the ocean on one side and spectacular mountain views on the other. There is a heiau at hole 16. You might get distracted by the ocean views and could probably spot a green sea turtle or a humpback whale if you looked carefully.

Phil Mickelson set the Po`ipu Golf Course record in the 2004 PGA Grand Slam of Golf. His score for the day: 59.

Po`ipu Bay offers a daily clinic for $35 and lessons for $40 per half-hour. The clubhouse has excellent pro shop locker facilites and club storage. If this place is good enough for the likes of Tiger Woods, Ernie Els, Vijay Singh and Phil Mickelson, it's good enough for you.

Grand Hyatt Resort & Spa has a professional golf shop in the hotel lobby. Here you can buy a variety of golf equipment and apparel. The shop is open from 8 am-6 pm.

Kiahuna Golf Club, 2545 Kiahuna Plantation Drive, Po`ipu, ☎ 808-742-9595, www.kiahunagolf.com. Greens fees $110 (with cart), 16 and under $75, after 2 pm $75; 18 holes, 6,885 yards, par 70. Robert Trent Jones, Jr. took great care in designing this course. It includes sites of historic interest such as a heiau, and the remains of a Portuguese house and crypt. Kiahuna has five sets of tees, even tees for junior players (the only junior tees in Hawaii). Players at all levels will enjoy the challenges posed by water hazards and tradewinds.

Kiahuna Golf Club, 10th hole

Kiahuna has a fully stocked pro shop. You can take golf lessons here and there's also a driving range on-site.

Kukuilono Golf Course, Papalina Road, Po`ipu, ☎ 808-332-9151; greens fees $7 per day, kids 17 and under $3 per day; cart fee $6 per nine holes; nine holes, 3,077 yards, par 36. Kukuilono Golf Course is a public course that was built in 1929 by Walter McBryde. It was the second course on Kaua`i, behind Wailua Golf Course. McBryde donated the land to the state and the golf course is now among the most beautiful and least expensive in the entire state. He's actually buried by the eighth hole. This is a great course for beginners and hackers alike. There aren't that many hazards. Experienced golfers will enjoy the views. The course overlooks the plains and ocean. Wind definitely becomes a factor here.

This area is also home to **Kukuilono Park**, which features stunning views and a small Japanese garden. Take a walk through when you're done with your round. Tee times start at 7 am sharp. Greens fees are an unbelievably low $7 per day. You can't beat it.

Biking

The best area for biking here is **Mahaulepu**. It's two miles from the end of Po`ipu Road. Keep heading east on the dirt road. You'll get to a main intersection, where you turn right. The trail passes sand dunes that were formed over thousands of years, heading east past a heiau (temple). There are also fossil remains (look, but don't touch) and archeological sites.

There are plenty of old dirt plantation roads in this area that are worth exploring on a mountain bike. The trails are fast and flat, making very easy and fun riding.

Regular road riding isn't bad in the area either. You can ride the 10-mile **Koloa Heritage Trail**, which winds from Koloa to the Po`ipu Resort area. There is a bit of traffic, especially heading toward Spouting Horn. Just be aware and use common sense. Make sure you have a lock with you because you're going to want to go for a swim.

**Outfitters Kaua`i**, Po`ipu Plaza, 2827A Po`ipu Road, Po`ipu, ☎ 888-742-9887, 808-742-9667, www.outfitterskauai.com, rents cruisers for $20 per day, mountain bikes starting at $39 for adults, or $20 for kids. They also carry baby seats. They give discounts for longer-term rentals. Ask before you reserve your bike. They're also friendly in the shop and like to tell folks where to go. They have maps available.

Some hotels and condo resorts offer bicycle rentals. Ask before you book your accommodations.

ATVs

Kaua`i ATV, 5330 Koloa Road, Koloa, ☎ 877-707-7088, 808-742-2734, has two tours in its repertoire. The first is a three-hour tour that takes you through sugar fields, former film locations and past Waita Reservoir. This tour costs $99. The second one is a four-hour tour through the Haupu Valley to Kahili Mountain. Along the way, you'll go through an old cane tunnel (headlights provided) and if it's been raining, you'll get down and dirty in the mud. There's an area they call the "mud splash" that's a lot of fun. You'll end up at Kahili Falls, which is a very pretty swimming area. If you're afraid of getting your clothes dirty, they do provide rental clothes. The four-hour tour costs $145 per person. You'll ride on a Yamaha ATV, with an option to ride in a two-person or six-person dune buggy. If you didn't bring your camera, they will have photo CDs of your tour available for purchase afterwards.

Po`ipu Beach

On Water

Beaches

Po`ipu Beach County Park

Two of the most popular, and safest, beaches are within the park: Brennecke's Beach and Po`ipu Beach. The park has a huge lawn area, with many palm trees. At Po`ipu Beach the waters are clear and safe for all kinds of activities: swimming, snorkeling, surfing and body boarding. There's a natural wading pool that's perfect for toddlers and younger children. It does get crowded with tourists and locals alike, especially on weekends. There are facilities here such as restrooms, parking, showers and lifeguards. Restaurants and convenience stores are also nearby. The area is lined with picnic pavilions, which make it an excellent spot for lunch.

If kids don't want to play in the water, there's a small playground at the park for their amusement.

Snorkel equipment, body boards, surfboards and other beach equipment can be rented at nearby Nukumoi Surf Company or Brennecke's. Plus, there's plenty of free parking available. This is a great spot to catch the sunset. The beach park is located at Hoowili and Po`ipu Beach Roads.

HAWAIIAN MONK SEALS & HONU

You may very well spot a Hawaiian monk seal at the beach. Remember that it's illegal to approach or harass this critically endangered animal. Visit www.kauaimonkseal.com for more information about these amazing animals.

Green sea turtles are also abundant in the area. They have been endangered since 1979. It is against the law to touch or otherwise harass them. If you see one while snorkeling, give it 10-15 feet of space.

Brennecke's Beach

This popular beach lies at the eastern end of Po`ipu Beach Country Park. The small beach is especially popular with surfers and body boarders. Don't let that discourage you from swimming. Surfers and body boarders are only permitted to do their thing well offshore, making the beach safer for swimmers and snorkelers.

Brennecke's Beach

The beach is named for Dr. Marvin Brennecke. He came to Kaua`i in 1931 and was the plantation doctor on Lihue Plantation. For years, he owned a home adjacent to the park. Over the years, the home became a landmark and was destroyed by Hurricaine Iwa in 1982. It was never rebuilt. The county later acquired the land to expand the park. The beach itself was decimated by Hurricane Iniki 10 years later.

Shipwreck Beach (Keoniloa Beach)

Shipwreck Beach was named after an unidentified ship that lay in the waters here until Hurricane Iwa destroyed its remains. It's a very popular site for experienced surfers, body boarders and windsurfers. Swimming at Shipwreck Beach is iffy at best because of the strong currents. There's a cliff that is a popular site with local fishermen. You'll even see kids jumping off the cliff into the water (not recommended). The beach is in front of the Grand Hyatt Resort & Spa. There's a public access way between the Hyatt and Po`ipu Bay Golf Course.

Mahaulepu Beach

Mahaulepu Beach

Mahaulepu Beach is a two-mile stretch of coastline that is made up of three smaller beaches: Gillin's Beach, Kawailoa Bay and Haula Beach. The area is pristine, as local residents have fought off development for years. A majority of the land is owned by Grove Farm Properties, which is in turn owned by former AOL/Time Warner Chairman Steve Case. The area is coveted not only for its beauty, but for its scientific and archeological significance. Geological history is preserved in the rock formations and there are fossils in the sand dunes. You can make a day out of exploring this beautiful area. It's well worth the time spent.

Starting at the easternmost end, **Haula Beach** is very secluded. The swimming here is pretty dangerous, but the scenery that surrounds you and the isolation from the hustle and bustle of the resort area makes the trip out here worthwhile.

Kawailoa Bay is one of the most romantic spots on the island. It's also another spot for windsurfers. **Gillin's Beach** is named after a former engineer at Koloa Sugar Plantation who built a house there in the 1940s. The original house is long gone, but there's a new house there that is available for vacation rentals (see *Vacation Rentals* later in this chapter). The area is not for swimming, but great for a romantic stroll along the beach.

Prince Kuhio Beach

This beach is located on the east side of Kuhio Shores Condominiums. It's a small beach with a rocky bottom. Snorkeling and diving are excellent here. It's very common to see green sea turtles. Swimming isn't so great because the bottom is too rocky.

Prince Kuhio Beach *(shorediving.com)*

Lawa`i Beach

Lawa`i Beach (Hawaiian Images)

On the west side of Kuhio Shores is Lawa`i Beach. It also fronts The Beach House Restaurant. This is another fantastic spot for snorkeling and is home to three major surf spots: **PK's**, **Centers** and **Acid Drop**. Surfers and body boarders frequent the area.

Snorkeling

Kaua`i Seariders Adventures, www.kauaiseariders.com, ☎ 808-332-7238, offers a three-hour tour on their rigid-hull inflatable. The tour includes snorkeling and lunch. Rates are $89 for adults and $69 for children ages five-12.

**SeaFun Kaua`i**, from Aloha Kaua`i Tours, ☎ 800 452-1113, www.alohakauaitours.com, offers guided snorkel tours. You'll

learn about the history of the island and the area on your way to Lawa`i Beach. You snorkel here for about 45 minutes, looking at butterfly fish, tangs and surgeon fish, wrasses and puffers. It's a good snorkel to get you started. Once you're warmed up, you head over to Prince Kuhio Beach for a more advanced snorkel.

Kaua`i Z Tours, Kukuiula Harbor, ☎ 888-998-6879, 808-742-7422, www.ztourz.com, has tours that specialize in snorkeling. They welcome novice snorkelers and take you to different locations along the south shore. Tours start at $84 per person. They also offer private charters.

If you want to snorkel on your own, you can pick up snorkeling gear virtually anywhere. **Nukumoi Surf Company**, ☎ 808-742-8019, across from Brennecke's Beach, rents snorkel gear (snorkel, mask and fins) for $5 a day and $15 a week. **Kaua`i Down Under**, at Sheraton Kaua`i Resort, and **Brennecke's Beach Center**, at Brennecke's Beach, also rent gear. Or you can check with your hotel or condo. Some places do have snorkel gear available for their guests.

The south shore offers some of the best snorkeling on Kaua`i because the water is so clear. There's very little runoff in these waters. It doesn't rain a lot on the south shore so visibility isn't affected.

You'll find that Po`ipu Beach Park has some good snorkeling to the right side of **Nukumoi Point**, the **tombolo area** (a narrow strip of sand dividing the ocean). It's full of turtles, tangs, butterfly fish and the full gamut of tropical fish.

Behind the Sheraton Kaua`i is **Kiahuna Beach**. The eastern end is protected for snorkeling. It is a bit rocky on the bottom.

Lawa`i Beach has excellent snorkeling. The reef is about 50 yards from shore and you'll find a cornucopia of tropical fish. Green turtles and the occasional Hawaiian monk seal come here to enjoy the sunshine. There's a sandy bottom near The Beach House Restaurant. This is the best spot to enter the water.

Prince Kuhio Park has snorkeling that's just as good as Lawa`i Beach. You will find that the reefs are deeper and more developed.

Brennecke's is very popular for a lot of water activities. If you plan to snorkel here, be on the lookout for body boarders. Also watch out for the undertow, which can get pretty strong.

Before you hit the water, you might want to bring a disposable underwater camera. For $12-$16 you can pick one up. The cameras are surprisingly easy to manage underwater and take decent pictures as long as the water's not too murky. You can buy one at Brennecke's Deli, Nukumoi Surf Co. and virtually any grocery store.

Surfing

Surf's up all along the South Shore! The Po`ipu area offers numerous places to surf, as the waters of the South Shore are much calmer than the North Shore. During the winter months, the waves tend to be very calm, so first time surfers won't be intimidated. In summer, the waters remain calm, with the occasional "south swell" coming on shore, but the waves are still pretty manageable for first-time surfers. Intermediate and advanced surfers will absolutely love the south swells. No matter what your level is, you will become addicted to surfing the world-class waves.

If you want to experience surfing on your own, the best spots are at Lawa`i Beach and a break called Lemon Drops.

Lawai Beach is home to the surf spot known as "Acid Drop." It looks easy from shore but it'll chop you up like "acid" once you get out there. It's also home to two other popular surf breaks, **PKs** and **Centers**. The breaks here are pretty localized, so if you don't know what you're doing out on the water, you're better off at Po`ipu Beach Park.

Board rentals are abundant along the beaches. A few good places to start for board rentals are **Nukumoi Surf Company**, 2100 Hoone Road Po`ipu, ☎ 808-742-8019, which rents soft boards for beginners at $5 per hour, $20 per day or $60 per week. Experienced surfers can rent fiberglass boards for $7.50 per hour, $30 per day or $80 per week.

There are plenty of places in the Po`ipu area that offer surf instruction. **Po`ipu Beach Surf School**, ☎ 808-652-9590, has private and group lessons available. The lessons are geared for beginners. They also rent boards.

Surfing lesson

Kaua`i Surf School runs their operation through Nukumoi Surf Shop. They break up your two-hour lesson with a half-hour of instruction on land, then you get to spend the next hour in the water putting what you learned to use. The final half-hour is spent with more practice. Lessons are held throughout the day in Po`ipu and cost $60 for a two-hour group lesson. A two-hour private one-on-one lesson is also available for $100. Call for reservations at ☎ 808-651-6032 or 808-742-8019.

If you really want to build up your surfing skills, you can take the seven-day **Kaua`i Surf Clinic**. It's meant for beginners and intermediate surfers, with each one-hour lesson building on what you learned the day before. You then practice in the water for the rest of the day. I could think of worse ways to spend a vacation. The clinics are held throughout the year. Call ☎ 808-651-6032 or 808-742-8019 for more information.

AUTHOR'S CHOICE ★ Perhaps the best known surf school is **Margo Oberg Surfing School**, Kapili Road, Po`ipu, ☎ 808-332-6100, 808-639-0708. Owned and operated by California native Margo Oberg, this school has been in operation since 1977. Margo is a former professional surfer and won the first of her seven Women's World Surfing titles when she was only 15. A 1½-hour group lesson starts at $60 per person. Two-hour private lessons are $100.

Aloha Surf Lessons, ☎ 808-639-8614, is owned and operated by Kaua`i's own professional surfer (one of Kaua`i's many professional surfers), Chava Greenlee. They have two-hour lessons. The first hour is instruction and the second hour is spent surfing on your own. Lessons are offered for beginners (kids are more than welcome to surf) all the way up to experts. The two-hour lesson is $50 per person. Private lessons are also available.

Garden Island Surf School, Hoonani Road, Po`ipu, ☎ 808-652-4841, www.gardenislandsufschool.com, has two-hour lessons but here you spend 1½ hours with personalized instruction and a half-hour on your own. They specialize in teaching beginners how to surf, but do offer instruction for intermediate and advanced surfers. The beginner lesson is $75 per person.

Body Boarding

The South Shore of Kaua`i is a body boarder's dream. The best time to body board here is in the summer, when the south swells create the juiciest waves. Of course, with that comes your warning about rip currents forming offshore. It's very common to see lifeguards and fire trucks making rescues during this time of year. Check with lifeguards about the conditions before you go out.

The best place to go body boarding is **Po`ipu Beach Park**. The break at **Brennecke's** on the eastern end of the beach park is forgiving and very easy.

There are plenty of places to rent body boards. You can start with **Nukumoi Surf Company**, 2100 Hoone Road, Po`ipu, ☎ 808-742-8019, which rents boards for $5 a day or $24 a week.

If you're renting a condo, you might want to check to see if they have body boards for your use. Some hotels also have body boards available for their guests.

Kayaking

In the winter months, the surf is too rough on the North Shore. This means that kayakers will come down to the Po`ipu area for the calm waters and great kayaking.

**Kayak Kaua`i**, Kuhio Highway, Wailua, ☎ 800-437-3507, 808-826-9844, does a tour of the South Shore. You launch in Po`ipu and paddle west past Spouting Horn, Lawa`i Valley, the unusual Nomilo Pond, and Wahiawa Cove to Port Allen. You paddle for over eight miles. It's not for the faint of heart. These tours are run from October-April (weather permitting). This is the prime time of year to see whales breaching the water as you paddle. Check with Kayak Kaua`i in advance, as they need a minimum of four people for the tour. This all-day excursion costs $145 per person.

**Outfitters Kaua`i**, 2827A Po`ipu Road, Po`ipu Plaza, ☎ 808-742-9667, 888-742-9887, also takes you on a journey along the South Shore from Po`ipu to Port Allen. This tour is eight miles as well. You launch from Kukuiula Harbor, pass Spouting Horn and land at Lawa`i Kai on the grounds of Allerton Gardens. You then continue on to Port Allen. It's run from mid-September through mid-May for $135 per person.

During the summer, Outfitters Kaua`i has an all-day excursion to the Na Pali coast. You'll meet at their office in Po`ipu, where you hop in a van to Haena. You launch there and paddle 15 grueling miles along the beautiful Na Pali coast to Polihale State Park. A van will meet you there and take you back to Po`ipu. You must be in excellent physical shape for this paddle. This tour costs $185 per person.

If you want to rent a kayak, Outfitters Kaua`i can help you out with that as well. They rent primarily for the Wailua or Huleia rivers at $40 per person per day.

Windsurfing

Windsurfing pro

If you're a beginner, windsurfing opportunities are a bit limited on the South Shore. Experienced windsurfers will have a field day in the area. Places like **Shipwreck's Beach** and all throughout the **Mahaulepu** area are great spots if you know what you're doing. If you're a beginner and want to learn, your best bet is to head up to **Anini Beach** on the North Shore and take lessons from **Windsurf Kaua`i**, ☎ 808-828-6838. Anini Beach is much more forgiving for beginners.

Snuba

**Snuba Tours of Kaua`i**, Po`ipu, ☎ 808-823-8912, www.snubakauai.com. Snuba? What's that? This is a shallow diving system that combines the best of the snorkeling and scuba worlds. It was created for people who like snorkeling and want to take it a step further underwater. You're attached to a floating scuba tank through a 20-foot air line that allows you to move around. You can also get closer to the deeper reefs and marine life. You do need basic swimming skills to snuba and have to be at least eight years old. They dive off of **Lawa`i Beach** in Po`ipu. During the 1½-hour tour, you spend about 30 minutes in the water. The cost is $65 per person.

Scuba

If you're going on a guided dive, one place they'll probably stop is at **Sheraton Caverns**. This is one amazing dive. There are three lava tubes that connect to a wall. There's a haven of marine life here. Octopi, turtes, eels, schools of tropical fish. This is paradise!

**Kaua`i Down Under**, Sheraton Kaua`i Resort, ☎ 808-742-9255, www.kauaidownunderscuba.com, has a number of dives for beginners and experienced divers. For beginners, they start you off in the pool for instruction and then send you into the ocean for a one-tank dive. If you want to get certified, they can help you with that as well. They offer guided dives, night dives and review dives. For experienced divers, you can stop by the shop to rent gear. The staff is pretty knowledgeable and will direct you to different dive sites.

Mana Divers, Ele`ele and Po`ipu, ☎ 877-348-3669, 808-335-0881, www.manadivers.com, has a number of opportunities for diving, even if you're a beginner. They offer introductory dive courses all the way through PADI (Professional Association of Diving Instructors) certification and specialty classes. The classes are geared more for the experienced diver. They offer Scuba Diver certification courses over two days, as well as a PADI Divemaster course. If you're staying at the Grand Hyatt Kaua`i in Po`ipu or Kaua`i Marriott in Lihu`e, they offer introductory classes in the pool.

Dive Kaua`i Scuba Center, 1038 Kuhio Highway, ☎ 808-822-0452, www.divekauai.com, has all of the gear you need. You can rent tanks, wetsuits, weight belts and much more. They offer introductory shore dives for $105 (one-tank dive) and $140 (two-tank dive). If you're already certified, they have shore dives and boat dives starting at $90. They also do night dives and offer PADI certification courses. They're certainly worth checking out if you have any interest in diving during your stay.

Seasport Divers boat

Seasport Divers, 2827 Po`ipu Road, Po`ipu, ☎ 808-832-9222, 808-742-9303, www.seasportdivers.com, offers dives for anyone and everyone. If you're a beginner, they have a class where they start you off in a pool, then head out on a one-tank shore dive or a two-tank boat trip. They offer shore dives at Koloa Landing. Experienced divers should check out the morning dives to various points along the South Shore. They also rent all the gear you need, including weight belts, tanks, regulators and wet suits

Fathom Five Divers, 3450 Po`ipu Road, ☎ 808-742-6991, starts out with introductory classes that include shore dives at either Koloa Landing or Tunnels on the North Shore. There are introductory boat dives as well. If you're already a certifies diver, there are a number of one- and two-tank boat dives. Dives are in the morning, afternoon or at night. During the summer, you can take the ultimate dive to Ni`ihau. Fathom Five will take you out on a three-tank dive to Lehua and other sites off the coast of Ni`ihau. They also have certifications for Padi Divemaster and Rescue Diver.

If you plan to dive on your own, **Po`ipu Beach**, **Lawa`i Beach** and **Koloa Landing** are good spots for shore dives. Po`ipu and Lawa`i Beaches are better for beginners, while Koloa Landing is more appropriate for experienced divers.

Whale-Watching

The South Shore of Kaua`i has plenty of whale-watching, both from land and sea. The best time to view whales is between November and March, with the peak season in February. The best places in the area are **Mahaulepu**, **Po`ipu Beach Park**, **Lawa`i Beach** and **Spouting Horn**.

If you want to get a little closer, you can take a whale-watching tour. Most launch from Port Allen (see *The West Shore*) and there are a few that launch from Po`ipu.

Kaua`i Seariders Adventures, www.kauaiseariders.com, ☎ 808-332-7238, has a three-hour tour on their rigid-hull inflatable. The tour includes snorkeling and lunch.

Kaua`i Z Tours, Kukuiula Harbor, ☎ 888-998-6879, 808-742-7422, www.ztourz.com, offers whale-watching during their snorkel tours. See *Snorkeling* for more information.

During the winter, **Na Pali Riders**, ☎ 808-742-6331, www.napaliriders.com, runs whale-watching tours out to Kipu Kai on their rigid-hull inflatable.

Sunset Cruises

There's nothing more romantic than watching the sunset whie you're sailing. There are plenty of sunset cruises. Most leave from Port Allen and head up the Na Pali Coast. However, there are a couple of companies that take the journey around the Po`ipu Coast.

Blue Dolphin Charters, ☎ 808-335-5553, 877-511-1311, Port Allen, www.kauaiboats.com, has a sunset cruise that sails around the Po`ipu area. This two-hour cruise includes dinner, drinks and live music and is available only in the summer. $95 per person. They also have a year-round cruise around Na Pali for $116 per person.

Blue Dolphin Charters

Captain Andy's, ☎ 800-535-0830, 808-335-6833, www.napali.com, Port Allen, takes you on their 55-foot catamaran for a sunset cruise along the South Shore off of Po`ipu. The ride takes you toward Maha-ulepu and Kipu Kai. This is a basic tour that includes cocktails, but the choices are limited. They do have musicians playing Hawaiian music throughout the cruise. $69 per person.

Captain Andy's catamaran

Fishing

Sport Fishing Kaua`i, ☎ 808-742-7013, www.fishing-kauai-hawaii.com, will take you on a trip to catch Pacific blue marlin, ahi (yellow fin tuna), and mahi-mahi. They have private or shared charters starting at $95. Even if you're a beginner, the crew will show you how to catch the big one.

Cast & Catch, ☎ 808-332-9707, has freshwater bass fishing guides that will take you to reservoirs around the island on their 18-foot bass boat. They'll also help you get your freshwater fishing license. **Waita Reservoir** is a good spot for largemouth bass, peacock bass and smallmouth bass.

Make sure that you have all of the proper licenses if you plan to do any freshwater fishing. Before your trip, you can go online to obtain a freshwater fishing license at www.ehawaii.gov/dlnr/fish/exe/fresh_main_page.cgi. You fill out the information, print, sign and you're all set. If you don't get a chance to do this before you leave for your trip, **Lihue Fishing Supply**, ☎ 808-245-4930, and **Waipouli Variety Store**, in Kapa`a, ☎ 808-822-1014, can handle it for you. Fees are $25 for a non-resident license, which is good for one-year. You can purchase a seven-day tourist license for $10 or a 30-day tourist license for $20.

Check with the Department of Land and Natural Resources, Division of Aquatic Resources office, at ☎ 808-274-3344, before you head out. You can also find them online at www.hawaii.gov/dlnr/dar/index.html.

■ Spas

AUTHOR'S CHOICE ★

Anara Spa, Grand Hyatt Resort & Spa, Po`ipu, ☎ 808-742-1234, is a huge 45,000-square-foot facility in the Grand Hyatt Kaua`i. They have four Jacuzzis, massage rooms that face a private garden, open lava rock showers. This elegant place will melt any stress away. You can get a massage, facial, body treatment or workout in the newly expanded fitness center. Anara Spa has a three-lane 25-foot swimming pool if you prefer to swim laps, as opposed to swimming in the open ocean. A café is on-site where you can munch on fruit, granola and salads. The staff and atmosphere give you a first-class spa experience you won't get anywhere else on the island.

Anara Spa

Pool at Anara Spa

If you don't want to venture to a

spa, **Kaua`i Massage**, ☎ 808-651-2572, offers massages. They'll bring their tables to you for Lomi-Lomi, Swedish, myofascial release or sports treatments.

■ Shopping

Shopping in the Po`ipu Resort area is an interesting experience. You have countless shops, farmer's markets, the market at Spouting Horn and shopping in Koloa Town and Po`ipu Shopping Village. There are also fine shops at resorts such as the Hyatt.

Old Koloa Town takes you back 150 years as you stroll through the area. As the sugar industry waned and tourism picked up, these old plantation buildings were renovated and turned into a quaint shopping experience.

There are a number of restaurants and services here in the center. **Tomcats Grille**, **Pizzetta** and **Lappert's Ice Cream** all consider Old Koloa Town home.

Carved turtle from Christian Riso

Christian Riso Fine Art & Framing, ☎ 808-742-2555, www.christianrisofineart.com, specializes in Hawaiian and tropical art. He represents artists such as Kim Starr and Kerry Oda.

At **Island Soap and Candleworks**, ☎ 808-742-1945, www.kauaisoap.com, you can see how they use local ingredients like macadamia nut and kukui nut oils to make soaps, lotions and other health and beauty products. My favorites are the Morning Mint and Hawaiian Sea soaps. Both smell great and are good for your skin. Open from 9 am-9 pm daily.

Work of Timothy Parsons at Kebanu Gallery

Kebanu Gallery, ☎ 808-742-2727, features fine pieces of pottery, sculpture, and hand-blown glass. The art is unique and attractive. **Crazy Shirts**,

☎ 808-742-9000 , www.crazyshirts.com, has quality t-shirts that are dyed with clever designs. The shirts are dyed in red dirt, beer, chocolate, wine and coffee.

Po`ipu Shopping Village is basically a strip mall. There are fine dining options like **Roy's**, **Keoki's Paradise** or **Puka Dogs**. There is also much shopping to be done.

Na Hoku Po`ipu Shopping Village, ☎ 808-742-7025, is part of a chain that's been around Hawaii since 1924. They create elegant tropical designs and have Tahitian pearls, diamonds, bracelets, or you can buy a Hawaiian slipper pendant.

Overboard Clothing, ☎ 808-742-1299, carries a nice selection of men's and women's swimwear, casual wear and accessories. They have brands such as Tommy Bahama, Tori Richard, Quicksilver and Kohala. Other Overboard stores are in Hanalei and Kapa`a.

Sand People, ☎ 808-742-2288 carries an eclectic mix of gifts. They also have casual clothing. Next door is **Sand Kids**, which is a children's shop with a variety of clothing, beachwear, games, toys and footwear.

Making Waves, ☎ 808-742-6899, features a large selection of swimwear and beach accessories for men, women, juniors and children. They carry the latest releases feom the top designers, such as Jantzen, Tommy Bahama and Roxy.

Kaleidescope Galleries of the Pacific (formerly Kahn Galleries), ☎ 808-822-3636, features the work of artists from Kaua`i and all over the globe. The gallery also has bronze sculptures and handcrafted koa pieces.

Sunthreads, ☎ 808-742-1115, is a small boutique with the latest in ready-to-wear ladies' and juniors' clothing, hats, and fashion jewelry. The hats are colorful and tasteful.

Honolua Surf Co., ☎ 808-742-9152, www.honoluasurf.com, is a surf apparel shop. You'll find clothes and accessories. There's also **Honolua Wahine**, ☎ 808-742-7567, which is a surf apparel shop just for women.

The shops at the **Grand Hyatt Resort & Spa** are notable. I was surprised to see such high-quality stores in a hotel. The stores here are generally open from 9 am-9 pm daily. You can stop at **Na Hoku** for diamonds, Tahitian pearls (also check out their shop in Po`ipu Village Shopping Center). They carry Cartier, Carrera and Jose Hess as well.

Collectors Fine Art of Hawaii has original wall art, handblown glass, bronze sculptures, as well as acrylic and wooden pieces by local and international artists. They also represent the fine art division of Disney, Inc.

Lamont's Gift Shop offers a wide range of clothing, accessories and jewelry, as well as a selection of gifts and sundries, snacks and cold drinks. The **Sandal Tree** has lots of fun and funky footwear for men and women. They carry stylish sandals and high heels, handbags and hats. They represent designers such as Arch, Donald Piner, Mephisto and many others.

Reyn's is the place to go for high-quality aloha shirts and aloha wear. For really nice Hawaiian quilts, check out the **Hawaiian Quilt Collection**, which carries bedspreads, wall quilts and ceramics.

Kohala Bay Collections is a great store if you want something sophisticated yet casual (perfect resort wear). They carry brands like Tommy Bahama, Tori Richard and Polo by Ralph Lauren.

Nukumoi Surf Shop, ☎ 808-742-8019, www.nukumoisurf.com, across from Brennecke's Beach, is the surf shop of the South Shore. They have everything you need, with a sweet selection of long boards, short boards and body boards. They also carry beach chairs, rash guards and a large selection of surf apparel.

Over by Spouting Horn is one of the better places to shop. It's an outdoor swap meet (**flea market**) with vendors selling jewelry, gifts, clothes and t-shirts. The souvenirs are of good quality and they tend to be much less expensive than most stores.

Groceries

If you need to pick up groceries, you're in luck. There are quite a number of places to try. And there's also a health food store in the area.

Brennecke's Beach Deli, 2100 Hoone Road, Po`ipu Beach, ☎ 808-742-1582, www.brenneckes.com, has a small store that carries film, batteries, beach equipment and everything else you'd need for your day at the beach. They also serve shave ice for the kids and sandwiches to go.

Sueoka Store, Koloa Road, Koloa ☎ 808-742-1611, is an old-time mom-and-pop grocery store that's been in business since 1916. They carry a variety of Kaua`i-made products such as Kaua`i coffee. They also sell Kaua`i-grown produce and flowers. Next door is **Sueoka's Snack Shop**, which serves plate lunches and other local foods.

Koloa Fish Market, ☎ 808-742-6199, is in Old Koloa Town, right across from Koloa Post Office. Here you can pick up all kinds of fresh seafood: smoked fish, ahi poke, sashimi, seared ahi. You can also get party pupu platters. Koloa Fish Market has some of the best plate lunches around. They have specials daily.

Big Save, ☎ 808-742-1614, also on Koloa Road and it's well stocked with anything you'd need for cooking a nice dinner.

Kukuiula Store, ☎ 808-742-1601, in Po`ipu Plaza (next to Outfitters Kaua`i), has all of the typical convenience store items plus anything and everything else that you might need for that picnic on the beach.

Koloa Natural Store, ☎ 808-742-8910, in Old Koloa Town, has a good selection of health food and organic items. This sure will save you time since you no longer have to head all the way up to Kapa`a to get health food.

Whaler's General Store, ☎ 808-742-9431, has a large selection of groceries, snacks, liquor, cosmetics, sundries, suntan lotion, film, gifts, souvenirs and beach accessories. They are located in Po`ipu Shopping Village.

Finally, the **farmers' markets** are all over the area throughout the week. Every day, there's a market held by the West Kaua`i Agricultural Association in Po`ipu. You can find it at Po`ipu Road and Cane Haul Road. The other daily market is at Koloa Bypass Road, held by the Koloa Haupu Growers. Monday at Koloa Ball Park, you should be ready to go right at noon. That's when the market starts and people start lining up beforehand to get in. It's kind of like a mad Christmas dash. Kalaheo Neighborhood Center, off of Papalina Road, hosts a market Tuesday at 3:30.

Where To Stay

Resort

AUTHOR'S CHOICE ★

Grand Hyatt Resort & Spa, 1571 Po`ipu Road, Po`ipu, ☎ 808-742-1234, hawaii.hyatt.com. From the moment you enter the lobby, you'll feel like royalty as you walk around this palatial hotel. It brings back the old-time feel of Kaua`i. It's simply a beautiful place to be. The lobby is open, which allows the breezes to come right in off the ocean. The 50-acre grounds are massive and pristine. Classically designed, the 602-room hotel takes you back to the 1920s.

The resort is very friendly to families. There's the **Camp Hyatt Program** for kids between the ages of 3½ and 12 for $70 per day or $45 for a half-day. Some of the activities include lei making, hula lessons and face painting. The Hyatt also has a special Night Camp until 10 pm.

Aerial view *(Hawaiian Images)*

The resort has several fabulous restaurants (see *Where to Eat* section). For golfers, **Po`ipu Bay Golf Course** is adjacent to the property, an award-winning course designed by Robert Trent Jones that hosts the

PGA Tour Grand Slam of Golf every November. For tennis players, there are four courts with regularly held lessons and clinics. **Anara Spa** has a 25-yard swimming pool, wellness classes a salon and massage and relaxation therapy.

Room at the Grand Hyatt

In front of the property is **Shipwreck Beach**. You can look out and see windsurfers, body boarders and surfers, maybe even a green sea turtle or humpback whale in the distance. The currents here aren't good for swimming, but the beach is just fine for sunbathing. There is an outdoor pool with a 150-foot waterslide, waterfalls, volleyball, and Jacuzzis. There are also five acres of saltwater swimming lagoons.

The rooms are spacious and luxurious, with marble sinks and bath. The rooms also have private lanais with ocean or garden views.

The Grand Hyatt is regularly labeled the finest resort in the state, and with good reason. If you have the opportunity and the budget, definitely do try it. It's worth every penny. There's so much here, you might have a hard time leaving. $400+.

Hotels

Aloha Estates

Aloha Estates at Kalaheo Plantation, 4579 Puuwai Road, Kalaheo, ☎ 808-332-7812. This 1926 plantation-style home provides very affordable accommodations. The property was recently renovated with new paint, windows and

Hibiscus Suite kitchen

fixtures. There are six rooms available starting at $45 per night. Five of the rooms have a small kitchenette and one, The Hibiscus Suite, has a full kitchen. The rooms, on the small side, have private bathrooms and color televisions. There's a two-night minimum stay. Under $100.

Pool at the Sheraton

Kaua`i Sheraton Hotel**, 2440 Po`ipu Beach Road, Po`ipu, ☎ 808-742-1661, www.sheraton-kauai.com, is another amazing hotel in the Po`ipu resort area. The 394 rooms are spread over 20 acres of lush landscaping. Fronting the hotel is **Kiahuna Beach, which offers decent swimming. You're also near Po`ipu Beach Park. The hotel is wrapping up a $24 million renovation on both the Garden and Ocean wings. When complete, all king-bed rooms in both wings will have four poster beds. In the Garden Wing, king beds and double beds will have quarter canopies. All rooms will have a 32-inch LCD flat screen television. The bathrooms will have new tiles and granite tops.

They have three tennis courts, spa and fitness center, several fine restaurants with great views, and two swimming pools. There's the Garden Pool and the Ocean Pool. The Ocean Pool is much nicer because it offers better views. For kids between five and 12, the **Keiki Aloha Club** offers activities five days a week; morning and afternoon sessions are available. The cost is $50 per day. You can still participate in the program even if you're not a guest at the property. In this case, a full day would cost $75 per child.

Kaua`i Sheraton

If you're interested in scuba diving, you can sign up for introductory lessons or boat dives. **Kaua`i Down Under** dive shop is on the premises for all of your diving needs. $200-$300.

AUTHOR'S CHOICE ★ **Kalaheo Inn**, 4444 Papalina Road, Kalaheo, ☎ 888-332-6023,www.kalaheoinn.com. This 14-unit inn is a great bargain and is perfect for the medium-budget traveler. There are studio, one- , two- and three-bedroom units, all clean, nicely furnished and comfortable. Each room comes with a kitchenette, except for the three-bedroom unit. That has a full kitchen. As a guest, you'll have access to barbecue grills, beach gear, snorkel gear, golf clubs, games and, sometimes, bananas grown on the property. The staff is wonderful and will go out of their way to accommodate you. Under $100-$200.

Kalaheo Inn

Condominiums

**Alihi Lani at Po`ipu Beach**, 2564 Hoonani Road, Po`ipu, ☎ 800-742-2260, 808-742-2233, www.poipuconnection.com. The two-bedroom, two-bathroom units in this complex are

Alihi Lani

roomy, with 1,150 square feet of living space. Each of the six units has excellent ocean views. The lanais are covered and huge. The living area is open, so you can feel the gentle tradewinds throughout your condo. The grounds are well maintained, and include a swimming pool and barbecue area. There is a four-night minimum. $200-$300.

**ResortQuest at Po`ipu Kai**, 1775 Po`ipu Road, Koloa, ☎ 877-997-6667, 808-742-7424, is made up of five individual communities with condominiums, townhouses and private homes. The units range from one to three bedrooms. Each unit has plenty of space to move around, with a fully equipped kitchen and a private lanai. Some buildings have their own swimming pool, spa and barbecue area. There are nine tennis courts on the property. The location is within a few minutes drive of Po`ipu Beach, which offers a nice way to spend the day. $200-$400.

ResortQuest at Po`ipu Kai

**Po`ipu Shores**, 1775 Pee Road, Po`ipu, ☎ 808-724-7700, 808-742-9720, www.castleresorts.com, has 39 one- to three-bedroom units available. All have oceanfront views. On-site, you'll find a swimming pool, sun deck and barbecue area. Like most Castle Resorts properties, this seems a bit overpriced. $200-$400+.

Po`ipu Shores

**Makahuena at Po`ipu**, 1661 Pee Road, Po`ipu, ☎ 808-742-2482, 808-742-2379, www.castleresorts.com, has one- to three-bedroom condos. All of the units are individually furnished, which makes it a challenge to know what you're going to get. Some of the apartments seem alright, others don't. All have a full kitchen, washer and dryer, data port, cable television, and, most important, a wet bar and private lanai. The rooms can overlook the gardens or you can have an ocean view. On the grounds, you'll find a barbecue area, tennis court, sun deck, swimming pool and hot tub. $200-$400+.

Makahuena at Po`ipu

AUTHOR'S CHOICE ★ **Kiahuna Plantation Resort by Outrigger**, 2253 Po`ipu Road, Po`ipu, ☎ 808-742-6411. This is one of the better bargains on the South Shore. There are 333 rooms on the property. Most have a garden view or partial ocean view. There are only a few with a full ocean view. All of

Kiahuna Plantation Resort

the rooms are spacious, nicely decorated and, as usual, the Outrigger staff is very responsive. It has 35 beautifully landscaped acres of gardens and tropical flowers located right on **Kiahuna Beach**. **Moir Garden** is on the property. Take a look at the renowned collection of orchids and cacti. There are nine tennis courts. Outrigger has seasonal children's programs available. You can dine at **Plantation Gardens Restaurant & Bar**. These are walk-up condominiums (no elevators). Two-night minimum stay. $200-$400+.

Room at Kiahuna Plantation Resort

Koloa Landing Cottages, 2704 Hoonani Road, ☎ 800-779-8773, www.koloa-landing.com, consists of five quaint cottages across from Koloa Landing. You're also within walking distance of Po`ipu Beach. There's the two-bedroom, two-bathroom Tea House, a spacious cottage that's beautifully furnished with Asian and Polynesian influences. Or you could stay in the Bamboo House, a bright studio with a full kitchen and queen-sized bed. The Hoonani House is a unique two-bedroom with a full bathroom. The two-bedroom Tiki House even has a thatched breakfast bar. Walking through the grounds is

The Tea House at Koloa Landing Cottages

a real treat, like walking through a tropical jungle. All of the units have wireless Internet access. $100-$300.

Turtle Cove Suites, ☎ 866-294-2733, www.kauaibeachrentals.com, has something for everyone. The location is excellent as it's alongside Waiomo Stream. The owners are art aficionados and it shows throughout the interior of the suites. The suites are sylish and meticulously decorated with Pacific Rim accents. There are four large suites on the property, each with a private lanai and ocean views. The sizes range from a 450-square-foot studio to an 1,120-square-foot oceanfront suite. The prices are affordable and suit most budgets. A pool and Jacuzzi are available for your use. $100-$300.

Turtle Cove Suites interior

Hideaway Cove Villas

Hideaway Cove Villas, 2307 Nalo Road, Po`ipu, ☎ 866-849-2426, 808-635-8785, www.hideaway-cove.com, has seven rooms spread over two buildings. The units range from studios to three-bedrooms. All have hardwood floors, very comfortable overstuffed furniture, four-poster beds, kitchenettes and private lanais. Even the smallest studio feels spacious. You also have use of beach gear (coolers, chairs, etc.) and barbecue grills. Overall, Hideaway Cove Villas is a good value. There's a two-night minimum. $100-$200.

Lanai at Hideaway Cove Villas

Living room at Hideaway Cove Villas

Kuhio Shores, 5050 Lawa`i Road, ☎ 800-367-8022, 808-742-7555, has one- and two-bedroom condos, all of which are oceanfront. You're in a prime location, literally at the region's best beach area. You're next to the Beach House restaurant as well, which is nice, but why go there if you already have such wonderful ocean views where you are? The ocean views really are spectacular. There really isn't much in the way of surrounding grounds. But it doesn't matter since you're so close to everything. The interiors are pleasant and roomy. Considering the location and the views, Kuhio Shores is a real steal. There's a four-night minimum stay. $100-$300.

Kuhio Shores

Whalers Cove - An Oceanfront Luxury Vacation Condo, 2640 Puuholo Road, ☎ 808-742-7571, www.whalers-cove.com. You're living in the lap of luxury here. There are one- and two-bedroom units, all of which are spacious, quiet and have oceanfront views. Each unit has two bathrooms and a full kitchen. The rooms are stunning, classically designed and decorated. Some have koa wood doors, which adds a nice touch. The heated pool and spa tub face the ocean, as does the barbecue area. It seems that everywhere you go, the ocean is right there. $400+.

Terrace at Whalers Cove

Whalers Cove from the water

Bed & Breakfasts

Gazebo at Bamboo Jungle

Bamboo Jungle, 3829 Waha Road, Kalaheo, ☎ 888-332-5515, www.kauaibedandbreakfast.com. Wow! What a quaint little spot. New owners really invested in the property and it shows. Whether it's the tastefully decorated rooms or the beautiful gardens on the property, you get the feeling that they really care. All rooms have private bathrooms. For the environmentally conscious, it might help to know that they use non-chemical cleaning and laundry products. The owners also installed a new solar hot water system, which gives everyone plenty of hot water. The small pool and Jacuzzi under a lava rock waterfall really adds a romantic touch. You can get a massage by the waterfall on the premises. Three- to five-night minimum stay. $100-$200.

Gardens & pool at Bamboo Jungle

**Po`ipu Inn Bed & Breakfast**, 2720 Hoonani Road, Po`ipu, ☎ 800-808-2330, 808-742-0100, is run by the same folks who run the Kaua`i Inn in Lihue. They put the same care and attention in here as they do with Kaua`i Inn. This is a charming plantation-style home. There are four one-bedroom units, each with a private bath. One room, the Plumeria Suite, has a Jacuzzi tub. They're wonderfully decorated to fit in with the plantation theme. It's located across from Waikomo Stream and a short walk from Koloa Landing. $100-$200.

Marjorie's Kaua`i Inn, 3307-D Hailima Road, Lawai, ☎ 800-717-8838, 808-332-8838, www.marjorieskauaiinn.com. These are spotless, affordable studios nestled on a cliff. The rooms are decorated with high-quality furnishings that evoke the spirit of old Hawaii. All rooms have a private bath, kitchenette, large lanai and cable television. There's also a pool and Jacuzzi available. If you stay in the Sunset View Room, you'll have your own Jacuzzi. This is a wonderful place for a quiet getaway. The word has spread about Marjorie's Kaua`i Inn and, since they only have three rooms, make sure you book well in advance. $100-$200.

Valley View Room at Marjorie's

Vacation Rentals

Gloria's Vacation Rentals, ☎ 808-742-2850, www.gloriasvacationrentals.com, as of press time, was undergoing a change of ownership. At any rate, you can still get a wonderful, bright one-bedroom cottage for as little as $110 per night. You could also opt for a four-bedroom house with swimming pool.

**Re/Max Kaua`i**, at Princeville Shopping Center, ☎ 877-838-8149, 808-826-9675, www.remaxkauai.com. Even though Re/Max Kaua`i is located in Princeville and they specialize in the Princeville area, they do have some condos and vacation home rentals in Po`ipu and Koloa. You can make your reservations through their online reservation system.

Kaua`i Vacation Rentals List, www.kauaivacationresorts.com, is a directory that lists hundreds of condominiums, secluded honeymoon cottages, oceanfront luxury homes and beachfront bungalows throughout the island. They have listings to fit all budgets, from $400 to $21,000 per week.

Garden Island Properties, ☎ 800-801-0378, ☎ 808-822-4871, www.kauaiproperties.com, handles vacation properties across the island. They have vacation rental homes, cottages and beach condos starting from $500 a week.

Kaua`i Vacation Rentals, ☎ 808-367-5025, ☎ 808-245-8841, www.kauaivacationrentals.com, has a large selection of vacation rental homes. Whether it's a cottage, bungalow, ocean-view condo, beachfront villa or luxurious oceanfront home, they'll probably have it in their inventory.

Garden Island Rentals, ☎ 800-247-5599, 808-742-9537, www.kauairentals.com, rents everything from condominiums to luxury oceanfront vacation homes. They have a large inventory of rentals in the Po`ipu area to choose from. If you want to rent a vacation home, keep in mind that there's a seven-day minimum.

Kailani House

Tropical Paradise Realty, ☎ 808-246-3737, www.tropicalparadiserealty.org, offers a vacation rental in a restored plantation-style home. The Old Koloa House is a charming three-bedroom, two-bathroom home in the middle of Koloa. The house once served as a bed and breakfast. The interior is quaint, with a touch of old Hawaii. The 1,575-square-foot space comes with an expansive, landscaped backyard that has mountain views. It's nicely landscapeda, with a lot of privacy. The location is great since you're near Koloa Town and Po`ipu Beach. $100-$200 per night.

Gillin's Beach House

Gillin's Beach House, ☎ 808-742-7561, www.gillinbeachhouse.com, sits on Gillin's Beach, which is named after a former engineer at Koloa Sugar Plantation who built a house on this site in the 1940s. The original house was destroyed by Hurricane Iniki, but the family decided to rebuild. They built a three-bedroom, two-bathroom house with a private water system, electricity, cellular telephone, television, dishwasher, and other standard appliances. The key here is seclusion. You're located in Mahaulepu, on a beautiful beach that's quite isolated. Still, you're not too far from civilization, only a few minutes from Po`ipu and Koloa Town. Rentals start at $2,600 per week.

Coastline Cottages, Po`ipu Beach, 4730 Lawa`i Beach Road, ☎ 866-641-6900, 808-742-9688, www.coastlinecottages.com, has oceanfront vacation rentals that range from an 800-square-foot studio to an oceanfront 3,200-square-foot, three-bedroom cottage. No matter which one you choose, you will have a private and relaxing getaway. All of the cottages are spacious and reflect the style of Hawaii in the 1930s and '40s. There is a private chef and massage therapist available. You'll also get Kiahuna Swim & Tennis Club privileges. $200-$400+ per night.

Beachfront rental

Garden Isle Cottages, Oceanfront, 2658 Puuholo Road, Koloa, ☎ 808-742-6717. All units are fully equipped with a

Omao Cottage

washer and dryer, color television and DVD player, plus full and mini kitchens The cottages are roomy and can accommodate your family. There's a double bed in the living room and a king bed in the bedroom. You also have a private lanai that looks out over the ocean. These oceanfront cottages are near Po`ipu Beach Park, which is perfect if you love to spend the day in the water. $100-$300 per night.

Camping

There are no state or county camping sites along the South Shore of Kaua`i. However, **Salt Pond Beach Park** does offer a great spot for camping and it's not too far from the Po`ipu Resort area. Just drive west on Kaumaulii Highway. It's run by the County of Kaua`i, so you'll need to get a county permit. To obtain a county permit, contact the Kaua`i County Parks Permit Section by calling ☎ 808-241-4463. Their hours are 8:15 am to 4:00 pm, Monday through Friday. You can also get a permit at the Kalaheo Neighborhood Center, ☎ 808-332-9770. However, they're only open between Monday-Friday between 8:30 am and 12:30 pm. Camping permit fees are $3 per adult, per night for non-residents and free for Hawaii residents.

Kahili Mountain Park, ☎ 808-742-9921, is run by the Seventh Day Adventists and they offer cabins on 197 acres of land upcountry starting at $55 per night. However, they accept reservations only from individuals and groups who are involved in humanitarian, educational, agricultural, and health care organizations or activities. For recreational purposes, they only accept members or groups from, or sponsored by, the Seventh-day Adventist Church.

■ Where To Eat

Pizzetta, Old Koloa Town, Koloa, ☎ 808-742 8881, www.pizzettarestaurant.com. Open daily from 11 am-10 pm. This is the first Pizzetta on Kaua`i (the second one is in Kapa`a). Over the years, Pizzetta has established a reputation for having the best pizza in the area. The menu is standard Italian: pizza, pastas, subs, panini, salads and dishes such as eggplant parmesan and chicken marsala. My favorite is the meatball sub. There are drink specials served daily from 3 to 6 pm. The only possible drawback is that Pizzetta can be packed at dinner time. If that's the case, they can deliver to Po`ipu, Omao, Kalaheo and Lawai. $15-$35.

AUTHOR'S CHOICE ★ **Puka Dog**, Po`ipu Shopping Village, Po`ipu, ☎ 808-742-6044, www.pukadog.com. Open Monday-Saturday from 10 am-6 pm. I know what you might be thinking. Seven dollars for a hot dog? Are you kidding me? I was every bit the skeptic myself upon hearing about these ridiculously expensive wieners. But I have to admit I was impressed. The difference is that they use fresh tropical fruit to create a unique hot dog. You can get mango relish, pineapple relish, even coconut relish with your dog. They even serve vegetarian hot dogs. You can get the standard ketchup and mustard and the hot dog will still be good, but I recommend you go for the mango relish. That alone is worth the money. Under $15.

Puka Dog

**Po`ipu Tropical Burgers**, Po`ipu Shopping Village, Po`ipu, ☎ 808-742-1808. Open daily from 6:30 am-9:30 pm. Reservations required for parties six or more. Po`ipu Tropical Burgers is run by the same folks who own Tropical Burgers & More in Kapa`a. I was not optimistic, since my experiences at Tropical Burgers & More were not pleasant. I don't know if it's because my expectations were low, but I was pleasantly surprised by the service. The burgers were much better here than at the Kapa`a branch. They serve breakfast, lunch and dinner. The breakfast menu consists of the standard eggs and waffles. Po`ipu Tropical Burgers also features live Hawaiin music from 6:30 to 8 pm on Sundays. Under $15-$35.

Brick Oven Pizza, Kaumualii Highway, Kalaheo, ☎ 808-332-8561. Open Tuesday-Sunday from 11 am-10 pm. I really like the atmosphere of Brick Oven Pizza. It's large, old and very open, with high ceilings. The tables have checkered tablecloths. Brick Oven Pizza does make decent pizza, but you can get better pizza elsewhere. I have tried the Italian sausage sandwich. They make their own sausage, and I do give them credit for trying, it's rather bland. Like ground pork with no spices whatsoever. The service wasn't terribly impressive. Under $15-$35.

**Roy's Po`ipu Bar & Grill**, Po`ipu Shopping Village, Po`ipu, ☎ 808-742-5000, www.roysrestaurant.com. Open daily from 5:30-9:30 pm. Roy's has long had a reputation throughout the state as one of the top fine-dining establishments. Chef Roy Yamaguchi's Hawaiian fusion cuisine really put the restaurant on the map. He started with his restaurant on Oahu, then quickly expanded to the neighbor islands and places like Philadelphia. Yes, even Philly can use a little Hawaiian fusion. Even though the location could be better (fine dining in a strip mall?), the food and service are still outstanding. The menu changes regularly, but will feature such classics as macadamia nut mahi mahi and, for dessert, you must have Roy's Chocolate Soufflé. $50+.

e.b.'s Eats, Po`ipu Shopping Village, Po`ipu, ☎ 808-742-1979. Open Monday-Saturday from 8 am-5 pm. e.b.'s Eats is a relatively new restaurant that has taken Kaua`i by storm. The restaurant initially opened in Lihu`e, where it was a huge success. So much so that e.b.'s moved to its new location in Po`ipu Shopping Village. It's a breakfast and lunch spot that offers a variety of coffees and baked goods. Breakfast can be as simple as a tasty English muffin breakfast sandwich or get something a little heavier like the mushroom meatloaf loco moco. Breakfast is served until 11 am. Then it's time for lunch. e.b.'s offers delicious salads, sandwiches, quiche (ask about the flavor of the day) or macaroni dishes. Under $15-$35.

Lappert's Ice Cream, Old Koloa Town, Koloa, ☎ 808-742-1272. Open daily from 10 am-9 pm. Here's another location for Lappert's ice cream. The ice cream is locally made, but that really doesn't justify the price. I never did understand what the fuss is about. It's mediocre, not great. Menu items include a variety of Hawaii-themed ice cream, coffee, cookies and brownies. Other locations are in Coconut Marketplace in Kapa`a, Princeville Shopping Center in Princeville and in Hanapepe. Under $15.

Taqueria Norteños, Po`ipu Plaza, 2827A Po`ipu Road, Po`ipu, ☎ 808-742-7222. Open every day except Wednesday from 11 am-9 pm. This hole in the wall is a great find. Cheap take-out Mexican food is perfect if you're on your way to the beach or returning to your condo from a long day out on the road. Did I mention cheap? All entrées are priced under $5. How can you beat that? The portions are huge and tasty. The cuisine is from the Sonara region in Northern Mexico. It can be hard to find this little take-out window. It's in Po`ipu Plaza, right next to Outfitters Kaua`i. Pick something up when you return your kayak. Under $15.

Taqueria Norteños burrito plate

Kalaheo Coffee Co. & Café, 2-2560 Kaumualii Highway, Kalaheo, ☎ 808-332-5858. Open daily for breakfast and lunch 6:30 am-2:30 pm. Dinner is served Wednesday-Saturday from 5:30. Located directly across from Brick Oven Pizza, this charming spot is a wonderful place to get breakfast. The café's location makes it perfect if you're on your way to Waimea Canyon. Breakfast serves up fantastic omelets, pancakes and Sweetbread French Toast. Lunch is pretty much made up of hot and cold sandwiches and salads. Coffee drinks are served all day. Parking can be a challenge here, especially in the morning. It can get crowded. Under $15-$35.

Casablanca, at Kiahuna Swim & Tennis Club, Po`ipu, ☎ 808-742-2929. Open Monday-Saturday 7:30 am-10 pm; Sunday 8 am-6 pm. This outdoor restaurant has an elegant, yet casual atmosphere. The view from the restaurant overlooks the tennis courts and garden area, which makes it fun to watch tennis players both good and bad go at it. On the menu you'll find healthy fare with Mediterranean/Italian influences. A few things on the menu that you might try are gazpacho and, for dinner, the lamb tangine is wonderful. Casablanca has belly dancing on Thursday nights to add to the Mediterranean flair. $15-$35.

Casablanca

AUTHOR'S CHOICE ★ **Joe's on the Green**, at Kiahuna Golf Course, ☎ 808-742-9696. Open daily for breakfast and lunch 7 am-2:30 pm; Happy Hour 3-5:30 pm; dinner Wednesday and Thursday 5:30-8:30 pm. Reservations recommended for dinner. After a hard round of golf, you're going to want to take a break and grab a bite to eat. Joe's is a casual stop for breakfast or lunch. Breakfast is good, with a standard (eggs, pancakes, etc.) menu that's done right. For lunch, Joe's serves up burgers, salads and sandwiches. Try the Asian barbecue ribs. The prices are right. Even if you're not a golf fan, Joe's is worth the stop. The service is excellent and the atmosphere is casual as you overlook Kiahuna Golf Course. Breakfast and lunch under $15, dinner $35-$50.

Joe's on the Green

Brennecke's Beach Broiler, 2100 Hoone Road, Po`ipu Beach, ☎ 888-384-8810, 808-742-7588, www.brenneckes.com.

Open daily 11 am-10 pm. Reservations recommended for dinner. Brennecke's is best known for two things. First, for its unbelievable ocean view. If you get a table on the second floor lanai, you'll overlook Po`ipu Beach Park. It's also known for its food. The food, however, could be better. It's a bit overpriced (you don't expect that ocean view to be free, do you?), and the quality is just mediocre. Lunch is much better, where you can get a prime rib sandwich or fish tacos. Brennecke's is a great place to come for a drink. Looking down on the beach makes for great people watching. Lunch $15-$35, dinner $35-$50.

Brennecke's Deli, 2100 Hoone Road, Po`ipu Beach, ☎ 808-742-1582, www.brenneckes.com. Open daily 8 am-8 pm. Here's the most convenient place to pick up something if you're planning on spending the day at Po`ipu Beach. Brennecke's Deli also has shave ice, which makes a nice treat for the kids. They serve up made-to-order sandwiches. You can eat there, as they have picnic tables and benches set up or you can take your lunch to go. For added convenience, you can pre-order by phone and pick it up. They offer daily picnic packages, so be sure to ask. Speaking of convenience, there's a small store that carries film, batteries, beach equipment and everything else you'd need for your day at the beach. Under $15.

Plantation Gardens Restaurant & Bar, 2253 Po`ipu Road, Po`ipu, ☎ 877-745-2824, 808-742-2121. Open for cocktails at 5 pm; dinner from 5:30 pm. Reservations recommended. Simple and elegant atmosphere set in an old plantation manager's estate. The interior is made of cherry wood floors, bamboo ceiling fans, in an open atmosphere. Be sure to check out the koa wood bar. It's beautiful. You're surrounded by the Moir Gardens. You can dine inside or on the lanai and feast on a more modern version of local cuisine. Traditional local food has a new twist with menu items like Seafood Laulau and Island Stir-fry. For dessert, try the Lilikoi Cheesecake or the Flourless Chocolate Cake. $35-$50.

Keoki's Paradise, Po`ipu Shopping Village, Po`ipu, ☎ 808-742-7535, www.keokisparadise.com. Open for dinner from 5 to 10 pm. Keoki's Paradise is not hard to find. Just follow the trail of tiki torches to the restaurant. The tropical theme is evident throughout the restaurant with bamboo, streams,

Keoki's Paradise

waterfalls and a thatched awning down to the staff's aloha shirts. The menu consists of mostly fish, but does have something for everyone. Carnivores will enjoy the Koloa Ribs or the Coconut Crusted Chicken. Entrées come with salad and bread, but don't fill up too much. You're going to want to save some room for Kimo's Hula Pie. The food is very good, although a little pricey. The Bamboo Grill is a bar in the restaurant, open from 11 am to 11 pm, with Hawaiian music on Thursday and Friday nights and Sunday afternoon. $15-$35.

AUTHOR'S CHOICE ★ **Beach House Restaurant**, 5022 Lawa`i Road, Po`ipu, ☎ 808-742-1424, www.the-beach-house.com. Open for cocktails at 5 pm; dinner 5:30-9 pm. Reservations highly recommended. The Beach House Restaurant has a reputation as one of the most romantic restaurants in the world. Readers from various publications statewide vote the Beach House the best restaurant on Kaua`i. It's very hard to disagree. Fine art adorns the walls, the sunsets are fabulous and the food is wonderful. The service is always first-rate. Back to the food, the menu is extensive, with fish and steak options. Your meal is artfully presented and excellent. Try to make reservations for a window seat. It will make your experience at The Beach House absolutely perfect. You must have the Molten Chocolate Desire for dessert. It's outrageous! $35-$50.

Dondero's Italian Restaurant, Grand Hyatt Kaua`i Resort & Spa, ☎ 808-240-6456, Serving dinner Tuesday-Saturday from 6 pm-10 pm. Reservations highly recommended. There's something about dining at the Grand Hyatt that makes any meal worthwhile. The setting here is romantic and elegant. You're under the stars overlooking Shipwreck Beach. The food and service are first-rate. The menu is Northern Italian, with pastas, lamb, osso bucco and beef dishes. The chocolate crême brulée is something to remember. Overall, Dondero's provides an unforgettable dining experience. If you want privacy, there's a private dining room for parties of up to 12 people. $35-$50.

Ilima Terrace Restaurant, at Grand Hyatt Kaua`i Resort & Spa, ☎ 808-240-6456. Open for breakfast and lunch 6 am-2 pm. Ilima Terrace offers a breakfast buffet every morning that's overpriced. Lunch is better, with sandwiches, burgers, salads and pizzas. However, this is a charming place to enjoy Sunday brunch. The menu is extensive and features made-to-order omelettes, quiche and crêpes. The Sunday Brunch is excellent and worth the money. You're in the same area as Tidepools, so the atmosphere is charming and you are seated overlooking the koi pond. Breakfast $15-$35, lunch $35-$50, Sunday brunch $15-$35.

Ilima Terrace

Tidepools Restaurant

Tidepools Seafood & Steak, at Grand Hyatt Resort & Spa, ☎ 808-240-6456. Open for cocktails starting at 5:30; dinner 6-10 pm. If you don't want the romance of Dondero's or you just want to be somewhere to relax and enjoy pupus and drinks, Tidepools is the place to go. The atmosphere is charming. It's a series of thatched huts on a koi pond. Tidepools is surrounded by waterfalls. The tables are spaced at a distance, giving you a bit more privacy. The Mango Lobster and Crab

Cake is delightful and the grilled mahi-mahi is fantastic. Tidepools also serves an excellent prime-rib. $50+.

Casa di Amici, 2301 Nalo Road, Po`ipu, ☎ 808-742-1555. Open daily for dinner from 6 pm. Reservations recommended. If you plan to venture to Casa di Amici, bring your cell phone. The restaurant is hard to find above Po`ipu Beach. But be sure not to miss this wonderful Italian restaurant with al fresco dining. The cuisine is a fusion of Italian with French influence. The result is excellent quality and highly creative. On the menu you'll find pork loin saltimbocca, mahogany-glazed salmon, panko-crusted tiger prawns, and paella prawn risotto. $35-$50.

Tomkats Grille, 5402 Koloa Road, Koloa, ☎ 808-742-8887. Open 7 am-10 pm; late night cocktails from 10 pm to last call. No, this place wasn't named after the pairing of Tom Cruise and Katie Holmes. It is the home of a really fun establishment. It's a lively atmosphere that's laid back. It's one of the few places in the Po`ipu area that has a true local feel to it. The food is good. It's standard American: burgers, sandwiches and the like. There are over two dozen beers on tap. Be aware that you may find a cat or two running around or sleeping in a chair. If you're allergic to cats, this may pose a problem. $15-$35.

Kalaheo Steak House, Papalina Road, Kalaheo, ☎ 808-332-9780. Open daily from 6-10 pm. Kalaheo Steak House offers tasty steaks that are reasonably priced. The atmosphere is casual and informal. It has a rustic feel with pine walls and black leather booths. They serve steaks, ribs, chicken and seafood. It's a very popular place with locals because the food is good, the portions are large and it's reasonably priced. It's one of the better deals in the area. They do not take reservations, so you will need to get to the restaurant early to secure a table. $15-$35.

Pomodoro Ristorante Italiano, Rainbow Plaza, Kalaheo , ☎ 808-332-5945. Open for dinner Monday-Saturday 5:30 pm-9:30 pm. Reservations recommended. When you drive though Kalaheo, you wouldn't think that there's a good Italian Restaurant anywhere nearby. Believe it or not, one does exist. Pomodoro Ristorante is a family-owned restaurant with an intimate, casual atmosphere. There are plenty of pastas on the menu to choose from. They also have other traditional

Italian dishes like chicken parmesan. The chicken saltimbocca is flavored just right with sage, cheese and prosciutto. The house specialty is lasagna, which is served as a huge portion. I was pleasantly surprised by the food and the service here. $15-$35.

**Po`ipu Beach Broiler**, 1941 Po`ipu Road, Po`ipu, ☎ 808-742-6433. Lunch 11:30-3 pm; dinner 5-10 pm; Happy Hour 2-5 pm daily. Po`ipu Beach Broiler has a very open and casual atmosphere. The lunch menu has sandwiches, salads and burgers. Dinner features seafood and steaks. The atmosphere is pleasant and service is good. Dinner seems overpriced, however. You're better off coming here for lunch or for a drink during Happy Hour. $35-$50.

Po`ipu Beach Broiler

**Po`ipu Bay Bar & Grill**, ☎ 808-240-6456. Open Monday-Saturday for breakfast and lunch from 7 am-2:30 pm; Sunday 7:30 am-2:30 pm; cocktails 10:30-5 pm daily. The restaurant overlooks the 18th hole of Po`ipu Bay Golf Course. There is indoor seating, as well as an open-air courtyard with spectacular mountain views. The menu features standard breakfast items and creative dishes like Dungeness Crab Hash. For lunch, PBGB's serves classics like Ahi Caesar Salad or their signature Crab Melt. $15-$35.

Pattaya Asian Café, Po`ipu Shopping Village, Po`ipu, ☎ 808-742-8818. Open Monday-Saturday 11:30 am-2:30 pm; dinner every evening from 5-9:30 pm. Pattaya has an extensive menu that features Thai, Vietnamese and Chinese cuisines. The meals are moderately priced and the service is good. They have a lot of good curries on the menu. I also enjoyed their Pad Thai. $15-$35.

Shells Restaurant, Sheraton Kaua`i Resort, ☎ 808-742-1661. Open daily for breakfast 6:30-10:30 am and dinner 6-9:30 pm. Reservations recommended. Shells has oceanfront dining with an outdoor lanai, as well as a spacious dining room with shell chandeliers. If you can, get an outdoor seat because the view is unbelievable. They serve a breakfast buffet in the morning for $20 per person or you can order à la carte. For dinner, there are plenty of fresh seafood dishes, plus steak and pasta. Breakfast $15-$35, dinner $50+.

■ Nightlife/Culture

The Point, at Sheraton Kaua`i, ☎ 808-742-1661, is a wonderful place to unwind with a cocktail. They're open from 11 am to midnight, serving pupus and light lunch. Entertainment ranges from contemporary Hawaiian to jazz, rock and Top 40 hits. Live entertainment is Thursday from 8:30 pm to 11:30 pm and on Friday and Saturday nights from 9:30 pm to 12:30 am.

Stevenson's Library

Stevenson's Library. This bar inside the Grand Hyatt in Po`ipu was named after Robert Lewis Stevenson. They have the best selection of cigars, Scotches and Ports. There's also live jazz every night and pool tables. It's a very comfortable place to be in. It's cozy and wood adorns everything. The furniture is comfortable. It decorated like an old study.

Seaview Terrace is in the Grand Hyatt Kaua`i Resort & Spa. The terrace has a sweeping view of Shipwreck Beach and Keoneloa Bay. The atmosphere is relaxed and open as the tradewinds come through. Seaview Terrace is open for cocktails from 4 to 8 pm. There's live entertainment every evening. It's a very pleasant place to stop for a drink on your way to dinner.

Inside **Keoki's Paradise**, ☎ 808-742-7535, is **The Bamboo Grill**. It's open from 11 am to 11 pm with Hawaiian music on

Thursday and Friday nights and Sunday afternoon. It seems to be a happening place pretty much every night. **Po`ipu Tropical Burgers** also features live Hawaiian music from 6:30 to 8 pm on Sundays.

Beach House Restaurant, ☎ 808-742-1424, has a sophisticated bar with seats that have great views of the beach and bay areas. Get here right when the bar opens at 5 pm to grab one of the prime seats. This is a great place to watch the sunset. The drink menu has everything. You can get a tropical frozen drink like lava flow or a mai-tai, or you might want to opt for a beer. The Beach House also carries an extensive wine list.

There's even some late night action in Koloa! **Tomkats Grille**, ☎ 808-742-8887, serves up late night drinks from 10 pm to last call. It's not a bad place to stop on your way home from dinner.

Hula

Po`ipu Shopping Village has Polynesian entertainment and dance at 5 pm on Tuesdays and Thursdays.

The **Grand Hyatt Resort & Spa** hosts free hula shows every Tuesday and Saturday at 7 pm.

The **Sheraton Kaua`i** has a sunset torch lighting ceremony with Hawaiian music and hula every evening from 5 to 6 pm.

Keiki Hula Show at the Grand Hyatt

Luaus

Drums of Paradise Hyatt Luau, Grand Hyatt Resort & Spa, ☎ 808-240-6456, www.hyatt-kauai.com, takes place on Sunday and Thursday at 5:30 pm. During the summer, luau is on Tuesday as well. Adults are charged $65 per person; children six-12 are $33. The luau here was a bit disappointing. The food is excellent, with your typical luau favorites like Kalua pig and lomi lomi salmon. The revue features music

Drums of Paradise Luau

from Tahiti, New Zealand, Samoa and the rest of Polynesia. The show itself was OK, but not noticeably better than other luaus.

Surf to Sunset Luau, Sheraton Kaua`i Resort, 2440 Hoonani Road, Po`ipu Beach, ☎ 808-742-8205, 808-742-1661. Monday and Friday at 5:30 pm. Traditional luau is $75 per person (children six-12 $37); Golden Circle Dinner is $87 per person (children six-12 $43). This is a traditional luau, which includes the lei greeting, a luau show and buffet. The Golden Circle Dinner also offers premium seating for the show and tableside beverage service. Upon arrival, you receive a shell lei greeting and have your picture taken with Po`ipu Beach in the background. That makes a very pretty picture. You can enjoy cocktails and mai tais and walk around the grounds to see local artisans who teach lei making, lauhala and coconut weaving.

Then the feast begins! The luau features kalua pig, lomi salmon, pipikaula, poke and poi, as well as Korean, Japanese and Chinese dishes. Before the show, they put on a fun pareo (sarong) fashion show that teaches you a few ways to tie your sarong. The show consists of traditional hula chants and dance, which gives you the feeling that you're experiencing a real Hawaiian luau, not something manufactured and overproduced.

Lihu`e

What to See

IN THIS CHAPTER

No matter where you're coming from or how you get to Kaua`i, odds are the first town you'll land in is Lihu`e. Lihu`e means "cold chill," a reference to the cold winds that blow across the lands. Today, Lihu`e is the home of Kaua`i's main airport, the main seaport, Nawiliwili Harbor, and Kaua`i's largest shopping mall, Kukui Grove Shopping Center. You'll also find big-box retail stores such as K-Mart, Wal-Mart and Costco here. Lihu`e is the county seat of Kaua`i. The area also includes Nawiliwili Harbor, and the residential towns of Puhi and Hanama`ulu.

Lihu`e was originally a small village in the ahupua`a (land district) of Puna. It remained a small town for years. After Captain Cook's landing in 1778, Waimea was the major port, until sugar became king. Once the sugar industry emerged in the 1800s, it became clear that Lihu`e's central location would be crucial to the area's growth.

The **Lihu`e Sugar Plantation** is central to the area's history. The plantation was established in the late 1840s by Henry Pierce, Supreme Court Justice William Lee and Charles Reed Bishop, businessman and husband of Bernice Pauahi Bishop, who was descended from Hawaiian royalty.

The plantation processed sugar at Lihu`e Mill, starting in 1851. The Lihu`e irrigation ditch was built by William Rice, bringing water from Kilohana Crater. This was the first irrigation ditch project in Hawai`i and it enabled the company to grow significantly over the next few years. The company acquired land at Ahukini and then built the company's second mill in Hanama`ulu. By the end of the century, the Lihu`e Plantation had 1,600 workers, mostly immigrants. The ditch systems eventually grew to 51 miles.

In the 1940s, World War II had an adverse effect on the industry and Lihu`e Mill was no exception. With labor shortages and blackouts, sugar production became extremely difficult. By the 1950s and '60s, the plantation camps were closed and turned into subdivision housing. The economy was phasing out sugar and developing tourism as its cash crop. One by one the sugar plantations closed their doors. Lihu`e Plantation was the last to close, in November 2000.

Today, **Hanama`ulu** has a population of over 3,000, mostly second- and third-generation immigrants from the plantation. Hanama`ulu is also known for Kalepa Ridge. There once was a large heiau called Kalauokamanu where humans were sacrificed. It was destroyed in 1855.

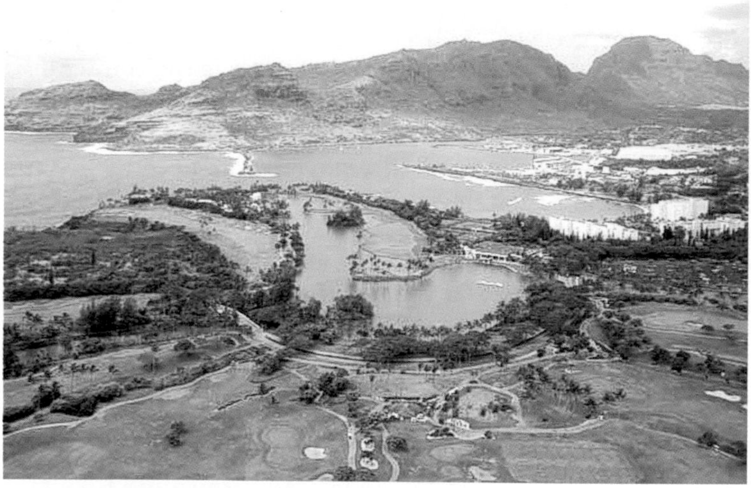

Nawiliwili Harbor

Nawiliwili Harbor was created in the 1930s. At the time, Waimea served as the island's main port, but since there were no deep waters in the area, Nawiliwili Bay was dredged. A lighthouse was first built on **Ninini Point** in 1906. It was rebuilt in 1923, which is the structure that still stands today.

Ninini Point

The lighthouse did have a close call in 1941, when a Japanese submarine attacked the entrance to the harbor. Fortunately, the shells were duds and damage to the area was limited.

Driving west from Lihu`e will take you through the residential area of **Puhi**. Puhi is home to a number of shops and Kaua`i Community College. Most notably, it is also where you will find **Kilohana**, a restored plantation estate.

Grove Farm Homestead Museum, 4050 Nawiliwili Road, ☎ 808-245-3202, is the restored plantation home and museum of George Wilcox. Wilcox was the son of Hanalei missionaries and went on to become one of the island's most successful sugar planters, and then a philanthropist. The home was built by Wilcox in 1864. It was turned into a museum in 1978. On the grounds, you'll find the Wilcox family home, a plantation office, workers' houses, gardens and livestock. The buildings feature furnishings from that period and a collection of artifacts. Guided tours are Monday, Wednesday and Thursday at 10 am and 1 pm for $5 per person. Reservations are required.

**Kaua`i Museum**, 4428 Rice Street, Lihu`e, www.kauaimuseum.org, ☎ 808-245-6931. Open Monday-Friday

9 am-4 pm, Saturday 10 am-4 pm. Admission is $7. Free admission the first Saturday of every month. Guided tours are held on Monday, Wednesday and Thursday at 10:30 am for $10. Call for reservations. The museum is housed in two buildings in downtown Lihu`e. The oldest, the Albert Wilcox Building, was built in 1924 as a public library. At first I didn't think I would spend too much time in this small space. Much to my surprise, I spent hours combing through the exhibits on different cultures that have had such a strong influence in Kaua`i: Japanese, Chinese, and Filipino. There's a collection of ancient Hawaiian artifacts such as poi pounders and weapons, furniture from the missionary era and World War II memorabilia. They also have an exhibit, with video, that documents Kaua`i's natural history from its beginning as a volcano (!), tracing its history to the Polynesian settlers and right up through World War II. There's also a contemporary gallery featuring the works of local artists. I highly recommend visiting the museum on a rainy day, or if you are in search of a new and different experience.

Wailua Falls

Wailua Falls was made famous when it was featured in the opening sequence of *Fantasy Island*. Ever since then, visitors have flocked to this 80-foot waterfall. The cliff over the pool was once a diving platform for the ali`i (royalty). It's very easy to see from the side of the road, which makes this your best chance to observe a waterfall without a long hike. To get there, take Highway 56 from Kapa`a to Hanama`ulu. Follow Ma`alo Road in

Hanama`ulu for about three miles. The waterfall will be on the right.

The **Alekoko**, or **Menehune, Fishpond** is near the Huleia National Wildlife Refuge. Fishponds were built at the time to provide a ready supply of fish in case ocean conditions prevented Hawaiians from fishing in their outrigger canoes. The fishpond gets its name from legends that say the large pond was built about 1,000 years ago by hundreds of Menehune. Stories say that the pond, which is made from a stone wall 900 feet long and five feet high, was completed in one night. They apparently managed this by lining up in a double row that was 25 miles long, extending to the village of Makaweli, and passing stones from hand to hand.

Menehune Fishpond

To see the Menehune Fishpond, drive inland along Hulemalu Road from Niumalu past Nawiliwili Harbor. The road rises above the Huleia Stream. Look for a turnoff and an overlook marked by a Hawai`i Visitor's Bureau warrior sign.

Huleia National Wildlife Refuge

Huleia National Wildlife Refuge is adjacent to the Menehune Fish Pond. The Huleia Refuge was established in 1973 to provide open, productive wetlands for endangered

Hawaiian waterbirds. The 241-acre refuge is in a relatively flat valley along the Huleia River, bordered by a steep, wooded hillside. This land was once used for taro and rice. Thirty-one species of birds, including endangered Hawaiian stilts, coots, moorhens, and ducks, can be found here. Of the 31 species, 18 are introduced, and there are no native mammals, reptiles or amphibians. It is believed, however, that the Hawaiian hoary bat might live in this area. The refuge is closed to the public, but it can be viewed from the Menehune Fishpond Overlook.

Kipu Falls

Kipu Falls is a popular stop for swimming. The falls are fed by the Huleia Stream on its way to Nawiliwili Bay. The pool is surrounded by a 20-foot rock wall. There are a couple of jumping areas and a rope swing, as well as a ladder for you to climb. It doesn't seem that high up when you're in the pool but, once you make it to the top, you might feel differently.

If you do go to Kipu Falls, there are a few things you should know. First of all, never, ever dive into the swimming area. Hitting your head on a rock would be bad. Very bad. Second, reef shoes would come in handy here. The area is full of rocks, which can be quite slippery.

Take Highway 50 west from Lihu`e. Turn left onto Kipu Road and you'll get to a dirt road just before the bridge. Turn left on the dirt road and take that until you reach the gate. Park outside the gate and you should see a trail that leads to the falls. It's about a five-minute hike.

Sightseeing Tours

Roberts Hawai`i Tours, ☎ 866-898-2519, www.robertshawaii.com, offers bus tours from your hotel to

Waimea Canyon. You'll stop at Spouting Horn and Hanapepe Valley along the way. Tours operate Sunday, Tuesday, Thursday and Saturday. The cost is $44 per person. Roberts also has a tour that stops at Fern Grotto and Opaeka`a Falls, as well as Waimea Canyon. This tour is available only on Sunday, Tuesday, Thursday and Saturday, for $64 per person.

Polynesian Adventure Tours, ☎ 808-246-0122, www.polyad.com, has two tours of Waimea Canyon as well. Their Waimea Canyon Experience Tour operates on Monday, Wednesday, Friday, Sunday. You stop at Spouting Horn, Hanapepe, and Fort Elizabeth, before reaching Waimea Canyon. The cost for this tour is $47 per person. They offer a second tour that allows you to see the Coconut Coast, including Opaeka`a Falls and Nawiliwili Harbor, for $68 per person.

Kaua`i Movie Tours van

Kaua`i Movie Tours, ☎ 800-628-8432 or 808-822-1192, www.hawaiimovietours.com, runs highly popular tours that take you around the island in their mobile theater, so you can visit the actual locations while you're watching scenes from the films in which they appear. The films and TV shows include *Jurassic Park*, *Raiders of the Lost Ark*, *South Pacific*, *Blue Hawai`i*, *Gilligan's Island*, *Fantasy Island* and about 30 others. They offer three different types of tours daily, starting at $111 per person.

Kilohana, ☎ 808-246-9529, has carriage rides, a railway tour and horse-drawn sugar cane tour. Kilohana encapsulates the grandeur and elegance of the bygone sugar plantation era. You will see how "the other half lived," mainly the plantation managers and their ilk. Albert Spencer Wilcox purchased the land from Lihu`e Plantation in 1896 and lived there with his wife until 1935. In 1936, Albert's nephew, Gaylord Wilcox and his wife, moved to Kaua`i from Honolulu to manage Grove Farm. They tore down the existing structure and replaced it

Kilohana carriage ride

with an English country home designed by architect Mark Potter.

In 1985, Kilohana was turned into a commercial property. The 15,000-square-foot mansion was restored. The courtyard became Gaylord's Restaurant and the bedrooms, carriage house and guest cottages were converted into shops.

You can stroll through the grounds on your own or take a carriage ride through the grounds. Or try a one-hour carriage ride in a sugar cane wagon pulled by Clydesdale horses.

Kilohana also has the new Kaua`i Plantation Railway, which is a recreation of the days when steam trains shuffled workers to the fields and brought the sugar cane to the mills. The Kaua`i Plantation Railway will take you through the grounds of Kilohana and through a working plantation where you'll see groves of mango, banana and papaya trees. among many others.

Sugar cane tour

The 20-minute carriage ride through the grounds is $12 for adults, $6 for children under 12. Kilohana also offers the tours from 11 am-6 pm Monday-Saturday and Sunday from 11 am-3 pm. The one-hour tour gives you an extensive look at the history of sugar from 1835 to the present day. This one is $29 for adults, $15 for children under 12. The Sugar Cane Tour is only on Monday, Tuesday and Thursday at 11 am and 2 pm. Reservations are required.

Lihu`e

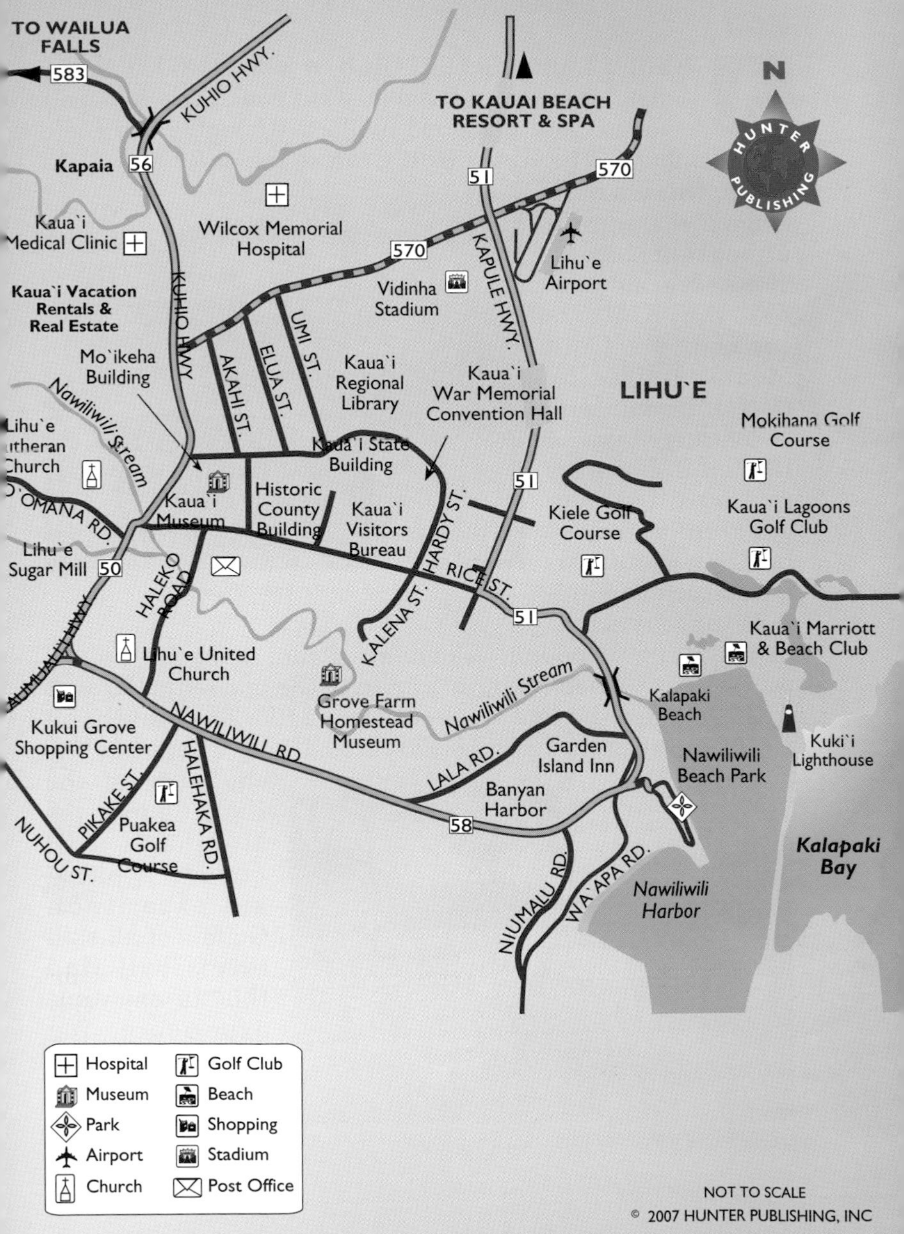

TO WAILUA FALLS
583
KUHIO HWY.
Kapaia
56
Kaua`i Medical Clinic
Wilcox Memorial Hospital
TO KAUAI BEACH RESORT & SPA
N
HUNTER PUBLISHING
51
570
570
Vidinha Stadium
KAPULE HWY.
Lihu`e Airport
Kaua`i Vacation Rentals & Real Estate
KUHIO HWY
Mo`ikeha Building
AKAHI ST.
ELUA ST.
UMI ST.
Kaua`i Regional Library
Kaua`i War Memorial Convention Hall
LIHU`E
Mokihana Golf Course
Nawiliwili Stream
Lihu`e Lutheran Church
Kaua`i State Building
Historic County Building
Kaua`i Museum
Kaua`i Visitors Bureau
HARDY ST.
51
Kiele Golf Course
Kaua`i Lagoons Golf Club
O`OMANA RD.
Lihu`e Sugar Mill
50
HALEKO ROAD
RICE ST.
KALENA ST.
51
Kaua`i Marriott & Beach Club
KAUMUALI`I HWY
Lihu`e United Church
Grove Farm Homestead Museum
Nawiliwili Stream
Kalapaki Beach
Kukui Grove Shopping Center
NAWILIWILI RD.
HALEHAKA RD.
Garden Island Inn
LALA RD.
Nawiliwili Beach Park
Kuki`i Lighthouse
PIKAKE ST.
Puakea Golf Course
Banyan Harbor
58
NUHOU ST.
NIUMALU RD.
WA`APA RD.
Kalapaki Bay
Nawiliwili Harbor
Hospital
Museum
Park
Airport
Church
Golf Club
Beach
Shopping
Stadium
Post Office
NOT TO SCALE
© 2007 HUNTER PUBLISHING, INC

■ Adventures

On Land

Golf

Kaua`i Lagoons Golf Club, ☎ 808-241-6000 for tee times, www.KauaiLagoonsGolf.com, has two golf courses, both designed by Jack Nicklaus, the Kiele and Mokihana. The **Kiele Golf Course** is par 72 and 7,070 yards. This is a challenging course with unbeatable ocean views. It's no wonder the Kiele is ranked a "Gold Medal" course by *Golf Magazine* and is considered one of the top five courses in Hawai`i. You're greeted at every hole by a white marble statue of an animal or mystical being: Happy Buddha, Elephant, Swan, Dragon, and, of course, The Golden Bear, in tribute to the master golfer who masterminded the course. Greens fees $195. The **Mokihana Golf Course** is par 72 and 6,900 yards. If you're not up for the challenge of the Kiele Course, the Mokihana will provide a pleasant experience. Golfers of all skill levels will find this an enjoyable experience. You have views of Mt. Wai`ale`ale, which is an incredible sight,

The Kiele Golf Course

The Mokihana Course

but you don't get the ocean views of the Kiele Course. Greens fees are $120.

Puakea Golf Course, 4150 Nuhou Street, Lihu`e, ☎ 866-773-5554, 808-245-8756, www.puakeagolf.com. Par 72; 6035 yards. Located across from Kukui Grove Shopping Center, Mount Haupu provides the backdrop for this course, designed by Robin Nelson. It opened in 2003, making it the newest course on the island. It is the most fun to play, especially if you're an intermediate player. You have mostly mountain views, but there is the occasional ocean view. You can play nine holes for $75 or all 18 holes for $125.

Puakea Golf Course, Hole 5

Tennis

There are two public courts in the Lihu`e area. **Lihu`e Country Park** has two lighted courts. They are on Hardy Street, between the Wilcox Elementary School and the Convention Hall (White Dome Building).

Puhi Park has two courts (without lights). You'll find them at the end of Nani Street in Puhi. If you're heading west on Kaumuali`i Highway just past Chiefess Kamakahele School, turn left on Nani Street. Courts are on the left, at the end of street.

Biking

One route that's great is the **Kalepa Ridge Trail**. It's a three-mile singletrack trail (three miles out and three back). It begins at the end of Hulei Road in Hanama`ulu and the ends with a grand view that overlooks the Wailua River. There are many other stunning view of the coastline, Kipu Ridge and Wai`ale`ale. The trail is appropriate for intermediate to advanced riders. There are some areas that will be too steep to ride, where you'll have to dismount and carry your bike. It's a dry dirt trail, so you should stay off the trail if it's wet.

To **rent a bike**, you can go to **Kaua`i Cycle and Tour**, 1379 Kuhio Highway in Kapa`a, ☎ 808-821-2115. They offer rentals starting at $15 a day. They also have maps and guided tours from $65 a day.

Stop by **Outfitters Kaua`i**, 2827A Po`ipu Rd, Po`ipu, ☎ 808-742-9667, www.outfitterskauai.com, to rent a bike and a car rack, throw the bikes on and go to town. They also offer bike maps to make it easier for you to find your way around.

Coming from Hanalei, you can rent one from **Pedal-N-Paddle**, ☎ 808-826-9069, www.pedalnpaddle.com, at Ching Young Village. They rent mountain bikes for $20 a day or $80 a week. Pedal-N-Paddle also has tandem bikes at $10 a day and cruisers for $10 a day or $30 a week.

ATVs

AUTHOR'S CHOICE ★ **Kipu Ranch Adventures**, ☎ 808-246-9288, www.kiputours.com. Their ATV tour is awesome, plain and simple. They start out teaching you the basics of ATV operation. You then ride through the 3,000 acres of Kipu Ranch, which still functions as a cattle ranch today. The friendly and knowledgeable guide will recount the history of the area. You'll also see where scenes were shot from *Jurassic Park*, *Raiders of the Lost Ark* and *Six Days, Seven Nights*. Kipu Ranch is an extraordinary place and the ATV tour is a fun and exciting way to explore the land. There's plenty of time to stop and take pictures. You'll want to because some of the scenery is striking, especially the view of Kipu Kai from the top of Mount Haupu. They have two tours: a three-hour tour for $109 per person and a four-hour tour over terrain that is a bit more challenging. It includes a stop at a waterfall and swimming area for $145 per person. If you don't want to ride on an ATV, they do have a two-passenger Yamaha Rhino and a four-passenger, guide-driven Kawasaki Mule available. This is an excellent option for families.

Ziplining

Kaua`i Backcountry zipline

**Kaua`i Backcountry Adventures**, Hanama`ulu, ☎ 808-270-0555, 808-245-2506, takes you through the old Lihu`e sugar cane plantation to a zipline course built on land that's not accessible to the general public. You start out with a short ride on their 4WD to the Lihu`e Plantation and the first zipline. You'll get safety information and gear before you start out on the seven ziplines down the mountainside. Some of the lines are really long and fun. You end with a deli lunch and a swim. Kaua`i Backcountry Adventures is a close second to Princeville Ranch Adventures for zipline tours. Both courses were fun and thoroughly enjoyable. The 3½-hour tour is $120 per person.

Just Live!, ☎ 808-482-1295, www.justlive.org, tends to gear their tours to corporations for teambuilding activities and youth and community building services. They do have tours for visitors, however, such as their Zipline Tree Top Tour. This consists of six ziplines, a 70-foot-high swinging bridge and, if that's not enough, a dual rope crossing that's 60 feet high. You zip over pine, eucalyptus, bamboo and mango trees. This tour is three hours and costs $99 per person.

For an added bonus, they have a unique Moonlight Zipline Tour. They provide headlamps so you can see where you're going. This one is held during the summer when there's a full moon.

If you want to get extreme about it, Just Live has a zipline tour that includes climbing a 60-foot rock wall and two spectacular zipline runs geared for the more adventurous types. This tour lasts 3½ hours and costs $115 per person.

On Water

Beaches

There are plenty of beaches in the Lihu`e area, which are great for sunbathing, surfing, snorkeling. The waters here tend to be much calmer than on the North Shore, even in the winter months.

Niumalu Beach Park is right near Nawiliwili Harbor. It's a small, three-acre park that has picnic tables, showers and restrooms. There's a boat ramp that's used to launch small boats, which makes kayaking and sailboarding popular here. It's also a popular place for picnics and campers. Camping is allowed with a County permit. To get here, follow Rice Street as it loops around at Kalapaki Beach and becomes Nawiliwili Road. Follow it past the Anchor Cove Shopping Plaza and bear left on Wa`apa.

Nawiliwili Park is located by Anchor Cove Shopping Center and Harbor Mall. The beach itself isn't very impressive. It's a favorite place for picnics, spearfishing, and shoreline fishermen as well as for beach volleyball There's a concrete wall that lines the area, so it's not pretty to look at. For swimming and sunbathing, you're better off going to nearby Kalapaki Beach.

Did you know that Nawiliwili means "the wili wili trees?" Hawaiians once used the orange and red seeds to make leis and the wood was light enough to be used for surfboards and canoes.

Kalapaki Beach is directly behind the Kaua`i Marriott Resort & Beach Club. It's a fine beach for swimming and surfing. There's an easy surf break that's perfect for beginners. You can get lessons there as well. On the downside, it is a crowded beach, mostly used by guests of the Marriott. Facilities include free parking, restrooms, and showers; food and drink are available at Kalapaki Beach Hut. There is no lifeguard. To get there, go to the entrance of the Marriott and turn right at the "Shoreline Access" sign.

Kalapaki Beach

Ninini Beach is north of Nawiliwili Harbor. Ninini is made up of two beaches separated by lava rock. It's a good spot for swimming and offers an excellent view of nearby mountain ranges and ships coming in and out of Nawiliwili Harbor. Both beaches are secluded and occasionally draw nudists to the area. Remember that nudity is illegal in Hawai`i. The smaller beach is a little rocky, while the larger one has a nice sandy bottom. The larger beach is much better for sunbathing, swimming and snorkeling.

To get there, take Ahukini Road, then turn right onto Kapule Highway. Turn left onto the unpaved road (the old Lihu`e Plantation Company Dirt Road) after half a mile. Turn left at the gate onto the paved road, then bear right when the road forks. Ninini Beach is at the end of the road, 1½ miles from the fork. There are no facilities and no lifeguards

Ahukini State Recreational Pier is a one-acre park at the end of Ahukini Road near the airport. This is a popular pole fishing spot with locals. It's also good for whale-watching during the winter months. The pier was used by cargo companies importing and exporting goods up until World War II.

Ahukini Pier *(shorediving.com)*

Hanumalu Beach Park is popular with locals for camping and picnics. Hanama`ulu Stream empties into the area and poor circulation causes the water to be murky. It's run by the Hawai`i Division of Land and Natural Resources. Swimming is prohibited in the area.

Nukolili Beach Park, a long sandy beach, is behind the Kaua`i Beach Resort. It is empty more often than not. The beach fronts part of Wailua Golf Course, so if you hear someone call "fore!" you'd better run for cover. The swimming conditions aren't great. The bottom is shallow and rocky. Strong currents form in high surf.

Kipu Kai, with Mt Haupu in the background

Kipu Kai is a small crescent beach that's one of the most beautiful on Kaua`i. Unfortunately, public access is extremely limited. You can get there by boat or through a private road in the estate. The last owner was cattle rancher John T. Waterhouse. Upon his death, Waterhouse bequeathed the land to the State of Hawai`i in 1984. He wanted the lands to be used as a nature and wildlife preserve. However, the land doesn't officially fall to the state until after the deaths of his nieces and nephews. You can get a glimpse of it through Kipu Ranch Adventure's ATV tour. They'll take you to the top of Mount Haupu. The stunning view below is Kipu Kai.

Snorkeling

Snorkel Tours

**SeaFun Kaua`i**, 1702 Haleukana Street, Lihu`e, ☎ 808-245-6400, has a four-hour snorkel tour that is perfect for beginners. You'll be provided with snorkel equipment and the tour is led by a marine biologist, who is eager to explain all of the mysterious marine life. They visit different beaches, depending on current ocean conditions, to provide the best possible experience for you. You'll also get basic instructions if you're new to snorkeling.

Captain Don's Sportfishing, Nawiliwili Harbor, ☎ 808-639-3012, www.captaindonsfishing.com. If you're looking for a private charter, check out Captain Don's Sportfishing. He'll take you out along Kaua`i's south shore. All equipment is provided, including flotation devices. Beginners are welcome, and Captain Don will give you with instructions if you need them. A three-hour trip will cost $375 and a four-hour run will be $475.

Places to Snorkel

If you want to go snorkeling on your own in the Lihu`e area, your best bets are **Kalapaki Beach** and **Ninini Beach**. The snorkeling in the area tends to be only fair at most times, but both beaches do have good snorkeling on very calm days. At Kalapaki, it tends to be calmer toward the eastern end of the beach.

You can pick up gear from **Kaua`i Beach Boys**, right at Kalapaki Beach. Free snorkeling instruction and tips are available with every rental, along with a snorkel map to direct you to the best snorkel spots on Kaua`i.

You should also stop at any of the rental shops listed above or at any grocer or pharmacy and pick up an underwater camera for about $12-$17. They are surprisingly easy to manage underwater. In order to take the best shots, you'll need to get pretty close. If the water's clear, you can certainly pick up the vibrant colors of reef fish.

Tubing

AUTHOR'S CHOICE

**Kaua`i Backcountry Adventures**, Hanama`ulu, ☎ 808-270-0555, 808-245-2506, takes you on a fun tubing adventure through the historic irrigation system of the former Lihu`e Plantation. This ditch and tunnel system that once irrigated vast sugar crops had been unused since sugar was taken out of production in 2000. Kaua`i Backcountry Adventures opened it up in January 2003 and it has been a popular tour on the island ever since. It's a very relaxing way to spend the afternoon as you travel through tunnels and down the ditch. After that, you're taken to a natural swimming hole for swimming and a deli lunch. My only complaint is that the tubing could have lasted a little longer. The guides are incredibly friendly and make sure that you're having a great time. You can tell they enjoy what they do. The tour lasts about three hours and is $99 per person.

Surfing

Kaua`i Beach Boys, ☎ 808-632-0071, offers 1½-hour lessons at Kalapaki Beach. They'll take you through the basics of surfing, safety and ocean knowledge. Then, you're in the water catching waves. The lessons are $65 and reservations are required. They also rent surfboards if you want to try it on your own. **Kalapaki Beach** is by far the best place to go for surfing in the area.

Boogie Boarding

The best place for boogie boarding in the Lihu`e area is also Kalapaki Beach. You can pick up a board at **Kaua`i Beach Boys**, ☎ 808-632-0071, which rents by the hour, day or week.

Kayaking

Aloha Canoes & Kayaks, ☎ 808-246-6804, takes you on a three-hour tour up the Huleia River, where you'll see the Menehune Fishpond and Kipu Ranch. From Kipu Ranch you hike to a waterfall and swimming area. The morning and afternoon tours cost $70 per person. There's a midday tour that includes lunch for $82 per person.

Ali`i Kayaks, Harbor Mall, ☎ 808-241-7700, has a one-hour guided kayak tour around Kalapaki Bay. If you have no idea what you're doing with a kayak, this is a good way to get introduced to the sport. Cost is $21 per person.

They also offer a tour of the Wailua River. Your guide will explain way the river is so revered in Hawaiian culture. You hike up to Secret Falls, where you have lunch. Plan on four miles of kayaking, and about 1½ miles of hiking. Tour duration is approximately 4½ hours and costs $104 per person.

Island Adventures, ☎ 808-246-6333, www.kauaifun.com, runs a kayak/hiking tour through Huleia National Wildlife Refuge. You paddle 2½ miles, then hike along an interesting forest trail full of exotic plantlife, birds and an occasional wild pig. After the hike, you hop on a van that takes you to a waterfall and swimming area. The cost is $89 per person for approximately three hours.

**Outfitters Kaua`i**, 2827A Po`ipu Rd, Po`ipu, ☎ 888-742-9887, 808-742-9667, runs kayak and hiking trips on the

Huleia River. You go through the Huleia National Wildlife Refuge, past Menehune Fishpond, as you paddle for about two miles up the river. You then tie up your kayak and hike three-quarters of a mile to Hidden Falls. You hike back to the river and then are picked up in a motorized canoe for the trip back. There's a morning tour that costs $94 per person. The afternoon tour includes lunch and costs $104 per person.

Kaua`i Beach Boys, ☎ 808-632-0071, rents double or single sit-on-top kayaks with life jackets and tall backrests. They're really meant to stay around the Kalapaki Beach area. The kayaks are just fine for a quick cruise, but not for a long haul.

**Ali`i Kayaks**, ☎ 808-241-7700, 3501 Rice Street, Harbor Mall, Lihu`e, will rent a kayak only if you're going to stay in Kalapaki Bay and the Huleia River. They do not rent for the Wailua River. Rentals run $15 and hour or $45 per day.

Canoeing

Aloha Canoes & Kayaks, ☎ 808-246-6804, shows you how to paddle a Hawaiian double hull canoe. You paddle around Kalapaki Bay, Nawiliwili Bay, Niumalu Bay and the Hulei'a River. The guides will give you a bit of a history lesson as well on the legends and myths of Kaua`i. The tours are held Monday, Wednesday and Friday. The 1½-hour tour is $60 per person. There's also a longer 3½-hour tour that includes some hiking and swimming for $82 per person. This one goes up the Huleia River, where you see the Menehune Fishpond, and to Kipu Ranch. A deli lunch is included.

Sailing

Kaua`i Beach Boys, at Kalapaki Beach, ☎ 808-632-0071, rents a small fleet of Hobie and Prindle catamarans on a daily basis for $90 per hour. They also offer sailing lessons and rides for $40 per person with a minimum of two people.

True Blue Charters, ☎ 808-246-6333, has a custom-built 42-foot trimaran that will take you on a private sunset cruise. They only do exclusive bookings and have a 20-person max.

Whale-Watching

True Blue Charters has a whale-watching tour during whale season for $59 per person. They also bring a marine naturalist on board to help narrate the tours.

Lahela Ocean Adventures, ☎ 808-635-4020, will take you out on their 34-foot Lahela sport fishing boat for a two-hour private whale-watching excursion. The boat holds up to six passengers and costs $299.

Captain Don's Sportfishing, www.captaindonsfishing.com, ☎ 808-639-3012, offers a 2½-hour whale-watching tour for $325 or $75 per person on shared trips. Captain Don will go where the whales go, so you won't miss a thing.

Fishing

Nawiliwili Harbor is home to most of the fishing charter companies on the island. Any one of these tours will offer deep sea fishing or bottom fishing.

Kai Bear, ☎ 808-652-4556, www.kaibear.com, has four- and six-hour shared charters ranging from $160 to $230. They also have four- , six- and eight-hour private charters starting at $800. They get you fishing within 15 minutes of leaving the slip on their 38- or 42-foot Bertrams. They also provide you with one custom-made Blue Water Rod and Penn International Gold two-speed reel and lures. Depending on the season, you can catch ahi (tuna), marlin, and mahi-mahi.

True Blue Charters, ☎ 808-246-6333, will provide you with all of the necessary items: bait, tackle, lures. Deep sea fishing includes marlin, tuna, wahoo, mahi-mahi and shark. Bottom fishing includes mackerel, rudder fish, wrasse, sea bass, and rainbow runner. Prices start at $139 per person for a four-hour trip or $179 for a six-hour trip. Eight-hour excursions are also available.

Breakaway Fishing Charters, ☎ 808-635-9456, is run by Captain Jeff Steiner, who offers private and shared charters. The tours last four to eight hours, with equipment and beverages provided. A four-hour shared tour starts at $115 per person and rates go up to $1,000 for an exclusive all-day charter. You can go trolling, bating or bottom fishing. At the end of your trip, Captain Jeff will fillet and divide fish.

Captain Don's Sportfishing, ☎ 808-639-3012, www.captaindonsfishing.com, will take you fishing aboard the *June Louise*, which is a 34-foot twin diesel. You be looking to catch mahimahi, ono and ahi. The captain will clean and fillet your catch for you. If you've finally caught the whopper that would look great over the fireplace back home, Captain Don will put you in touch with the taxidermists to get it mounted. A four-hour shared charter costs $125 per person and goes up to $875 for an eight-hour private charter.

Lahela Ocean Adventures, ☎ 808-635-4020, will take you to catch marlin, mahi-mahi or tuna. After your trip, they can have your trophy catch mounted and shipped to you or they will fillet portions of your catch. They do four- , six- or eight-hour private and shared tours starting at $425.

If you just want to pick up a pole and see what happens, you can go to **Ahukini State Recreational Pier**. It's a small, one-acre park at the southern end of Hanama`ulu Bay. It's a popular place for pole fishing. The bay is a Marine Protected Area and is regulated by the state. If you plan on spearfishing or net fishing in the area, check with the Department of Land and Natural Resources for more information at ☎ 808-274-3344 or write Division of Aquatic Resources, 3060 Eiwa Street, Room 306, Lihu`e, HI 96766. To get to the pier, drive to the end of Ahukini Road (Highway 570) off Kuhio Highway (Highway 56) in Lihu`e.

Another popular spot for pole fishermen is **Nawiliwili Park**, right next to Kalapaki Beach. If anything, it's convenient. You literally just drive up, drop your line and see what happens.

Stop by **Lihu`e Fishing Supply**, 2985 Kalena Street, ☎ 808-245-4930, for any fishing supplies you need.

In the Air

Helicopter Tours

AUTHOR'S CHOICE ★ **Jack Harter Helicopters**, ☎ 888-245-2001, 808-245-3774, www.helicopters-kauai.com. Jack Harter is the guy who started it all. He began the first helicopter service in 1962. He's no longer doing tours, but he does make sure you are in good, capable hands. One thing that the company is known for is their detailed and accurate information. I found the narration insightful and accurate. The company has two planes. The ASTAR is roomy and comfortable, with huge windows for everyone to get a good view. Their Hughes 500 helicopter is a four-passenger helicopter that is flown with the doors off for that extra sense of adventure. Both have a two-way communication system, which allows a dialog between you and the pilot.

They have two tours. A 60-minute one for $229 per person covers all the major areas, such as Nawiliwili Harbor and the Menehune Fishpond, Waimea Canyon, Na Pali, Mt. Wai`ale`ale and Manawaiopuna Falls in Hanapepe Valley. They also have a 90-minute tour for $299 per person that follows the same route, but is much slower to allow more photo opportunities.

Will Squyers Helicopter Tours, ☎ 888-245-4354, 808-245-8881, 808-245-7541, www.willsquyres.com, flies in air-conditioned ASTAR 350s with custom windows to maximize viewing. The pilots are knowledgeable and the company loves to highlight its perfect safety record. The 55-minute tour takes you to Waimea Canyon, Mount Wai`ale`ale, Alakai Swamp, Wailua Falls and the Na Pali Coast. It costs $219.

Will Squyers Helicopter Tours

Safari Helicopter Tours, ☎ 800-326-3356, 808-246-0136, www.safariair.com. This family-owned company flies air-conditioned ASTAR 350B2-7 helicopters that have forward-facing seats with more legroom, a soundproof cabin with Bose stereo headsets and a two-way intercom system between pilot and passengers. You have unobstructed views while a four-camera video system records your flight. The Deluxe Waterfall Safari is 55 minutes at $224 per person. Check Safari's website before you book for potential savings.

**Island Helicopters Kaua`i**, ☎ 808-245-8588, www.islandhelicopters.com, has two new six-passenger ASTAR helicopters. All offer smooth and stable flight with forward-facing seats, extra-large windows, state-of-the-art CD stereo systems and two-way communication between pilot and passengers. The main attraction is the "Kaua`i Grand" tour, which pretty much follows the same route as the other helicopter companies – Manawaiopuna Falls in the Hanapepe Valley (as seen in the movie *Jurassic Park*) Olokele Canyon, Waimea Canyon, the Na Pali Coast and, weather permitting, on to Mount Wai`ale`ale. This 50-minute flight costs $250 per person. It's not a bad tour, but you can do better elsewhere.

Blue Hawaiian Helicopters, ☎ 800-745-2583, 808-245-5800, www.bluehawaiian.com, only offers one tour. The 50-minute ECO Adventure flies on an ECO-Star helicopter, which gives you more room and less noise. It also has a two-way communication system and large windows that are great for photos. Your tour starts in Lihu`e and heads to Hanapepe Valley, and Mana Waiapuna, the waterfalls featured in *Jurassic Park*. Then it's on to Waimea Canyon and the Na Pali Coast. The narration is pretty good, but the helicopter's the real star. This 50-minute flight is $219 per person.

**Air Kaua`i Helicopters,** ☎ 808-246-4666, www.airkauai.com, flies one tour that lasts for about 60 minutes through Hanapepe Valley, Waimea Canyon, the Na Pali Coast and Mount Wai`ale`ale. The ASTAR helicopters are equipped with Bose Acoustic Stereo headsets, providing two-way communication. The tour costs $195 per person. Be sure to book in advance.

Heli USA Airways, ☎ 808-826-6591, www.heliusahawaii.com, does one tour out of Lihu`e Airport. All of their tours start you off with a video presentation. Then you climb aboard their ASTAR helicopter and fly around the island. You head into Hanapepe Valley, Waimea Canyon, Na Pali Cliffs, pass Bali Hai and Hanalei Valley. This tour is only 45 minutes and is $169.

Air Tours

**Wings Over Kaua`i,** ☎ 808-635-0815, www.wingsoverkauai.com. If riding in a helicopter doesn't appeal to you, perhaps a four-seat Cessna 172 Skyhawk will. Wings Over Kaua`i offers informative airplane tours. You cruise above waterfalls, the Waimea Canyon, and the Na Pali coastline. The rates for tours start at $86 per person for a 30-minute flight with a two-person minimum. The rates go up to $130 for a 70-minute tour.

**Air Ventures Kaua`i,** ☎ 866-464-7864, 808-651-0679, www.airventureskauai.com, is another option if you don't want to take a helicopter. They fly in a Maule MXT7-180 STOL aircraft. The pilot is very knowledgeable and makes the tour fun. For $69, you can book a 40-minute tour that takes a different route from Lihu`e Airport up the east coast of the island, where you see Sleeping Giant and Kilauea Lighthouse. The 60-minute tour circles the island, going over Waimea, the Na Pali Coast, Hanalei Valley and Kilauea Lighthouse. The rate for this one is $99. If you go to their website, you can get discounted rates on their flights, as well as discounted air/boat tour combos.

Kaua`i Aero Tours, ☎ 808-639-9893. If I had to sum up this tour in one word, it would have to be "Wow!" You fly in a Classic Citabria that was specifically designed for acrobatics. Not only will you see the sights of the island, but you also fly acrobatic loops, barrel rolls and other maneuvers. The pilot will even let you take the stick. They can only take one person at a time. Tours range from 30 to 60 minutes; prices start at $125.

Tropical Bi-Planes, ☎ 808-246-9123, www.tropicalbiplanes.com. If you ever wanted to ride in a plane with a classic look and feel, here's your chance. Tropical Biplanes, operated by Fly Kaua`i, runs tours in its 2002 WACO WMF Super bi-plane. You even get the nostalgic cloth helmet and goggles. Fortunately, the plane is modern, so you get a headset that provides two-way communication. The open cockpit gives you a feeling of freedom as you fly around Waimea Canyon and up the Na Pali Coast. They have 30- and 45-minute rides that travel either to the North Shore or along the South Shore, for $178 and $267 per couple, respectively. They also have a 60-minute ride that travels along the South Shore, up to the Na Pali coastline, Hanalei and Princeville for $356.

■ Spas & Health Clubs

Alexander Day Spa & Salon, Kaua`i Marriott, ☎ 808-246-4918, www.alexanderspa.com. The Kaua`i Marriott Resort & Beach Club's full-service day spa offers facials, body wraps and a wide variety of massages at the spa or on the beach. The salon will take care of all your beauty needs, and it doesn't even have to be your wedding day.

Mana Massage, ☎ 808-822-4746, www.manamassage.com. You'll find an eclectic mix of healing techniques at Mana Massage. They combine Hawaiian lomi lomi, myofascial release, hot lava stone, deep tissue and sports massage, among many others. You leave feeling lighter and more relaxed. You can find them inside the **Kaua`i Athletic Center** or in Wailua overlooking the Wailua River. They'll even come to you.

Kaua`i Athletic Club, Kukui Grove Professional Bldg, 4370 Kukui Grove Street, Lihu`e, ☎ 808-245-5381. Open Monday through Friday from 5:30 am to 9 pm and Saturday and Sunday from 8 am to 5 pm. If you can't help yourself and HAVE to get to the gym, the Kaua`i Athletic Club has free weights, Cybex machines and treadmills for your use. There are also five racquetball courts. You can get a daily membership for $12 or weekly membership for $45.

■ Shopping

Kukui Grove Shopping Center in Lihu`e is the largest mall on Kaua`i. There's a free shuttle that will take you from Nawiliwili Pier to the shopping center. One shop that's worth the trip is the **Kaua`i Products Store**, ☎ 808-246-6753. This is a great place to buy unique gifts that you find only on Kaua`i. They have everything from soaps, clothes and guava jams to Ni`ihau shell leis and coffee. There are also fine koa work, bamboo furniture, bronze sculptures and Hawaiian quilts to appreciate and purchase.

If you're on your way to the airport and didn't have a chance to do any shopping, there's still hope. Near Lihu`e Airport on Kuhio Highway is **Kaua`i Fruit & Flower**, 3-4684 Kuhio Highway, ☎ 800-943-3108, 808-245-1814. Pick up pineapples and papayas here that are already approved and inspected so you can check the boxes in as baggage or ship them home. They also ship flowers, leis, coffee and gift baskets.

For alohawear that screams Hawai`i, you must stop by **Hilo Hattie**, 3252 Kuhio Highway and Ahukini Road, ☎ 808-245-3404, www.hilohattie.com. They also have literally thousands of souvenirs (some are pretty tacky, some are not) to take home. You'll find everything Hawaiiana:

books, lighters, keychains, food, mugs, tiki items, t-shirts and a whole lot more.

After you tour the **Kaua`i Museum**, ☎ 808-245-6931, have a look at the **Edith Wilcox Gift Shop** in the museum, where you'll find Kaua`i crafts such as Ni`ihau shell leis, woodwork, lauhala weavings, a selection of historic books, cards, ornaments, ceramics, koa and coconut products.

Two Frogs Hugging

Two Frogs Hugging, 3215 Kuhio Hwy, ☎ 808-246-8777, the store you can't miss on Kuhio Highway, is a fun stop to peruse the handcrafted home accessories, Asian antiques and furniture.

Right by the Marriott, there are the Harbor Mall and Anchor Cove Shopping Centers. They're across the street from each other. At **Harbor Mall**, there are stores such as **Yong's Aloha Fashion**, which has a decent selection of alohawear, **Sandra's Crafts**, and **Human Rites Tattoo** – if you want a permanent reminder of your stay on Kaua`i.

Over at **Anchor Cove Shopping Center**, there's **Seven Seas Trading Company**, ☎ 808-632-2200, www.sevenseastradingcompany.com, which carries locally made and designed wooden bowls and boxes, jewelry, photography, artwork and clothing.

Carved marble box, Seven Seas Trading

Honolua Surf Company, Anchor Cove, ☎ 808-246-3636, www.honoluasurf.com, is a fine place to pick up surf apparel such as board shorts, swimwear and accessories. They also have a store in Po`ipu.

Kaua`i Recycling for the Arts

For truly unique jewelry and art, check out **Kaua`i Recycling for the Arts**, 3460 Ahukini Road, Lihu`e, ☎ 808-632-0555. It's a non-profit organization that takes recycled glass and creates art. There are free tours and demonstrations of the studio Tuesday-Friday from 9 am to 1 pm. Call ahead to reserve a tour.

Kilohana has a number of excellent shops hidden within the main house and elsewhere on the grounds. There is **The Country Store**, ☎ 808-246-2778, on the ground level of the main house. It sells gifts and collectibles made from koa, pottery pieces.

Grandes Gems & Gallery, ☎ 808-245-3445, specializes in Tahitian black pearls, opals, tanzanite, Chinese gambling chips and a unique selection of jewelry.

The Artisans Room, ☎ 808-245-9352, is on the lower floor of the main house. Here you can see the work of recognized artists. They have a fine collection of originals, prints and sculptures.

Clayworks at Kilohana, ☎ 808-245-2529, is a working ceramics studio and gallery. You can buy pieces that were created by Kaua`i artists here. You can even create your own work of art during studio hours. They also offer workshops and classes. Call for more information.

Clayworks at Kilohana

**Kaua`i Nursery & Landscape**, 3-1550 Kaumuali`i Highway, Lihu`e, ☎ 888-345-7747, 808-245-7747, www.kauainursery.com, sells certified plants that can be shipped to the mainland, such as orchids, plumeria, ginger and many others.

If quilting is of interest, be sure to check out **Kapaia Stitchery**, Kuhio Highway and Ma`alo Road, ☎ 808-245-2281. Here you will find Hawaiian quilts, fabrics and designs. Or you can pick up aloha fabrics and create your own alohawear.

If you want a bottle of wine to celebrate a special occasion, or just to enjoy, visit **The Wine Garden**, 4495 Puhi Road, Puhi Village Plaza, ☎ 808-245-5766. They have a full selection of vintage wines from California, Italy, Portugal, Germany and France. They also carry sparkling wines, ports and champagne. They're open Tuesday through Saturday from 10 am to 6:30 pm.

For necessities like suntan lotion, slippers, or film, you can stop by **K-Mart**, Nawiliwili Road, Lihu`e, ☎ 808-245-7742, or **Wal-Mart**, ☎ 808-246-1599.

Groceries

There are a few grocery stores in Lihu`e. There's the **Big Save** on Rice Street in Lihu`e, just behind the Kaua`i Museum. There's also a **Star Market** at Kukui Grove Center. Finally, after a long wait, **Costco** opened its doors to the public in October 2006. The store is in the Kukui Grove Shopping Center.

Don't forget about the **Kaua`i County Farmer's Market**, which happens every Friday at 3 pm in the Vidnha Stadium parking lot. There's also a private farmer's market on Mondays at 3 pm at Kukui Grove Shopping Center.

■ Where to Stay

Resorts

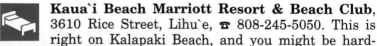

**Kaua`i Beach Marriott Resort & Beach Club**, 3610 Rice Street, Lihu`e, ☎ 808-245-5050. This is right on Kalapaki Beach, and you might be hard-pressed to find a good reason to leave the resort area to see the rest of the island. You have world-class golf in the Mokihana and Kiele golf courses nearby. You have a variety of restaurants, or bars. There are five tennis courts on the property, shopping and a fitness center. What else do you need? You could take a swim in the dazzling 26,000-square-foot circular pool, complete with cascading waterfalls. Or you could walk around the 800 acres of property.

Kaua`i Beach Marriott pools

The resort is stunning and well-manicured. There are statues, lagoons, waterfalls and fountains just about everywhere you look. The rooms are decent, with either garden views or views of Kalapaki Beach. There are also some time-share units in this resort, and don't be surprised if you're asked to sit through a time-share presentation while you're there.

Kaua`i Beach Marriott

It's very family-friendly. There's a program for children aged five-12 called Kalapaki Kids. For $45 for a full day, kids get to participate in different activities including lessons in Hawaiian culture, garden explorations, hula lessons, Hawaiian crafts, `ukulele lessons and more. The program includes a lunch, snack and a Kalapaki Kids T-shirt. $400+.

**Hilton Kaua`i Beach Hotel & Resort**, formerly Radisson Kaua`i Beach Resort, 4331 Kaua`i Beach Drive, Lihu`e, ☎ 808-245-1955, www.kauaibeachhotelandresort.com. The Kaua`i Hotel & Resort sits right on the beach. The beach is pretty, but is not good for swimming. But you're close to Lydgate State Park, which makes up for it. At the very least, you have a nice beach to walk on at sunrise or sunset. The

Hilton Kaua`i Beach

rooms are wonderfully decorated and fresh from a major renovation. Each room has a lana`i with ocean, lagoon, garden, mountain, or pool views. There's the Alolani Spa and Fitness Center, featuring a sauna and cardiovascular equipment. At press time, there are a number of renovations going on, so it's difficult to give the hotel a fair assessment. Most of the renovations were in the pools. Be aware that there is a "resort fee" of $10.95, which pays for services such as wireless Internet access. $200-$400.

Hotels

Tip Top Motel, 3173 Akahi Street, Lihu`e, ☎ 808-245-2333, is the place to stay if you're here for one night or if you just want a cheap place and don't plan on spending much time in your room. The rooms are small and have concrete walls. Sometimes the rooms are very clean, sometimes not. The Tip Top has been owned by the same family since 1916. There are 34 units, each with air conditioning and a television. Under $100.

Motel Lani, 4240 Rice Street, Lihu`e, ☎ 808-245-2965. For the price, you can't beat it. There are only nine rooms. It's a good place to stay if you're on a budget and want very simple accommodations. The rooms are very small, clean and barely furnished (most likely because furniture would make the room feel too cramped). There aren't televisions in the rooms, but you didn't come all this way to watch television, did you? Another plus for the hotel is that it's centrally located in Lihu`e. Under $100.

Kaua`i Palms

**Kaua`i Palms Hotel**, formerly Hale Lihu`e Motel, 2931 Kalena St, ☎ 808-246-0908, www.kauaipalmshotel.com. Here's the best value on Kaua`i, hands down. They recently changed hands and the new ownership has invested quite a bit to make sure you get the most bang for your buck. The grounds are newly landscaped, the hotel is newly painted, and the rooms now have flat screen televisions. The rooms are small but nicely decorated. The grounds are charming, with a feel of the old-plantation era. Rates are as low as $65 a night, which makes for a great deal. If you're hungry, there's no need to worry. You're within walking distance of at least a dozen restaurants in Lihu`e.

On the downside, the Kaua`i Palms is not secluded by any means. It's right off of Rice Street, so you may experience an uncomfortable night. If you're immune to traffic noise, it shouldn't be a problem. If you're a light sleeper, you might want to reconsider staying here. Under $100.

**The Kaua`i Inn**, 2430 Hulemalu Road, ☎ 800-808-2330, 808-245-9000, www.kauai-inn.com. This family-run place was one of the first hotels on Kaua`i. In the 1960s, you could see people like John Wayne and Lee Marvin hanging out by the pool. The location is excellent. You're near the airport and Kalapaki Beach. The rooms are pleasant and are equipped with microwaves, refrigerators, telephones, cable TVs, and king beds. Many have private lana`is, with ocean and mountain views. The Inn offers poolside complimentary continental breakfast, barbecues and horseshoes. $100-$200.

Garden Island Inn, 3445 Wilcox Road, Lihu`e, ☎ 800-648-0154, 808-245-7227, www.gardenislandinn.com, is near Kalapaki Beach and within easy driving distance of other parts of the island. The grounds are well kept; tropical flowers, banana trees and papaya trees surround the property.

Garden Island Inn

The 21 rooms were recently renovated to create a bright and comfortable atmosphere. The rooms include tropical flower arrangements, a refrigerator, microwave, coffeemaker, air-conditioning, television, phone, and ocean view. Boogie boards and snorkeling gear are provided, along with beach gear, ice chests and golf clubs. The Garden Island Inn provides a relaxed setting at a fantastic price. $100-$200.

Condos

Castle Kaha Lani, formerly Aston Kaha Lani, 4460 Nehe Road, Lihu`e, ☎ 800-367-5004, 808-822-9331, www.castleresorts.com. This 74 unit establishment is 50 to 100 yards from the ocean. You'll find the lana`is to be incredibly spacious. The condos as well, with 1,400 square feet of living space. The rooms are very comfortable. They have full kitchens. There is a heated swimming pool, sun deck, barbecue area, tennis court and putting green on the property. The only downside is that the beach isn't swim-friendly. Dangerous rip tides tend to form in the area. At least you're near Lydgate State Beach Park. Wailua Golf Course also borders the property.

Castle Kaha Lani

Banyan Harbor Resort, 3411 Wilcox Road, Lihu`e, ☎ 800-422-6926, 808-245-7333, www.vacation-kauai.com, has 148 one- and two-bedroom condominiums near Kalapaki Beach. All of the units have fully stocked kitchens and a washer/dryer unit. Not all of them have air conditioning. If you really want it, you have to ask. On-site, there's a pool that's heated in the winter, tennis, shuffleboard and barbecue grills. You're also very close to the golf courses at Kaua`i Lagoons. It's a fine value in a central location. $100-$200.

Castle Kaha Lani

Vacation Rentals

Kaua`i Vacation Rentals List, www.kauaivacationresorts.com. This is a directory that lists hundreds of condominiums, secluded honeymoon cottages, oceanfront luxury homes and beachfront bungalows throughout the island. They have listings to fit all budgets, from $400 to $21,000 per week.

Kaua`i Vacation Rentals, ☎ 808-367-5025, 808-245-8841, www.kauaivacationrentals.com, has a large selection of vacation rental homes. Whether it's a cottage, bungalow, ocean-view condo, beachfront villa or luxurious oceanfront home, they probably have it in their inventory.

Garden Island Properties, ☎ 800-801-0378, 808-822-4871, www.kauaiproperties.com, handles vacation properties across the island. They have vacation rental homes, cottages and beach condos starting from $500 a week.

Prosser Realty, 4379 Rice Street, Lihu`e, ☎ 800-767-4707, 808-245-4711, www.prosser-realty.com, has vacation rentals all over the island. They have properties ranging from budget-priced condominiums to incredibly luxurious homes.

Camping

To camp on Kaua`i, you need to get a permit. Depending on where you plan on camping, you either have to go through the state or county to get a permit.

If you plan on camping at Hanama`ulu Beach Park or Niumalu Beach Park, you have to go though the Kaua`i County Division Parks of Recreation. To obtain a county permit, contact the Kaua`i County Parks Permit Section by calling ☎ 808-241-4463. Their hours are 8:15 am to 4 pm Monday through Friday. Camping permit fees are $3 per adult, per night for non-residents and free for Hawai`i residents.

If you need to pick up **camping gear**, I recommend that you buy it at **K-mart** or **Wal-Mart** in Lihu`e. Both stores have gear that's cheap. For food, stop by **Big Save** in Lihu`e or **Star Market** at Kukui Grove Shopping Center.

If you want to **rent your gear**, you have to go all the way to **Pedal-N-Paddle** in the Ching Young Shopping Village in Hanalei, ☎ 808-826-9069. They offer daily and weekly rates for two-person tents, single-burner stoves and sleeping bags. **Kayak Kaua`i**, also in Hanalei, offers daily and weekly rental rates for day packs, backpacks, two-person tents, stoves and sleeping bags.

■ Where To Eat

JJ's Broiler, Anchor Cove, ☎ 808-246-4422, 888-246-4422. Open 11 am-10 pm. Serving lunch and dinner daily. Reservations are recommended for dinner, especially if you want to sit outside. JJ's Broiler is well known for its fantastic location overlooking Kalapaki Beach and for the food. They serve fresh fish, steak, sandwiches and pasta. The food is good and reasonably priced, and you can't beat the location. Lunch $14-$35, dinner $35-$50.

Aroma's, Harbor Mall second floor, ☎ 808-245-9192. Hours are Tuesday to Friday from 7 am to 9:30 pm, Saturday and Sunday from 8 am to 9:30 pm. Breakfast is served from 7 to 11 am, lunch 11:30 to 4:30 and dinner from 5:30 to closing. Reservations are recommended for lunch and dinner. There's a lot going on at this lively spot. The menu is an eclectic mix of influences, from Italian to Pacific Rim. It includes steaks, osso bucco and a vegetarian tofu stir fry, which is excellent. Breakfast under $15, lunch $15-$35, dinner $35-$50.

AUTHOR'S CHOICE ★ **Café Portofino**, Kaua`i Beach Marriott Resort & Beach Club, ☎ 808-245-2121. Open for dinner nightly 5-9 pm. If you're looking for a true Italian experience, come to Café Portofino. The menu is strictly Northern Italian and the restaurant sits above Kalapaki Beach, so you have delightful views of the ocean. The atmosphere is comfortable and romantic. On the menu, you can get eggplant parmesan, a wide variety of pastas, osso bucco, chicken or steak. $35-$50.

Dani's Restaurant, 4201 Rice Street, Lihu`e, ☎ 808-245-4991. Open Monday-Friday 5 am-1:30 pm, Saturday 5 am-1 pm. This is a place to go for breakfast and a cheap, local lunch. They serve mostly standard breakfast fare in the morning and plate lunches in the afternoon. The food quality isn't bad, considering the prices. You can get Kalua pig, laulau, teriyaki chicken or steak, beef stew or tripe stew. Under $15.

Deli & Bread Connection, Kukui Grove Center, ☎ 808-245-7115. Hours are Monday-Thursday 9:30 am to 7 pm, Friday 9:30 am to 9 pm, Saturday 9:30 am to 7 pm, Sunday 10 am to 6 pm. There's a reason the Deli & Bread Connection is always packed at lunch. They serve healthy and appetizing soups, sandwiches and baked goods. They serve a delicious meatloaf on occasion. It's not always available, but do try it if available. Under $15.

Duke's Kaua`i, Marriott Resort & Beach Club, ☎ 808-246-9599. Open daily 11:30 am-midnight. Duke's is a tribute to surfing's first icon, Duke Kahanamoku. It's a popular place with locals and tourists alike. Situated on Kalapaki Beach, it's hard not to come here and have a good time. The food is enjoyable, the atmosphere is nice, and the crowd tends to be lively. Duke's has live Hawaiian entertainment nightly. $15-$35.

Duke's Kaua`i

Gaylord's at Kilohana

Gaylord's Restaurant, at Kilohana, 3-2087 Kaumuali`i Highway, ☎ 808-245-9593, www.gaylordskauai.com. Open for breakfast 7:45-10 am, lunch 11 am-2 pm, dinner 5:30-9 pm. The restaurant is in a pleasant, open atmosphere that evokes the old plantation days The breakfast buffet isn't all that exciting, with standard fare, such as eggs, fruit, sweet rolls, and Portuguese sausage. Sunday brunch is also served from 8 am to 2:30 pm. The menu includes made-to-order eggs, pancakes, salad, and kalua pork hash. It's reasonably priced. For lunch and dinner, the food is fine, though the service is often less than ideal. Breakfast under $15, lunch $15-$35, dinner $35-$50, Sunday brunch $15-$35.

AUTHOR'S CHOICE ★ **Hamura's Saimin Stand**, 2956 Kress Street, Lihu`e, ☎ 808-245-3271 Open Monday-Thursday from 10 am-11 pm; Friday and Saturday from 10 am-midnight; Sunday from 10 am-9 pm. Hamura's is a local legend. The place looks like a hole in the wall, the menu is basic, and the saimin is fabulous. You've never had saimin until you've been to Hamura's. Under $15.

Hamura's Saimin

AUTHOR'S CHOICE ★ **Hanama`ulu Restaurant Tea House & Ara's Sushi Bar**, 3-4291 Kuhio Highway, Hanama`ulu, ☎ 808-245-2511. A family-owned restaurant for more than 60 years, this is a favorite with locals. It's great if you're looking for something off the beaten path. The interior is something else: authentic Japanese teahouses, stone paths, fish ponds are all here. Chinese and Japanese food is served. The service is fantastic and the food is full of flavor. Lunch $15-$35, dinner $35-$50.

AUTHOR'S CHOICE ★ **Colenti's**, Kukui Grove Shopping Center, ☎ 808-246-4940. The atmosphere here is that of a typical pizza joint, with cheap table booths and plastic benches. All that's missing is the red checkered tablecloth. The food is excellent. If you want to get a slice of pizza, this is the place to go. It's about as good as anything I've had. Their meatball parmesan sandwich is also something special. The service is friendly, and the food is reasonably priced. Under $15-$35.

**Ki`ibo Restaurant**, 2991 Umi Street, ☎ 808-245-2650. Open Monday-Saturday for lunch 11 am-1:30 pm; dinner 5:30-9 pm. Ki`ibo features cuisine such as shrimp or vegetable tempura, a variety of sushi, fresh sashimi, beef, chicken or pork teriyaki. You can also pick up a lunch bento (Japanese boxed lunch) for $5.25, which is cheap and easy. The service is fast and courteous, the food is inexpensive and good. A great value overall! Under $15.

A meal from La Bamba

La Bamba Mexican Restaurant, Kukui Grove Shopping Center, Lihu`e, ☎ 808-245-5972. Open daily 11 am-9 pm. Substantial portions of all the hearty standards ensure that no one goes hungry, and you'd be hard-pressed to finish off a plate of chiles rellenos or aromatic fajitas in one sitting. It's even more trying given that all entrées come with sides of beans and rice. Still, no one complains since the abundance of food only makes the affordable prices that much better. Lunch under $15, dinner $15-$35.

Ma's Family Restaurant, 4277 Halenani Street, Lihu`e, ☎ 808-245-3142. Open from 5 am to 1 pm, Monday through Friday, and from 5 am on Saturday and Sunday. This family restaurant has been at it for over 40 years and is a Kaua`i institution. They have a reputation for their large, tasty and inexpensive breakfasts and lunches. Ma's is great for plate lunches. Under $15. Cash only.

Oki Diner, 4491 Rice Street, Lihu`e, ☎ 808-245-5899. Open daily 6 am-3 am. Their pancakes are good, but not as good at at Tip Top Café.The service is OK at times, at other times not acceptable. The plate lunches are worth coming here for. The hours obviously work well if you're a night owl.

Rob's Good Time Grill, Rice Shopping Center, Lihu`e, ☎ 808-821-2205. Open for lunch and dinner 11 am-9 pm; Happy Hour 2-7 pm. This is a fun sportsbar. The food isn't bad and the drinks are plentiful. They offer a typical bar menu: burgers, sandwiches and pupus. Overall, it's an enjoyable place that won't break your budget. Under $15-$35.

Naupaka Terrace Steakhouse, Hilton Kaua`i Beach Resort, ☎ 808-245-1955. Open for dinner 6:30-9:30 pm. Naupaka Terrace is on the beach. They feature steak and seafood. The real reason to come here is for the prime rib and crab buffet. The atmosphere is pleasant, with ocean and pool views. The service could improve but, other than that, Naupaka Terrace makes for a pleasant dining experience.

Naupaka Terrace Restaurant

Tip Top Café & Bakery, 3173 Akahi St, Lihu`e, ☎ 808-245-2333. There is one reason to come here and one reason alone: banana macadamia nut pancakes. Need I say more? Tip Top Café has been known for years as a great place for pancakes. It's been around since 1916, so they've had some time to perfect that recipe. For lunch, typical local fare is featured on the menu and they are well known for oxtail soup.

The conveyor belt at Genki Sushi

Genki Sushi, Kukui Grove Shopping Center, ☎ 808-632-2450. Hours are Sunday-Thursday from 11 am to 9 pm, Friday and Saturday from 10:30 am to 10 pm. At Genki Sushi, it's not about the sushi. It's more about the novelty of having your sushi served on a conveyor belt. Seriously, the sushi goes round and round until someone takes it. It's the little things in life that are amusing. The sushi is surprisingly good and is reasonably priced. Under $15.

■ Nightlife/Culture

They say that Kaua`i doesn't have much of a nightlife, but one does actually exist in the Lihu`e area. There are a few bars that are open late worth checking out.

Rob's Good Time Grill, ☎ 808-821-2205, in the Rice Shopping Center, Lihu`e, is a fun sportsbar. The food isn't bad. It's one of the few places on Kaua`i that stays open late (until 2 am). They have seven televisions so you can catch your game, live entertainment, karaoke and dancing. There are a couple of pool tables. The menu is your typical bar menu: burgers, sandwiches and pupus. Overall, it's a enjoyable place that won't break your budget.

Duke's Canoe Club and Barefoot Bar, on Kalapaki Beach at the Kaua`i Marriott Resort & Beach Club, is a bar that features contemporary Hawaiian music on Friday nights. A Hawaiian trio plays upstairs every night. The menu is mostly American with a Hawaiian touch.

Kukui's Restaurant, also at the Marriott, has a sunset hula show on Saturday and a torch-lighting ceremony on Monday and Thursday.

Kukui's

You can try out the **Lihu`e Bowling Center** at the Rice Shopping Center in Lihu`e, ☎ 808-245-5263. They have pool tables and a karaoke lounge.

Nawiliwili Tavern, ☎ 808-245-1781, can be considered the best dive bar on Kaua`i. There's a mix of locals and tourists. This does have a neighborhood bar feel to it. They serve pupus and plate-lunch dinners, staying open until 1 am. Drop by for a cold one and get into a dart or pool game, or watch sports on satellite TV.

Kuikui Grove Cinema, ☎ 808-245-5055, at Kukui Grove Shopping Center, has first-run features on four screens.

Hula Show

Kaua`i's beloved **Auntie Bev** gives a free hula show at Harbor Mall. The show is every Wednesday at 12:15 pm. It's free to the public.

Luaus

The imu ceremony

Luau Kilohana, 3-2087 Kaumuali`i Highway, Lihu`e, ☎ 808-245-9593. Tuesday and Thursday nights at 5 pm. Adults are $65, children four-12 are $35. Luau Kilohana is held on the 30-acre grounds of Kilohana, a former plantation manager's estate. The luau begins at 5 pm, with cultural activities on the grounds. You can tour the estate, or check out any one of the demonstrations about Hawaiian culture and the history of the sugar industry in Kaua`i.

At 6:15, there's an imu ceremony, where the roasted pig is uncovered, and then feasting begins. The food is cooked at Gaylord's, the fine dining restaurant on the estate grounds. The menu includes Kalua pig, lomi-lomi salmon, teriyaki beef, pineapple chicken, poi, sweet potatoes and, for dessert, haupia (coconut custard). During dinner, you're entertained with hula and Hawaiian music.

Then you're guided to the show – a Polynesian revue complete with Samoan fire knife dancing. The show also features an homage to the first sugar cane train in Hawai`i.

Index